'AS THE REDS GO MARCHING ON . . .'

The Author

Pseudonymous Richard Kurt is 27 and was brought up in Urmston, Manchester. Educated at Manchester Grammar, Manchester University and Manchester United, he gave up teaching European history and took up writing United history. His first book, *United We Stood*, was published in 1994 and he continues to contribute to every edition of *Red Issue* under the moniker 'Red-Eye'. He has also written for *The Independent*, *The Game* and *Four Four Two* and is currently Press Officer for the I.M.U.S.A.

'AS THE REDS GO MARCHING ON ...'

The Unofficial Story of United's '94/'95 Season

Richard Kurt

MAINSTREAM
PUBLISHING

EDINBURGH AND LONDON

This book is dedicated to Emma, Alan Godwin and
'Captain' Jason Davies, ex-R.S., without whom I wouldn't have
been at liberty to write it.

First published in Great Britain in 1995 by
MAINSTREAM PUBLISHING COMPANY (EDINBURGH) LTD
7 Albany Street
Edinburgh EH1 3UG

ISBN 1 85158 719 5

A catalogue record for this book is available from the British Library

Typeset in Bembo by Litho Link Ltd, Welshpool, Powys

Printed and bound in Great Britain by Butler & Tanner Ltd, Frome

CONTENTS

Acknowledgments	6	Villa at Home	118
Introduction	7	City Away	122
The Story So Far . . .	9	Leeds at Home	128
Blackburn Away	9	Norwich Away	136
Newcastle Away	13	Everton Away	139
Newcastle at Home	16	Ipswich at Home	143
Barcelona Away	19	Wimbledon Away	147
Aston Villa Away	30	QPR at Home	151
City at Home	34	Spurs at Home	154
Palace at Home	39	Liverpool Away	157
Gothenberg Away	42	Arsenal at Home	161
Arsenal Away	54	Croydon Magistrates Away	164
Norwich at Home	59	Leeds at Home (league)	168
Galatasaray at Home	62	Palace at Villa Park	175
QPR Away	67	Leicester Away	184
Forest at Home	72	Chelsea at Home	187
Chelsea Away	76	Coventry Away	192
Leicester at Home	79	Sheffield Wednesday at Home	196
Southampton Away	82	Southampton at Home	200
Coventry at Home	87	West Ham Away	204
Sheffield United Away	91	Everton at Wembley	213
Newcastle Away	94	Afterword	220
Blackburn at Home	101	Further Reading	223
Palace Away	106		
Wrexham at Home	113		

ACKNOWLEDGMENTS

Particular thanks to the following, without whom . . .
Chris Robinson, John Daniels, Pete Boyle, Andy Mitten, Bob and Co. at the club and Bill, John, Richard and Lorraine at Mainstream.

Thanks to those whose info and opinions helped shape the contents:
Chris, John, Pete and Andy; Johnny Flacks, Andy Walsh, 'Jim Morrison'; Duncan, Robbie and Mark; Peter Pete, John Paul, Fergus and Southy; Dave Kirkwood, Grant Cass, Jamie Smith, Steve Black, 'Bert' Foulds; Rob Hatcliffe, Mick B. and Phil H., Andy Pollard, Tony Jordan, Jason Davies, Tony Knott, James Grieve, Adam Thomas, Lance and the missus; Neil and Ian at the club; Jim White, Andy Edwards, Angela Powers, Michael Crick; Laurence and Ben; Salford Jim; and those whose names I didn't catch who told their stories.

Thanks for past help in getting this far to:
Graham Beech, Sara and Emma, Nick Hornby, David Meek, Andy Spinoza, Paul Simpson, Juliette Wills, David Lacey, Jim White, Mike Sweeney.

Ta for special transport to:
'Steve and Rob Tours', Des Wright, Jane at 'Vanessa' show.

No thanks at all to:
Roy Evans, Francis Lee, MUFC stewards in Barca.

Honourable exemptions from tabloid-slaggings:
Ian Whitell, Paul Walker, Steve Millar.

Illustrations courtesy of:
Bert Foulds, Drastic, 'Jim Morrison', Adrian Longden, Pete Boyle, UF Productions, *Red Attitude*, Jim Phelan of Exotica.

Cover pictures courtesy of:
Jim Phelan of Exotica.

INTRODUCTION

I DID HAVE A good reason for writing this book, apart from the fact that the advance was a big help when wadding out to grasping ticket touts. Flicking listlessly through the dismal array of end-of-season books last summer, I thought that there must be a better way of recording a United season, one that reflects *our* experience and not some jobbing journalist's. The result is in your hands – an attempt to capture the year as we felt it at the time. As you'll see, each bit was written as soon as it happened - which makes for some wry reading with hindsight – so that the book allows you to follow the season 'as live'. I've also tried to give individual matches their proper weight, writing what I suppose is a mini-essay for each. After all, each United game dominates the day on which it's played and shapes much of the previous and subsequent days too . . . for any true, match-going Red, a United game is an overwhelming influence on our week. So to me it's a travesty to see a game in which we've all invested so much cash and emotion reduced to a 50-word summary in a poxy annual.

Not that this is just a collection of match reports; I hope you'll appreciate that there's a lot more to the book than merely the games. It is supposed to contain everything of significance that happened to us and I apologise now for the piles of stuff I have no doubt forgotten to include or never found out about in the first place. However, no apologies will be forthcoming for the completely biased content or the appalling lapses in taste or the fruitier language or the generalised insults that doubtless tar many an innocent.

As you'll see, this account kicks off with the visit to Ewood Park last October, for reasons more than mere symbolism. I didn't get asked to do the book until a couple of days before the game and didn't feel I could do justice to what went before, much of which I'd already forgotten about because it was so tedious. To me, the real character of the 94/95 season didn't start to emerge until that game. Before Ewood, the European Cup had dominated all else, culminating in that scintillating night against Barca on 19 October, overshadowing our domestic endeavours and leading us into temptation . . . 'we're gonna win the European Cup' we sang, laughably. Since then, the reality of the season emerged as our Euro adventure turned sour and the domestic game became our all. So, before 23 October was just a prologue – the plot began in earnest that vibrant Sunday afternoon. Handily, this spared me disinterring that god-awful trio of awayday disasters too . . .

Sorry about the unhappy ending – but then, this is only the latest chapter of the United saga. Jim White took you through the triumphs of '94, I've tried to lace the traumas of '95 with enough bile and black humour to keep you going and I trust that Andy Mitten's book on '96 will provide the joyous dénouement of this trilogy we all deserve. If my publisher doesn't take too much of a hammering on this one, I hope to be able to relate our 1997 European Cup victory to you, as the Reds go marching on . . .

With repeated thanks to those whose support, opinions and information helped shape this book,

Richard Kurt
Wembley Coach Park
May 1995

THE STORY SO FAR . . .

BLINDED BY THE LIGHT reflected from the gleaming European Cup, United have been cruising, domestically at least, on autopilot. Somehow we have contrived to win all our home games without conceding a goal but only the Liverpool win was even vaguely memorable, or vaguely atmospheric. Away from home, three dismal defeats on the trot have spoken volumes about our Euro-obsession, though in the wake of our draw with Barca, the obsession still appears well-warranted. Heading up to Ewood Park, ready to put our title challenge back on the rails, we lay fourth, two points behind Rovers and seven behind the runaway Toons. With the league top two as our next opponents – and with our European dream about to turn into a bed-wetting nightmare – this seems as telling a place as any to start . . .

23 October: BLACKBURN ROVERS AWAY

Final Score: Rovers 2 UNITED 4

Scorers: Eric 45 (*pen*), Andrei 51 & 81, Hughsey 66

Attendance: 30,060

IT'S ALWAYS BEEN EASY enough to hate Blackburn and their part-time, whippet-abusing, inbred fans without any further help from their players. Their 'senior vice-president' is doing more damage to the football economy than Thatcher did to the nation's; their manager is the one person even more hated by Reds than Kevin Keegan; 50 per cent of their support have miraculously emerged from their two-up two-down hovels just in time to latch on to the glory-hunting bandwagon that has rattled down the town's cobbled streets.

Happily for Reds of the venom-spitting persuasion, they have compounded their ugliness by signing a collection of eminently loathable characters. Batty, the archetypal Tyke with a face designed for adornment with spider-web tattoo; Sutton, all swaggering, hook-nosed posturing with a price tag to match his apparent off-field ego; and Shearer himself, whose choosing of Rovers over United surely demonstrates either his idiocy or his avarice, his song hijacked by Reds to be definitively reinterpreted as 'There's only one greedy bastard'.

Tim Sherwood as captain perfectly encapsulated how Blackburn have managed to combine City-style bitterness with Dalglishean whingeing when he said last May that Rovers' four points against us were proof that they were clearly the better team and should've been champions. The poor lad clearly had difficulty understanding the concept of league football – on his reckoning, United should have won at least eight titles in the Eighties. Still, working on the Sherwood System, I guess that makes good old part-time fishermen Trelleborgs a better team than Rovers, doesn't it? Not that Dalglish admitted any such truth after their Swedish humiliation, although he did memorably claim that 'Trelleborgs did nothing that surprised us'. Oh yeah?! When Trelly's second goal went in, your wasted defenders looked pretty f*cking shell-shocked to me . . .

The thousands of Reds packed into the Darwen End at four o'clock were naturally glad to help remind Rovers of their daytrip to Europe whilst also, in the spirit of knowledgeable enquiry, asking our rural friends where they were exactly when Blackburn were shit. Up a whippet or down at Maine Road, presumably. The vibe was sensational, imbued as it was by the afterglow from Wednesday and compounded in power by our sheer numbers. The rumours that Rovers were going to cut the away allocation just for this game proved to be largely unfounded and we were left to revel in the biggest Army awayday thus far. There would be no suffering in silence in exec-dominated hell as at April's fixture - 'revenge served cold', the Red speciality of the house, was to be gorged on by a feeding frenzy of thousands.

Throughout the first half, United enjoyed even more possession of the vocal stage than the team did of the ball. The home support, although at least audible to us unlike the pathetically timid mice at Hillsborough, were utterly outsung – they did just enough to give us something to react to, including the odd Munich wave, without ever stepping out of their role of very minor supporting actor.

They had their ten seconds of glory as Warhurst, collared-up in blatant Eric-idol mode, fluked their opener. There was much post-match talk of Rovers' 'bad luck' but how often would you expect to see such a conjunction of misfortune that allowed that one to go in? We had 60 per cent of the ball but carried only 40 per cent of the threat until the 44th minute, when God let down his keks and deluged Rovers in brown ones.

Of course it wasn't a penalty, or even a yellow card offence – that just made the enraptured singing of *Cheerio, cheerio* as Berg slunk off all the sweeter. What is it these days with United and penalties? In the darker days of the Eighties, it was a standing terrace assumption that penalties weren't even worth appealing for. Some sort of cosmic sliding scale was in operation back then that meant that every unjust penalty for Liverpool at Anfield had to be paid for elsewhere by United being denied one. Suddenly, now that Eric takes them, we get penalties gift-wrapped special delivery whenever we want them. At Wembley, at Elland Road and now at Ewood – perhaps God just likes Eric's technique so much that he can't help himself. One-one, Rovers down to ten men, and the first sustained 'oo-ah' of the day. Somewhere deep in King Kenny's stomach an ulcer grows ever more bilious.

The local wildlife spent the break growling and howling like their furry girlfriends up on the moors; the specimens who were penned up above us in the Darwen also provided the half-time entertainment with some formation spitting, as promised on page 28 of the match programme. Sky's shot of the week award should have gone to the Red six rows in front of the scoreboard who landed a direct hit on the nose of a miscreant's wife with a particularly sweaty pie. The team were to ensure that there was some egg on the Rovers faces to go with it five minutes later.

After Hendry's spawny header escaped Peter's flailing clutches – when we asked for performances like last season's, we didn't expect Schmeichel to deliver quite so literally – we had hardly begun the traditional post-goal rallying cry when Andrei delivered his Cossack sword-thrust. Watching the Sky re-run at nine reveals so many delights that you miss from the terraces; the heartbreak in Andy Gray's voice as Kan-Kan peeled away was wonderful. He knew, as we and the increasingly comatose home fans did, that Blackburn were dead in the water from that moment on. Hughesy's chip for the third, described by *The Guardian* as 'exquisitely nonchalant' and as 'fookin' killer' by my neighbour, was delicious enough but watching the telly in post-match euphoria, how fitting it seemed that Le Saux was at fault, given that he had got away with studding Keano's neck earlier – many of us missed that, so thank you Sky. Your services to televisual violence are much appreciated.

Faced with the conjunction of that goal and a full-throated three minute rendition of *3-2 to the Champions* that reverberated in every corner, Rovers and their fans melted away into the night. A glorious spell of *olé* football, taking the possessional piss in what was perhaps a deliberate homage to the Selhurst Spring Show, was crowned by a delightful goal, pedantically disallowed as Incey did his Nigerian impression in the goalmouth. 'Paul Ince is the Governor' filled the rain-spattered air as Rovers chased sprinting shadows whilst the matadors tormented and teased. Rovers reverted to bad sportsmanship, refusing to stop play for a Hughsey knock and failing to return possession afterwards, thus prompting Guvnor Ince to lecture Warhurst on the requirements of being a gentleman – though I'm not sure shouting 'dickhead! dickhead!' into his face was the way Professor Higgins would have done it.

The fourth that sealed their first home defeat for 13 months gave the scoreline the correct rout-like proportions, Andrei seeming to have the ball glued to his instep as he rounded Flowers and nutmegged his shot through the ugliest man on the pitch. Cue ten minutes of Cossack-dancing on the seats, raucous demands of Alan Shearer to remind us of the scoreline, yet more Pet Shop Boys and finally some fond bidding of farewells to the rapidly emptying Walkersteel garden shed. At the whistle, jubilant Reds piled out to mount the railings by the church and coach park to begin a night of awayday celebration that had been long overdue. With the Newcastle double-header and the Nou Camp to come, had we turned the corner just in time?

The media chose to concentrate on the 44th minute, of course, implying that what followed was inevitable and meaningless because of the numerical disadvantage so cruelly suffered by Rovers. Welcome to life at the top, you arriviste whingers. How many times in the past have United been so reduced and yet still come through? When you've got a good team that keeps its cool but uses its inbuilt passion, you can overcome such adversity. Rovers, remember, were actually ahead – a champion side in such a position should be able to organize, inspire and hold on for at least a draw, especially at home. The burning sense of injustice should drive you on. United won a cup final against formidable champions in just such circumstances and we weren't even in the lead at the time. Just last season, it could be said that we only beat Charlton *because* of the red card, such was the extra force we seemed to derive from being 'up against it'. If Blackburn are such a superior team as Tim Sherwood seems to think, they should've done much better - certainly better than allowing a team without Giggs or an in-form Cantona and with a makeshift half-injured full back to score three in 30 minutes. Spend less time moaning and brooding on your inferiority complex and you might actually win a trophy one day.

Team: Schmeichel; Irwin, Bruce, Pallister, Sharpe, Kanchelskis, Keane, Ince, Butt (McClair), Cantona, Hughes

26 October: NEWCASTLE AWAY – FIZZY POP CUP RD 3

Final Score: Newcastle 2 UNITED YOUTH TEAM 0

Attendance: 34,178

ALEX 'TINKERBELL' FERGUSON, AS he was once derogatorily known, hasn't always pleased the faithful with his selection policies. Rare, too, are the occasions when he manages to hoodwink the rest of the country with cunning team-picking stunts. But on a still, cool night in Newcastle, as over 3,500 Reds piled into the Milburn paddock to join 800 confrères across the stadium, he succeeded in giving us all an unexpected thrill. Someone at the Club had briefed the papers the previous night that United would field a close to full strength team, omitting three or four 'stars' but otherwise seeking to take the Geordies on near-level terms. The press faithfully reproduced this as gospel and Keegan prepared his over-hyped side accordingly – but with less than an hour to go till kick-off, Fergie revealed his true hand in top Newman and Redford *Sting*-style. The kids were back in full force with only Bruce, Pally and the Bogman from the firsts to look after the young whipper-snappers, plus reserve Choccy back to reprise his teacher role from the Vale Park game. Keegan later admitted we'd completely cocked-up his careful designs whilst we Reds on the terraces revelled in our good fortune. We were obviously going to lose – so it was party time. Eh?! Step into the surreal Twilight Zone that was United's League Cup campaign.

A fanzine editor signed off his 'phone call to me that afternoon thus: 'Of course I'm going – I just hope we lose'. That summed up the world of the Absurd we had entered. Nobody wanted United to progress in the League Cup. It would cause extra fixture congestion and injuries - besides, we had bigger fish to fry – and United should not need League Cup triumphs to get into Europe. And yet, as long as United remained in it, we the faithful would have to keep going. As long as a United first team is in action, even if it's supplied direct from the schoolyard, we had a duty to be there whatever we felt about the competition. Sure, it would have been Absolutely Fabulous if the sweeties from the youth team had gone onto Wembley but realistically, it wasn't going to happen. Thus it came about that hundreds of Reds spent eight hours and 30 quid travelling to see a bunch of boys almost certainly lose, and lose with our blessing. Mad, masochistic Mancs on tour - part two.

As it happens, those two away trips with the OT kindergarten turned out to be highlights of the early season despite all that. Vale Park had been a genuine terrace classic for those 3,000 who made it; within minutes of the team announcement at St James' Park, a frisson rippled through the paddock as if the throng had decided as one to make this a Port Vale revival meeting. Pete Boyle took up his mid-terrace position, perched his bum on a convenient post and proceeded to lead a willing, buzzing Red regiment through a rapidly improvised Geordie-baiting songbook. Beardsley and Keegan, unwisely emerging to take a look at the Red crowd, were greeted with *There's only one Quasimodo* and *One-nil to the baseball bat*, setting a tasteful tone for the rest of the night. The home crowd, of whom we expected so much, were pitiful. The St James' Roar is actually something between a squeak and a whisper − I've heard 10,000 at Roker Park make more noise. As for the ground, alleged to be a temple of football since redevelopment, it held only disappointment; it works like OT-in-reverse, looking so imposing from the outside, perched magisterially on its hill, but soulless and prosaic inside.

United were on a winner, of course. If the kids lost, there would be no shame since that is what you would expect from a mismatched clash between the reserve Teens and the league leader Toons. Nor would Newcastle have gained anything psychologically to benefit them for the up-coming league match with the big boys themselves. And if the Geordies lost, or won unconvincingly, the fillip for us would be immense, the damage to the hype-merchants intense. How gratifying it was to see Newcastle play in such an increasingly nervous fashion as to make it plain that they understood all the above only too well. Who knows how they'd have handled us had either McClair's snapshot or Brucey's header gone in within the opening 20 minutes. Newcastle should count themselves fortunate that the boys up-front were not quite at Vale Park sharpness; as it was, the match unfurled predictably with the Geordies dominating possession but becoming frantic in the area as the clock marched forward. The boys in Red, successfully shaking off the shame of having to wear girlie white socks, harried and chased and snapped with almost religious zeal, provoking the exasperated Geordie cloggers into incidents of violent child-abuse. 'Incey's gonna get you' warned enraged Reds as Beresford committed yet another gratuitous foul on Davies . . . and, of course, he did three days later.

The paddock Reds, meanwhile, partied on like the dudes they are. All the greatest hits from Port Vale were reprised as the Toons squirmed to hear they were being 'outclassed by the youth team'; the abysmal showing of the home fans led us to demand plaintively 'where's yer famous atmosphere?' but it seemed that the locals were too busy staring in open-mouthed wonder at us to respond. When a few Geordies to our left attempted to mount a response, their feeble – and indecipherable – effort produced much Manc merriment and a hearty reply, 'If you can't talk proper, shut yer mouth'. Ironic self-deprecation AND regional triumphalism in one line – what genius. Similarly, check the intellectual content of us singing this: 'If you hate Byker Grove, clap your hands' followed by a stirring rendition of the 'Corrie' theme tune and a paen to Bet Lynch. Childish pap culture referencing? Certainly not – more a mass-appeal encapsulation of Manchester's effortless cultural and historical superiority over the Geordie semi-savages. We give the world free trade, industry, top pop and Granada whilst the Geordies give us Lindisfarne and brown ale. Ta very much . . . What with a half-time entertainment of the Boyle Chorus Marching Chant, the Lee Sharpe Song and several throaty run-throughs of *25 years and won f*ck all*, the Red Army left the Toon 'Army' in no doubt as to who were the true champions. The two Geordie goals in the last eight minutes saved the home crowd from complete embarrassment but scarcely put us off our stride – the locals looked upon us with admiring gazes as they left after the whistle, knowing they'd seen the best. And we knew for our part that better was to come – Saturday would surely see us settle our account with the brown-ale breathed pretenders. 'Of that, there can be no doubt – aa-haa!' (c.Steve Coogan, another example of Red cultural hegemony . . .)

Team: Walsh; Neville, Irwin (Sharpe, Tomlinson), Bruce, Pallister, Gillespie, Beckham, McClair, Butt, Scholes, Davies

(NB: The only true black spot of the night – Sharpe was injured and would miss Barca away amongst others.)

29 October: NEWCASTLE AT HOME

Final Score: UNITED 2 Newcastle 0

Scorers: Pallister 11, Gillespie 77

Attendance: 43,795

WHEN THEY HANDED OUT the fixture cards back in August, 21 autumn days had stood out from the start, 21 days in which we were to face our city rivals, both of our main prospective title challengers and the double header against our Nou Camp nemesis. (That we ended up having another clash with the Geordies thrown in too was just a light entertainment bonus.) And to put the impending Barca fiasco into perspective, if you had been told pre-season that we were only going to lose one of those five epic clashes, wouldn't you have been largely satisfied? Without wanting to get too Biblical here, surely sometimes we are guilty of ignoring our blessings and dwelling on our occasional misfortunes – notwithstanding the Catalan catastrophe, these were three magnificent weeks.

If we had answered the questions about our away form by putting Rovers to the sword, then Newcastle's visit gave us the opportunity to silence the home-based Cassandras. Let's be honest; in five league homes, we had yet to get a sniff of the bubbles of last year's vintage. We had a 100 per cent home league record and were yet to concede a goal but we were going home with appetites unfulfilled – the gourmet feasts of '93/'94 had been replaced by a succession of Chicken McNugget performances. To some extent this was a function of the poverty of the opposition we'd faced, in that only the prospect of Liverpudlian blood had set our taste buds tingling so far. If we couldn't get turned on by such dullish opponents, it was no surprise that the players seemed to be struggling to keep their ends up too. But Newcastle at home was an entirely different scenario.

This wasn't just a case of avenging the honour of the defeated kids from midweek, delectable though it was to see Incey sort out the child-abusers and one of the kids themselves score the Geordie-slaying second. Nor was it simply a 'six-pointer' crunch clash, although it would have undoubtedly been seriously grim news had we slipped to ten points behind. This had become a match of symbolic import - supposedly the champions-past versus the champions-to-be, a team imperceptibly moving past its peak against another on their way up the summit to replace them. Such had been the tabloid-driven hype behind the 'Toon Army' (which had, in fact, been decimated by St James' redevelopment) and Keegan's Wunderteam (which hadn't, in truth, played well since the 4-2 against Chelsea) that Reds were left feeling WE had something to prove. As if Double Winners need to prove anything to trophy-less cheeky pups like Newcastle! Actually the tabloids, whose Geordie-hype was motivated by the frenzied search for novelty and change and driven on by their hunting pack mentality, had done us a favour. Within minutes of the kick-off, it was clear that the Reds were simmering with righteous passion – this was not going to be another of those habitual pre-Europe play-it-safe days.

Newcastle were without the shin-splintered Cole, thus providing Keegan with a sad, ready-made excuse for his post-match interview, even though it was clear from what we'd witnessed on Wednesday that Cole's seam was currently all mined out. Besides, this is what happens when you rely on one goal-hanger so much; when he disappears, your threat vanishes with it. Keegan said they were toothless up front but neglected to mention they were all gums at the back and rotting cavities in midfield. A United team packed with lions, tigers and, er, other wild animals with big gnashers seized the game in their jaws and savaged it. Hughes, Ince and Pally, who made up the rod of iron that is United's backbone, were God-like, whilst Dieu himself alongside trusty sidekick Andrei sliced up Geordie defenders at will – in particular leaving the gypsy Peacock dazed and confused, wishing he was tucked up in his caravan. Only the brilliance of Srnicek denied us the cricket score that our second half showing deserved.

Once we were ahead, any tensions in the team dissolved; after months of watching Pally head forward for corners to no avail, how pleasant a shock to see him bury Giggsy's one good ball of the day in devastating style. The Toon Army (*sic*) in the corner slowly sank into silence, unable to provide the lift that their predecessors had done the previous autumn, whilst K and East Lower finally began to unite to produce the wall of sound of which they're so obviously capable. United had, at last, rediscovered their tactical touch from yesteryear, happy to allow Geordies 50 per cent of useless, directionless possession before whipping their retreating arses on the break. Until United went two-up, Newcastle only managed two decent chances (which were comprehensively bollocksed-up by the hapless Sellars), a damning indictment of their failure to invent, create or challenge.

Within 20 minutes of the restart, the Reds were refusing to let the Geordies have the ball at all, presumably bored witless by Newcastle's hopeless fannying about; raid after raid was launched down the flanks, inspiring the home crowd to slide the volume fader ever upwards towards eleven. Hughes 'scored' but Giggs's corner was wrongly adjudged to have gone out; Ince hit the woodwork yet again with his now traditional second half thunderflash. By this point, the Geordie fans might as well have gone home and taken their redundant attack with them for all the help they were to their team; there was no response to a massed chorus of *Outclassed by the champions*' but then, what response could there be?

With Giggs the only disappointing performer, Alex pulled yet another substitution master-stroke à la Choccy and the Scouse by throwing Gillespie on for the shagged-out Welshman. With what seemed like immediate effect, the precocious Ulsterman won the game, avenged the kids and entered our dreams. Floating angelically across the edge of the box right under the approving gaze of the heavenly Eric himself, he contemptuously brushed off two dolts with a dummy before shooting sensationally into the far corner. Keith had truly arrived at last, both into our's and the nation's consciousness – how many teenagers get two goals into *MOTD*'s Goal of the Month in the space of a few days? You'd almost say he was Giggsian in impact, if that wasn't currently such an insult.

A third should have followed after Keane capped a stunning display by tackling on his line, hurtling down the field and delivering his trademark low, arcing ball only for Hughes to shoot over the bar. When Keano breaks into full flight like that, there's few more inspirational sights for the Red eye. And perhaps a third might have come as a result of the red card Howey should've had; he'd done what most mortals do after 80 minutes of having the piss taken by Andrei *viz* manhandled him to the ground. No card was produced but we could afford to show some generosity to a team who couldn't even stick the ball in the net after the offside whistle had gone, Mathie giving the West Stand Boys a late laugh with his embarrassing finish.

The point hadn't just been made; it had been slammed home until blood spurted out. United were back, and back at their best. A faint cry of 'Top of the league' from departing Geordies was smothered by a stadium-wide trumpeting of 'Campiones' – the team had made it clear that they intended for us to be able to continue singing that song for many a year yet.

Team: Schmeichel; Keane, Bruce, Pallister, Irwin, Kanchelskis, McClair, Ince, Giggs (Gillespie), Cantona, Hughes

2 *November:* BARCELONA AWAY – UEFA CHAMPIONS LEAGUE

Final Score: Barcelona 4 UNITED 0

Attendance: 114,273

TO SAY THAT WE were looking forward to this would be some understatement: as the first sentence of the first *Red Issue* of 94/95 put it, '74 Days To Go To Barcelona'. Everything else beforehand was just a stage-warmer for the main event; the merely domestic, at least until the end of October, seemed almost embarrassingly unloved and neglected in comparison. Even the previous Euro-ties shrunk in the shadow of the Nou Camp, the return to Istanbul in any case being joined by only 150 of the hardiest souls. Our 2-2 draw with Barca at Old Trafford, thrillsome and epic though it was, remained very much the junior partner of the double-header. It had proved – or so we thought – that we would at least be able to live with the Catalan giants. The real acid test, however, was this. If we could go there and get something, would any other Euro-giant stadium hold any fears for us?

But that's the football side: as one Red invader remarked, 'bugger the football – where's the crack?' Meaning the Gaelic 'craic' rather than those Moss Side rocks, of course. For, thankfully as it turned out, what inspired such fervent anticipation was not so much the 90 minutes on the pitch but the event, the sense of occasion, the booze-drenched voyaging and the camaraderie of the Red tribal gatherings in Barca and Lloret. And if you were a true Red, you had to do your best to be able to say 'I was there'. Because fixtures like this are what United are supposed to be about: this is what we waited 26 years to win the league to achieve. 'Bring on Spaniards by the score . . .' as the song goes – and your Juves and Milans and Bayerns. If we are the 'greatest team the world has ever seen', the Nou Camp is where we're supposed to be – Las Ramblas is where we're meant to pass out in a coma, not the 'Farmer's Arms' in some grotty provincial hovel.

Your correspondent, in a stupidly noble attempt to do the right 'journalistic' thing and experience Euro trips of both official and unofficial varieties, flew with the Club. Yet whatever route you travelled, getting the full picture would be impossible. Barca was a city of 7,000 stories, all of different itineraries, fluctuating fortunes and varying levels of debauchery. So all you can do is offer a selection of glimpses of the Barca experience as reported at the time by me, other

Red Issue correspondents, their counterparts at *Red News* and *Red Attitude* and others. I'll leave the literary-travel-writing stuff for the IFK trip . . .

Getting to Barcelona was one thing, getting a match ticket quite another. As if it wasn't tricky enough securing the cash, the time off work and the spousal approval, MUFC produced several of their own hoops through which desperate Reds had to jump, as *Red Issue* co-editor Veg scathingly outlined in his editorials.

Taking only 3,500 tickets for the game in Barcelona is daft. Rumour has it that United were offered as many tickets as they wanted for the game. They could quite easily have sold 10,000 tickets for the game; instead, by only taking such a pathetically small number, they have actually increased the potential for trouble, precisely what they claim their restrictions are designed to avoid. As it is now, there will no doubt be pockets of United fans all round the ground; there will still be 10,000 of us there, just in different parts of the ground. Will whoever at United who took the decision to have only 3,500 tickets, accept their share of the blame if there is trouble inside the Nou Camp, or will they use any such incident as a convenient excuse to justify their position? Ever since they relented for Rotterdam, United have sold tickets for all our European away games, to official members with confirmed travel details. Why have they suddenly changed their position now? The events of last November should not be allowed to cloud the fact that until Istanbul, the record of United fans abroad had been an excellent one. Can't they understand that people want more than 90 minutes football, a two hour sightseeing tour and a demonstration of local folk dancing when they follow the team abroad at great personal expense?

For many of course, the home leg is but a prelude to the game in Barcelona itself. A game for which United in ostrich-like fashion continue to bury their heads in the proverbial sand and refuse to issue tickets to anyone who makes their own way to Catalonia. United's intransigence and disregard for their hard-core supporters in this matter is shameful. Using the events in Istanbul last year as an excuse not to release tickets to independent travellers, they have priced their two-day trips at a figure at which it is hard to believe they are not guilty of rampant profiteering. £265 for a flight and one night's hotel accommodation is ridiculous. Miss Ellie's Travel, whose very trips United have done so much to scupper in recent days, were able to offer an extra night's accommodation for £16 less. United are, of course, citing supposed Football Association and UEFA recommendations as the excuse for not repeating their European ticket policy of previous years. If it is the condition, as they claim, that all away supporters are only allowed tickets in conjunction with travelling on official club trips, why did they break with this rule for the game against Gothenburg at Old Trafford? Tickets were on open sale for that game 'till kick off; any potential Gothenburg hooligans could have purchased tickets for any section of the ground. When the FA have been contacted on this matter, they admit that the restricted ticket policy is only a recommendation.

Assuming that readers had negotiated the MUFC obstacle course and booked their passage, if not their ticket, *Red Issue* offered my own 'indispensable' – if not entirely reliable – guide to Barca, which tendered some of the advice not forthcoming from Judith Chalmers.

Clearly, if you're trying to get the barman to run you a tab till next week – i.e. after your departure – or to get into some señorita's knickers, attempt the odd Catalan phrase or say something insulting about Madrid and you'll get a long way. However, once inside the Nou Camp, you might want to enrage local sensibilities by either the obvious – chanting 'Real Madrid' or 'Español' – or more subtly, by singing 'Franco, Franco, Generalissimo Franco' or even 'Jordi Pujol . . . is a wanker, is a wanker'. Pujol is Catalonia's President, named Jordi after a local saint. Johann Cruyff even named his son Jordi too – what a cocksucker!

The old city is stuffed full of churches and museums; the Cathedral of Gaudi is worth seeing if only as a demonstration of what a drugged-out architect can do with a year's supply of acid tabs and a load of knock-off concrete. You are, of course, better off heading for the Ramblas, infested with annoying street entertainers but also fit 'chicks', pot sellers and cool drinkeries – best of all, it runs through the massive, dodgy red light district where the real Barca skulks.

Those whose drinking tastes go further than Spanish lager to include slurping a certain kind of wine might at first find the haughty black-stockinged señoritas downtown a little intimidating . . . quirks to beware of: many Spanish girls are happy to perform whatever the time of month, so watch out when you're diving.

Red Issue, superbly true to its non-PC form, had unwittingly got Anglo-Catalan relations off to a cracking start.

> Boarding the plane to Barcelona, it was apparent that the girl sat behind us was a native Catalonian and she was soon to provide us with much amusement. Picking up a nearby freebie Spanish newspaper, the front page caught my eye, dominated as it was by photos of United fans on the piss abroad. Jools spotted with great delight the only two English words in the accompanying Spanish text – RED ISSUE. We couldn't turn around quickly enough to ask the Lolita behind us to translate. With a wry smile, reasons for which soon became apparent, she began to describe in very good English the Spanish journalist's distaste for claims made in *Red Issue*'s 'Guide to Barcelona' that local girls take it up the Gary Glitter in order to maintain their technical virginity. Upon completing the article the girl, still smirking mischievously voiced her own opinion that the information was 'not true and very bad'.

Fortunately, some of our less facetious ambassadors were on hand to learn a few cultural lessons on arrival when they visited the Nou Camp on Tuesday to soak up some Barca history.

> For 375 pesetas we then treated ourselves to a visit to the Museum and a sneak preview of the Stadium. From the outside, the Nou Camp does not grab the imagination, at a push it could even be mistaken for a multi-storey car park. Walking up the outside ramp, through the museum and out into the sunlight through, you get your first sight of what must surely be one of, if not the greatest sporting arenas in the world. In the warmth of a November morning with only Jordi Cruyff lapping the pitch, the Nou Camp still manages to take the breath away. What would it be like in less than 36 hours time with over 100,000 devoted Catalans filling its skyscraping tiers? A visit to the museum only goes to confirm what you've already suspected. Namely that the marketing men at Old Trafford should be sued under the Trade Descriptions Act. Our claims to be 'The World's Greatest Football Club' ring hollow once you've made a visit to this citadel.
>
> Calling Old Trafford the 'Theatre of Dreams' is rather like comparing The Royal Exchange with the London Palladium; the same performances might take place within its walls, but there the comparison ends.

Meanwhile, back in Manchester, some of us still hadn't left yet. On Wednesday morning, I was at Ringway, soaking up the bad vibes as bitterly as a Blue.

Apparently, the club ended up running a total of twelve planes to Barcelona, of which seven left on the day of the game itself from Manchester. By 10 a.m., terminal 1 at Manchester airport was filled with seven sprawling queues of Reds, as if seeking entry through check-in desk turnstiles to an invisible stadium. A brief sociological scan of the Red-shirted hordes revealed the official party to be a strangely skewed cross-section of an Old Trafford crowd - the young girls, grannies, Club Classy smarties and family groups were all there in abundance but 'the lads' were somehow under-strength. Resignedly realising that UF tours had probably creamed off the *Red Issue*-type elite, I prepared myself for a day of tedium. In the departure lounge, a few disparate cries of 'K stand's Barmy Army' went up, met with even fewer desultory replies of 'J stand, J stand' which served only to confirm that most of you, dear readers, were elsewhere.

At midday, a frisson of distaste rippled through the lounge as Martin Edwards pranced through; as he headed for his scheduled flight, an irate K Stander shouted over, 'So it's all right for YOU to travel unofficial, is it?' Fartin' had the grace to blush before scuttling off as the air filled with bitter denunciations of the entire Barcelona-trip scenario. I hesitate to call the trip a 'rip off' but when you compare the prices with either UF tours or the going rate for Barcelona mini-breaks, you can only conclude that someone, somewhere was making a pile out of us. In today's paper, I see an ad: four nights in decent accommodation in central Barcelona including flights for £154. The official day-trip cost more than that just for the flight. Johnny Flacks from the FSA was there, still fuming about the treatment meted out on Sunday to United supporters by Brittany Ferries. He is currently compiling a dossier on the entire subject of clubs and monopoly travel schemes and had calculated that someone was making close to £70 a head profit on the daytrip alone. The club, naturally, had licensed the whole deal to a third party so that no-one can know who exactly is making what; they are allowed to get away with this enforced monopoly by hiding behind the UEFA rules which were never meant to sanctify such rampant profiteering. One soft lad thought the extra cost was justified by the fact that 'security' had been provided but we worked out, after slyly questioning the suits themselves, that this extra cost amounted to £3 a head. What a racket - Al Capone would have been impressed.

Ah, the suits. Half-a-dozen to a plane, seemingly selected from an assortment of dodgy night-club doorways and various primary schoolyards, such was the disparity in age and appearance. As they strutted around the terminal, they exuded authority and responsibility in their natty sports casualwear – 'Aha!'. By the end of the day, it was clear that the only things that distinguished them from us were a) their blazers and b) their ability to get some duty free on the plane back. Their only 'authority' was over us; the varieties of Spanish officialdom treated them with utter disdain. They had less clout than your average package holiday tour rep; had they not been there, it wouldn't have made the slightest difference to the day's events.

At least the 'officials' had guaranteed tickets. Several thousand already in Barca and Lloret had come out on a wing and a prayer and were duly horrified to discover that the Nou Camp had actually sold out for the first time since the early Eighties. A testament to the pulling power of United, for sure, but one those lads could have done without at the time. Even those on supposedly respectable though unofficial tours found that once they'd crossed the Channel, the phrase 'guaranteed ticket' became translated to 'a ticket if we can find a few touts'.

> We'd all got knocked back from the Miss Ellie fall-out but got picked up by this other local firm as a group. Well past Calais with no tickets yet seen, we were getting suspicious to say the least. When we kept stopping for the tour rep to confer with dodgy-looking Spaniards on street corners, we knew the score. 'You'll get your tickets today at three/six/nine, tomorrow at ten/twelve/two . . .' On the day of the game, the bloke actually promised us tickets 'mañana'. This was the point at which we started discussing amongst ourselves when would be the best time to beat the living shit out of him . . . (Dave K.)

Barcelona became Rumour Central, outstripping even Manchester's capability to circulate porkies as the search for the golden ticket became ever-increasingly desperate.

TOP TEN RUMOURS HEARD IN BARCELONA

1. It's pay on the gate.
2. If we cause trouble they'll have to let us in.

3. Tickets go on open sale at 9.00 am.
4. If we behave they'll have to let us in.
5. Tickets go on open sale at midday.
6. 4.00pm.
7. Barcelona haven't sold out for 8/9/10/11/12 years.
8. It's a sell out.
9. They're going to round us up and put us in the empty paddock they've set aside.
10. They're going to round us up and put us next door to watch it on the big screen.

In the meantime, what else to do but party on? The Boyle had arrived on the Ramblas, a shot in the arm to any flagging revellers, and with thousands of buzzing Reds swarming all over Barca central, singing, supping and stripping were the order of the day.

A 'phone call to a mate in Barcelona resulted in the black news that he had been unsuccessful in securing tickets but he'd met some great lads whom he'd spent the whole day with. One of them hadn't stopped singing all day. 'Is he called Peter, by any chance?' I asked. 'Yes, how did you know that?' 'Pure luck,' I said, 'but I hope he kept his clothes on.'

Tearing ourselves away from the bar, we headed for the Ramblas in search of wine, women and song. We found Peter Boyle.

Just off what will surely become one of the most celebrated thoroughfares in United travelling history, Pete was doing his bit. Outside a bar whose name will forever escape me, at the entrance to the Placa Reial, the celebrated streaker was leading 150 or so Reds in renditions of his best hits. Far from alarming the locals, the sight of so many drunk Mancunians 'Drinking to Eric The King', drew a small crowd keen to witness this unique English ritual. As Boyle led the younger generation, the old more Euro-experienced Reds amongst the crowd tried to out-do each other with songs from battles and matches past. Not unnaturally, the scousers came in for it.

Night quickly arrived and thus it was time to start the body abuse again. By now clearly everybody who wasn't travelling official was in town, and the bar-crawls, sing-songs, and drunkenness had really started. Practically every Red you've ever met at United was here. All you had to do was walk around the centre and you would recognise ten or twenty people.

Now you really can't get away from Sticky Vicky. Just when you think you are safe, up she pops in the bar you're drinking at. The early evening had been spent watching Q.P. Ha ha ha ha, beating the Dirties and baiting the Scouse lad whose nose was still swollen from baiting us the night before. Everyone's heard the joke of the Duchess of York hiding the jewellery and Princess Margaret saving the Land Rover. Well, in the next bar, a woman of approximately 50, the original Shirley Lapper, just walked in and to dimming lights, and dodgy music took off her clothes. Nothing more unusual than a weekend at the Ritz you might think, but this was merely a prelude to an extraordinary act, during which (using Cockney rhyming slang) she was almost literally pulling rabbits from her 'hat'. Golf balls, snooker balls, tennis balls, chicken eggs, love eggs, razor blades and enough bunting to decorate a VE Day street party. But no f*cking tickets.

Kick-off approached, the time to get your head sorted and stagger to the Nou Camp, before battling through police cordons and Barca's 'Noixos' into the ground. For our most famed Blackpool Red, though, it was a journey too far.

By half past six some people were already returning to the hotel, unable to get into the Nou Camp, with tales of baton charges and heavy policing. One particularly inebriated Red had already given up his ticket to a fellow Red, his inability to see further than the end of his nose meant it unlikely he would get into the ground never mind see the game. At eleven o'clock the next morning he was still not fully aware of the scale of our defeat.

Whilst Mick prepared to spend a restful night on the bar floor, the ticketless tried their luck at the increasingly frenzied turnstiles.

. . . several clever jibs into the stadium were unsuccessful. One bloke managed to get in the official section and hid in the toilets for over an hour before dashing up the stairs when the attendant had disappeared. Another Red easily got in claiming that hooligans had robbed him of his ticket whilst his wife stood next to him crying her eyes out. Drunken Dave, sporting a Cantona Cup Final wig got in, but we think was too pissed to realise it.

So we were in: 3,500 officials and God knows how many jibbers, unofficials and free-loaders, mostly up in the heavens of the fourth tier, staring down at the hellish visions way below on the pitch that would soon be conjured up by the Catalonian wizards.

You have to admit that your first sight of the Nou Camp as you emerge through the boca into the top tier is breathtaking. TV pix and photos don't do it justice – it is truly awe-inspiring. Old Trafford is in comparison a nicely-shaped foothill next to the Himalayan mountain that is the Nou Camp. It partially compensated for having to spend so much time cooped up in their crappy concourse served by 'facilities' that would disgrace the Endsleigh sheds. Outside the ground, way way below, we could spy the suits pacing shabbily around the car park. Stories circulated about the rank wankiness of the official trips; those who'd arrived on Tuesday told of cancelled trips and tours, handicapped fans having to fend for themselves and even a suit who couldn't find his own hotel. Lads who'd been with UF tours before and had expected 'superior' packaging from the official trips said they'd never make the mistake again. Still, at least we were there and in; I wondered how the 'independents' were faring in their quest to gain entry – at least they'd have a good time getting here.

Kick off approached – we looked good spread across the top tier in a manner that brought back reminiscences of Rotterdam. Replays of the 2-2 shimmered on the giant screen as Barca fans slowly filled out the enormous bowl. The cage to our right, presumably UF tours, created a volume of noise out of all proportion to its size but the performance of 'our' 3,000 was patchy at best, provoking some in the cage below to shout 'make some f*cking noise you twats'. By the 60th minute, no one was shouting anything beyond the odd encouragement to Giggs to head for the San Siro. What can you say? I don't want to talk about it. It was like being forced to watch your girlfriend being gang raped by Leeds fans. Stunned and horrified, we just wanted to get back to the plane, go home and mourn.

A touch harsh on some of our 'supporters', perhaps? Then try this verdict from an 'unofficial', waylaid into the official section.

Barca fans suggested to us that we might want to make our way into the official United section; till my dying days I'll wonder why we took up their suggestion. The police were more than happy to let us transfer into the United section where we found ourselves sat in an aisle watching the game surrounded by the biggest bunch of wankers

I've ever had the displeasure to watch a game with. Is one of the conditions of being allowed on the official trip, that the participants should not utter a word in support of their team during the game and must have spent a minimum of 50 quid in the souvenir shop before boarding the plane? Forget what went on on the pitch, for me the game was lost the moment Ferguson left Schmeichel off the team sheet, but that's his job and without him we wouldn't even have been in the Nou Camp. The biggest disappointment came in the behaviour of those supporters. Instead of supporting their (and I use the word hesitatingly) team they spent the time bickering about who should be sat where, and slagging Giggs off. Thirty minutes after the end of the game with the stadium empty except for those of us kept behind, the morons who'd made the official trip decided to finally exercise their vocal chords as we were being led out of the ground.

It had been a grim half-hour detention at the end, for sure. Sat in stunned silence as if scarcely able to believe the mauling we had just witnessed by the Barcelonian lions in the amphitheatre below, a final insult came as a Barca boy emerged in the next stand waving a 'Barca-Leeds' flag. Some dimly realised that there would be more Barca-English love-ins to come once we were home: you could almost see the Barca flags at Maine Road already. The sole laugh of the night was provided by a cartoonish skirmish in the right end, after everyone had left, featuring a drum, a trumpet, a flag and a couple of pissed-up and pissed-off Reds. It was, as Veg wrote, a bit too early yet for the departing officials to be singing *Always Look On The Bright Side*.

After a few drinks, however, that San Miguel brightness is blinding: what we'd seen was a one-off, right? We drank to that . . .

Back home I was asked how I felt. 'To quote Brendan Behan', I replied, 'my liver is like the sole of a hobnailed boot'. The downside was obviously the performance on the pitch. The result was shocking. I left the ground in despair, in agony over what I had just seen, non-plussed at the effect that Schmeichel's non-inclusion had on the side. I met up with a group of lads walking away from the ground, avoiding the mass of celebrating Barcelona fans on their mopeds. This group all said the same thing:- 'Don't worry, we'll never play that badly against top opposition again'. So, I banished the pessimistic thoughts and contemplated where the next beer was going to come from. After all, I thought we'd still qualify – so whose round was it?'

So within the hour, the Ramblas was full of Reds singing 'We only lost four-nil' with beery, cheesy grins, making the most of the black humoured opportunities. What better excuse for the most disgraceful night of physical excesses too? Amidst the next day hangovers came the stories illustrating the Mancunian sang-froid and general savvy even in defeat.

Never have I seen so many ill-looking and wrecked people collected in one room. Bloodshot eyes, sore heads and aching limbs seemed compulsory and all looked as though they had, or were on the verge, of being sick. Phil, a legend in his own bathtub, had been singing all night in La Ramblas, off his head (he'd even stripped half naked). The bar he was in was closing and they wanted to bring the table he was standing (and singing) on into the bar. He wouldn't get off and despite the barman asking him to shut up carried on. The barman came back and chucked a bucket of cold water over him, to which Phil, cool as anything, literally, didn't blink and carried on with the next verse. As Phil told me: 'It was the first shower I've had all holiday'.

We settled down for drinks around midday, to be greeted by the injured from the night before. 'Fighting with the locals/police' we enquired when one lad appeared with fresh stitches in his chin. Nothing so dramatic it turned out. He'd fallen flat on his face, whilst climbing over a hotel balcony nine floors up, trying to escape the headmaster of a Maidenhead school for girls, one of whose pupils he'd been about to get to know a lot better in the biblical sense. If we thought he looked a mess though, we should apparently have seen the girl, who ran through a plate glass door trying to escape her headmaster.

I came across two Cockney Reds down by the harbour who'd been at the 'Marsella', overdoing it on the hallucinogenic *absinthe*. They'd built these two enormous piles out of rubbish and bottles and were shouting at passers-by: 'Do you want to ride on our elephants?' Anyway, this girl comes up trying to be smart and says, 'I don't want to ride them but can I just pat them on the trunk?' Quick as a flash, one of them whips out his pecker and says 'Awlright, but don't go stuffing any peanuts up it'. Stoned as f*ck but as staunch as ever. (Salford Jim)

We came home to the worst set of headlines we'd ever seen, wearily ready to hear 'Barcelona' sung at us for the next six months. We'd been ripped off, humiliated and beaten by the Lloret police; we'd been let down by some of our support and embarrassed by the comparative ineptitude of some of our players and the manager. Yet, come the end-of-year fan surveys, what will win the Best Awayday of the Year award? In spite of everything, more than 7,000 Red Army invaders had had the hedonistic trip of a lifetime. You figure it out . . .

Team: Walsh; Parker, Bruce, Pallister, Irwin, Kanchelskis, Butt, Keane, Ince, Hughes, Giggs (Scholes).

6 November: ASTON VILLA AWAY

Final Score: Villa 1 UNITED 2

Scorers: Incey 44, Andrei 50

Attendance: 32,136

TWO BLOKES GO INTO a pub, get the shit kicked out of them, have ten pints each to dull the pain and stagger out in the small hours. They proceed to start on each other; one gets the better of the other but ends up in the gutter after being suckered by two bottle blows to the head. That's Villa and United, that is.

Actually, Villa were the best possible opponents we could have had in the wake of the Catalonian catastrophe, being the only team in the country feeling even more depressed than ours. A side largely composed of increasingly sad old men, they had been living complacently on the fading glories of their Fizzy Pop triumph, rousing themselves for a last hurrah against Inter before subsiding back into a slow slide towards retirement. They reminded you of the United of autumn '86, an outfit subsumed in *fin-de-siècle* decadence, headed by a manager whose haunted appearance indicated a man who can feel his contract disintegrating in his hands. If United were to continue their tradition of bouncing back from Euro-cockups with domestic triumphs, we couldn't have asked for better than the team humbled by 'mighty' Trabzonspor.

Thanks to the Holte End rebuilding, United only received a pathetic allocation of 500 – it was scant consolation for the ticketless that even the Club Class brigade found it difficult to get in. As usual, Red ingenuity had produced a sprinkling of our lads throughout the stadium but nothing on the scale of, say, Portman Road. Some familiar faces were notable by their absence, still nursing the wounds to wallet and pride caused by Romario & Co. and thus forced to spend the afternoon back in Manc with Andy 'n' Martin for company. This was not a vintage Red Army awayday . . .

As has become routine, we had stunning pre-match news to digest – both Hughes and Peter were out injured, joining Parker and Sharpe on the casualty roster. Hughesy had some sort of neck trouble, presumably caused by whiplash from watching Barca players streaking supersonically around him whereas Peter had turned his ankle training that morning. Poor shell-shocked Walsh was in, as was Scholesy, getting a richly-deserved start at last. Oh, for the joy of a settled side – we'd become so used to an injury-free team over the last two seasons that this constant juggling has been a bit of a culture shock. Then within minutes of the kick-off, the ungainly, Palmeresque Ehiogu butted Butt and the toothless Nicky was off. A paranoid pessimist's delight – now both our only decent Nou Camp performers were off and the lumbering McClair was on to do his impression of a Villa player *viz* too old, too slow and too tired.

It soon transpired that, hopeless as Choccy was, he played no worse than anyone else. For most of the first half, the men-in-black certainly appeared to have dressed for mourning; woeful passing, sad shooting and tearduct-pricking losses of possession ensued. They looked nervous, as if half-expecting Romario to pop out from under someone's shorts for a rematch. Fortunately, Villa were almost as bad. Saunders seemed determined to prove that selling him was the only decent decision Souness ever made; Atkinson did his best to ensure that he was removed from the tabloid list of Fergie targets. Their 'fans' were dreadful, utterly silent until their freaky goal spun off Brucey in the 28th minute for what seemed to be the hundredth deflected goal conceded this year. Even then, our vocalising platoons were still able to cut through the muffled Villa efforts, especially after Paul Ince dispelled the Stygian gloom with a gorgeously well-hung blast past the hideous Spink just before the break. As stewards waded into the Holte to turf out Reds whose only crime had been to celebrate the goal and then be attacked by Brummie half-wits, 'Paul Ince is the Governor' received yet more airplay, a testament to his total dominance of the season so far.

We came back to our seats to a rendition of *Four-nil, Barcelona* from the Brummie wits (*sic*) – no doubt we shall have to endure months of tedious references to that infamous night. City and the Scouse had already begun their carnivals the previous day, both displaying 'FCB' banners and City's North Stand in particular spending more of their time singing about Barca than their own team – but then there's little new in Bluenoses being more obsessed with us than their own lads. Andrei silenced the Villa hordes and their filthy Midlands accents by drilling home yet another nutmeg with total ferocity in the 50th minute following Eric's cunning dummy (which we were sure was quite intentional . . .)

Two-one to the champions – and the attacking half of the team promptly shut down for repairs, presumably. Cantona and Giggs had been at their most peripheral in any event, the latter contriving to miss a sitter with four minutes left; the new wunderkind Gillespie hardly had a chance to impress when he came on. The rest of the game became a Stalingrad defence as the pressure and crowd volume ratcheted inexorably upwards as the desperation increased. Walsh blossomed remarkably into that most lovable of creatures, the certain-goal-stopper, whilst Keane proved he is almost the best full back at the Club. As late as the 92nd minute, Villa were still creating and wasting the sort of chances that United would've buried by the shovel-load. But this is the trouble with old bastards like Villa – they simply can't stick it in anymore. Like any other pensioner after spunking up once, there's no way they can manage it again that day. They'll be needing incontinence pads soon too, judging by their leakages at the back. Somebody please put Ron and his decrepit regime out of their misery, it's too painful to watch.

Amidst the outpourings of relief on the coach back that the lads had fulfilled Incey's promise to win it, there was also agitated discussion of the post-Barca landscape. The Sunday papers had been full of transfer talk, with Fergie quoted as being after two English players and with the usual list of suspects appended. The previous Sunday, Channel 4 had noted that Inter were claiming to have received a definite bid for Bergkamp from us; the latest gossip was that Stan Collymore was on his way. Taking all that in conjunction with the rumours swirling around Hughesy's contract negotiations and the renewed AC interest in Giggs, the future looked about as muddy as the OT pitch after Saturday's rugby mauling. Hughes had just published his autobiography that week, seeming to draw a symbolic line under the past and was now seeking a three year deal to secure his Red future. The Club, though, had other ideas.

After the game, an insider told me that MUFC were absolutely determined that Hughes would have to sign a one year rolling option deal, just like Robbo's old one, or else he'd be leaving – they were in no mood to compromise. 'If it's good enough for Captain Marvel, it should be good enough for Sparky' was the final word in the debate. A battery of reasonable explanations preceded this: he was getting more prone to injury, he was the oldest and thus most sacrificable foreigner, the PLC would demand that no money-loss be risked and, after all, if he continued to produce the goods there would be no question of further options not being granted.

But logic does not rule in situations like this. Hughes wanted security and must have felt he deserved it after all he'd done for the club. Remember he cost us nothing and we even made a profit on the Barca deals. His last season was his best ever and his game, based on strength and ball skill rather than speed, should not suffer unduly from the ageing process. Moreover, Robbo had only been put on rolling deals at the age of 35 – wasn't it an insult to offer the same to a 31-year-old at his peak? But above all, beyond all rational argument, he is Hughsey. The Red Dragon. Sparky. The Strettie Hero. The Lion King who is the embodiment of the Red Devil Spirit. So what if things went wrong and the Club 'wasted' half-a-million, for example? The overwhelming opinion amongst fans seemed to be that we pay for all this – and we say Hughsey must stay. Just give him what he wants because if he leaves for a Premiership rival, we will never forgive the board – vengeance will be sought.

Arriving in Manchester with the glow of three stolen points to warm the cockles of Red hearts, you nevertheless sensed a cold storm on the horizon. Beyond the immediate challenge offered by the rejuvenated Bitters on Thursday, beyond even the crunch tie in Goteborg in a fortnight . . . somewhere ahead lay the prospect that this great side might be on the verge of a minor break-up caused by Euro-obsessed Fergie tinkering and that, once broken, the reassembled pieces would never work as effectively again. Bbrrrr – shut that door, Isla . . .

Team: Walsh; Keane, Bruce, Pallister, Irwin, Kanchelskis, Ince, Butt (McClair), Giggs, Cantona, Scholes (Gillespie)

10 November: MANCHESTER CITY AT HOME

Final Score: UNITED 5 Bitters 0

Scorers: Eric 24, Andrei 44, 47 & 88, Hughes 70

Attendance: 43,738

LIKE MANY OTHER RED pessimists, I'm prone to bricking it before a Manchester derby. However well we're playing and however appallingly City are flailing about, we seem to prepare for the worst and pray for the best. In retrospect, it should've been obvious that this game was only ever going to go one way – although no-one could have foreseen quite how spectacularly. All the traditional indicators of victory were in place; United under pressure to bounce back from some disaster at home or abroad, City players both past and present mouthing off in the press a week in advance, Sky cameras ready to capture yet another Blue humiliation et cetera, et cetera. This year's Terry Phelan Award for Premature Vocal Ejaculation went to Mike Summerbee, the Fat Smugness himself, who whilst squatting behind the Sky Sports desk predicted that his son would lead the Bluenoses to certain triumph. His utter post-thrashing dejection on camera was indeed a picture to savour. When will the Bitters learn that pre-match bullshitting is the occupation of the terminally class-less? As usual, Reds kept their heads down and concentrated on letting their feet do the talking on the night itself. Mouthy Magoos were left struggling to extract their size ten club feet from their gobs. Ha, ha, ha.

A Thursday night is, of course, no time for a football game, as Don Revie once famously declared; nevertheless, the pre-game buzz was the best there'd been for weeks. As knots of Bitters bolted down Matt Busby Way, Umbro jackets zipped tight to the top to conceal their colours in memory of April's forecourt shenanigans, vibrant Reds packed under the restaurants to mount a 30-minute vocal picket. Everywhere in the vicinity, people seemed to be racing to the stadium rather than engaging in the usual Warwick Road shuffle.

The news was good. No Coton or Curle for City; Peter and Hughes back for us with Keane continuing at right back, scotching worrying rumours that May might be fit again to gift his favourite team a few goals. Choccy had wormed his way back in thanks to Nicky Butt's dental disaster (whilst Giggs had somehow kept his place in the team as well as in Behr's bed) but so towering were to be the

34

performances of the King, Governor and Cossack Prince that we could have carried half-a-dozen passengers and still won.

The Bitters packed into the corner were as disappointing as their team. Where was the famous Kippax wit of which we hear so much, or the lustful anthemic singing that spawned Oasis, or even just the simple Rags-reviling temper tantrums which we enjoy so much? They registered their presence for the first ten minutes, admittedly, but save for a late and slightly-amusing cry of 'f*ck off back to London' towards K stand, that was it. Man City FC – outsung by Port Vale. . .

Indeed, for ten minutes at least, it appeared that the boys in blue were attempting to give us a serious game. They fizzed eagerly about, peppering Peter with useless 30-yarders from time to time, resembling a bunch of ten year old trialists desperately trying to impress a visiting scout. They certainly seemed pumped up, as if the pre-match sustenance had been bowls of crack rocks supplied by the Moss Side denizens; early assaults on Hughes and Giggs were typical of a side half of whom ended up in the book. The assembled Magoos growled with satisfaction. And then, after toying absent-mindedly with these little boys for quarter of an hour, the men in Red simply seized them by the throat and throttled the life out of them.

Something lit Incey's fuse – he virtually exploded in the midfield, maiming three Blues at least for the rest of the night. They retreated in terror as the Governor took control. Eric, at last, bloomed into the full Technicolour star that we'd been waiting weeks to see, unveiling his full array of demonic tricks for the camera. Even he was upstaged by the Best Supporting Actor, Andrei Kanchelskis, revelling in his favourite role of Natural Born Killer – Of Full-Backs; by the night's end, Phelan had been scattered in bloody pieces across the turf whilst the no-mark on the other flank had simply disappeared, vaporized by the death-ray passes and lazer-beam runs that United produced at will.

Eric's clean, beautiful, virginal opener was the best of the night, supplied by his new on-pitch best friend Andrei and featuring an ankle-flick of outrageous brilliance. Within minutes it became obvious that this was going to be a question of 'How many?' such was United's geometrically expanding dominance. With huge irony, we deployed the old Barca one-two – killer goals just before and after the break which crushed any remaining traces of morale or fight in the Blue ranks. Andrei's first, again from a link-up with Eric, was predictable in both its occurrence and execution. For the third goal in a row, the Ukrainian had gone for the maximum piss-take, the nutmegged goal, this time deflected in by the hapless Giggs-assaulter

Edghill. Is some Far Eastern betting syndicate running a fixed odds scam on Kanchelskis nutmeg-goals or what? The third, again from the Foreign Legion double act, was a crowd-prick-teaser of the most delicious kind. This was to be no efficient settling for 2-0 like last April; we were being promised something special, something historic, and we all had the same figure in mind.

It goes without saying that the OT crowd is near its best for any derby but as the second half progressed and K stand took to its feet in increasing delirium, the atmosphere was becoming intoxicatingly rarefied – my brothers and I almost blacked out in the final minutes, such was the charged quality of the air we were gulping. Naturally, the renditions of '18 Years' and the like were frenziedly full-throated, interspersed with the odd display of Manc irony as in the clarion cry of 'City are back' from the entire stadium. City very sportingly helped raise the temperature still further by indulging in attempts at fisticuffs, savagely late tackles and general skullduggery - but always when Red backs were turned. In face-to-face confrontation, as noted by E.T. Horton later, the Bluebottles were on full display; Summerbee's terrified surrender in the corner to Ince, for example, had lower F stand in hysterics, so typical was it of City's abject inferiority. The Bluenosed infiltrators who were ejected from the North Lower at 3-0 must have been relieved to escape witnessing such a night of shame.

As United began to turn easy defence into stunning attack within seconds in the style of true double-winners vintage, Hughesy netted the fourth with the arrogance that we love and the rest of Britain hates, picking himself off the floor, dusting himself down and casually booting the ball home as if he were in a back garden kick around. The wag who shouted 'Bring Butt on for Schmeichel' was a tad previous; for a few moments, it looked as if the Reds were content with their night's torture session – even a City goal became a possibility as the snarling Beagrie drove forward repeatedly. We, by contrast, needed the fifth as much as if it were a winner and did our vocal best to transmit this to the players. Fortunately, Andrei had personal ambition enough to grant our wish – his last-gasp hat-trick sealer completed a night of pinball impressions for Tracey and a seismic evening of history for us. The ecstatic grin as wide as the Volga on Andrei's face at that moment will never be erased from the collective Red memory; Andrei is lovable enough as he is but that night he'd have had 40,000 volunteers to bear his babies. The Nou Camp nightmare had been banished from our minds, we had moved into second and were only two points adrift of a stuttering Newcastle. But above all that, we had beaten City 5-0 – and any Red Manc understands exactly what that means.

If, in tabloid terminology, the Barca defeat was 'a mauling, a thrashing, a humiliation', what then was this? A wholesale genocidal massacre perhaps? As the fifth rifled home, heads filled with happy metaphorical visions of Bluenoses impaled on spears, pleading for mercy as Sparky and Ince took turns to mangle City genitals with their hobnailed boots. To say that this was a 'historic derby win' is to damn it with faint praise; this was a once-in-a-century, life-affirming orgasm-fest of almost unparalleled proportions. If City ever recover from this virtual execution, it will be to live on as useless vegetables, to be forever pitied. . . so no change there then. Those poor underprivileged Bluenoses had had barely a week to celebrate their impromptu twinning with the Catalans only to be given a sudden, devastating taste of what we felt like the previous week – but much, much worse. This was repaying their premature schadenfreude with maximum high-street-banks compound interest. After all, at least we didn't have real Barca fans around us to take the piss for the next six months. But the Bitterman can rest assured that be he at work, rest or play, the diligent Red will never let him forget this night, until such a time as the result might be avenged. Computer projections suggest that this might occur sometime in the 2090s. Welcome to the hell that is the rest of your life, my Blue-hued friends.

History matters. As a former history teacher, I would say that, but this is a city that has a proper pride and respect for its past; moreover, most footie fans have an encyclopaedic knowledge and understanding of their clubs' histories that would impress AJP Taylor. During those 18 minutes when the score stood tantalisingly at 4-0, 43,000 heads contained but one thought. We didn't chant 'We want five' for reasons of greed or ritual – we sought the exorcising of demons from the soul.

Let me inject a personal note. I don't want to come over all Nick Hornby (it would mess up his nice shiny head) but one of my greatest childhood traumas was the 4-0 defeat in the League Cup at City back in November '75. I was only eight but I can still recall word-for-word the vivid description my father brought home after being out in town that night; he described the howling desolation he had seen in men's faces, the atmosphere of grisly doom in Stretford and how even the cars of returning Reds crawling through Manc at hearse-pace seemed to transmit the depression of their occupants. To me, it was as if the Club itself had been mortally wounded, and all of us with it – I skived two days off school but still suffered the consequences from the mini-Bitters for months afterwards.

September 1989: you're older, you 'understand' and as an adult you can handle your grief a little more maturely - though not much. The deficit is four goals again but this time the inclusion of the number five in the scoreline makes it even worse. For the next five years, you face the witty Bitter T-shirts commemorating the fluke result; never mind that this was their one victory in the last 20 attempts, the sheer dominance of that score provided the Blues with their lifeline. However brilliant we were, however many times we stuffed them, however many trophies we won, the Bluenose could always resort to his lifetime maxim – '5-1'. And you know what? Even though I wrote in *United We Stood* that Bertie Magoo's addiction to this Maine Road Mantra was the most telling indictment possible of Blue inferiority, every time I heard or saw the numbers '5' and '1' together, I felt a little stabbing pain inside – it's either my soul or possibly my bile duct. Whatever, now I can admit it, and so can you – five years down the road, it still grated the edges of the Red heart.

So, if you are a neutral reading this, can you now understand why Old Trafford abandoned its customary reserve and grabbed each other by the pork sword that night, so to speak? In the stroke of a Kanchelskis instep, the unfulfilled desire of many a lifetime had at last been delivered to us. Yes, yes, we'd had three-nils and three-ones in which we'd played them off the park and planet; yes, we'd knocked them out of cups, robbed them of title-winning points and helped get them relegated; and yes, the timing, manner and importance of last year's double victories will probably never be surpassed. But the fact remains that most of us had never seen City properly slaughtered with a scoreline to reflect it in our lives; instead, since our promotion, we've had to endure two four-goal stuffings and live with years of the resultant taunts. You would think that the hatful of derby victories would amply compensate but it didn't quite, did it? As in *The Princess and the Pea*, Reds-in-the-bed could still feel that 5-1 or 4-0 niggling, even under the layers of subsequent derby wins. Now, thanks to the inspiration of Eric, Incey and Andrei, we regal Reds, the Kings of Manchester in perpetuity, had got our fairytale ending – for a 5-0 win demolishes all that went before it. A generation of Bitter Blues will now be haunted by the memory of the demolition derby; Moss Side urchins, when they reach puberty and finally learn to count to ten, will stay in remedial classes because they can't bring themselves to utter the word 'five'; and TV directors worried about offending family viewers will be heartened to see Red crowds at derbies giving up the two-fingered salute in favour of the five-digit wave. Mmmm . . . '5-0'. It has a lovely ring to it, doesn't it? With Zen-like simplicity, it perfectly encapsulates the imbalance of forces in Mancunian football. As the West Stand Boys would have it, 'City - you're so shit it's unbelievable.'

Team: Schmeichel; Keane, Irwin, Bruce, Pallister, Cantona, Ince, McClair, Hughes, Kanchelskis, Giggs (Scholes)

NB: Andrei's was the first league hat-trick by a Red since Hughsey's against Millwall six years ago and the first by a Red in a derby since 1960; the 5-0 win was United's biggest ever in a derby and the joint biggest win by any Fergie United team.

19 November: CRYSTAL PALACE AT HOME

Final Score: UNITED 3 Palace 0

Scorers: Irwin 8, Eric 34, Andrei 50

Attendance: 43,788

FEW PROSPECTIVE FIXTURES MAKE the heart sink faster or the knob grow softer than any tie against Palace – Wembley '90 and Selhurst '93 excepted of course. Nine November days separated one of the most intense fixtures, City, from perhaps the most mundane. On the same principle that a thousand monkeys with typewriters will eventually write *Hamlet*, Danny Baker once managed to coin a telling description – that Crystal Palace are 'a horrible, second-rate, suburban joke-club'. (Back to the bananas now, Danny.) With a mini-European Cup Final to come in just four days, it was hardly surprising that Reds' minds seemed to be focused elsewhere and perhaps understandable that vocal chords were being rested for greater efforts to come.

Furthermore, as if that wasn't enough to deflate the atmosphere, the prospects for the day looked a little murky. Palace were coming off four straight wins and were playing impeccably, away in particular; United players would surely be trying to keep some kegs of powder dry for Wednesday; finally, Ferguson was being forced to field virtually a Coca Cola Cup side. Injuries and Brucey's suspension meant Choccy, Neville, Davies and – gulp – May would be starting, to be joined by two more kids within the hour. What better opportunity for the rest of the League than to have a preoccupied, semi-Reserves United face a young, resurgent team of harriers like Palace?

Within minutes of kick-off, the omens grew even darker. Schmeichel retired hurt after ripping back muscles to be replaced by a young Pilkington, himself already deputising on the bench for Walsh. Simultaneously, half-drunken latecomers like myself realised something far worse. That referee looked familiar from past nightmares . . . Well, burn my bollocks, it's Brian 'Forest' Hill. Prepare thyself for denied penalties and disallowed goals, the end is nigh.

An Apology. Readers of *United We Stood* or any United fanzine could be forgiven for thinking that we Reds recognise Hill as the spawn of Satan, a man to be headbutted on sight etc etc. We now wish to withdraw all past venomous insults, having realised that Mr Hill is indeed a fine specimen of British refereeing ability and is welcome to officiate at any United games he likes. What remarkable eyesight and insight he must possess to have been the only man in the stadium who didn't reckon the Bogman's 'tackle' on Armstrong to be a red card assault. Again, his ability to judge that Pilkington was still holding the ball inside the area despite appearing to be on his way to the touchline with it was most creditworthy. Come back soon, y'all.

We were already one up before Hill displayed his legendary proficiency after Denis had spun in a free kick off the Palace wall only seconds after Peter had hobbled off: it began to look as if Luck had decided to be our Lady tonight after all. As the first half progressed, something rather bizarre seemed to be happening; instead of the crowd getting turned on first and then inspiring the players to sparkle, as is the usual scenario, the OT occupants remained resolutely unmoved by the opener and continued to be content to let the visitors make the vocal running. This seemed only to spur the red shirts on even more, as if they were determined to shake us out of our sloth and forcibly open our non-singing throats. Davies and Andrei above all seized the roles of cheerleaders, dancing prettily down the flanks with increasing effect until Eric imperiously thundered home the second into the Stretford goal. Still, we were rather purring like cats instead of roaring as lions but when Andrei picked up Hughsey's devastating chest-flick early in the second half before racing 50 yards to score thrillingly, we all climaxed in crescendo.

Until that point, Palace had continued to buzz about annoyingly like Sarf London wideboys window-cleaning at traffic lights. Pilks had made what looked like a Banksian save from Preece whilst Armstrong had fortuitously hit the bar; David May for much of the first half looked like a sad schoolboy who closes his eyes when he heads the ball, his clearances spinning off in all directions, none of them safe. But at 3-0, Palace were at 'Game Over' stage with no coins left to play. In symbolic recognition, Fergie pulled Andrei off to give Gillespie a run and United proceeded to take the piss for the next quarter of an hour before finally closing down the afternoon's entertainment with over 20 minutes to go.

Symbolic, too, were the crowd dynamics during the second half. Palace were only ever silent during that 15 minutes of *olé* football after the third goal and managed to muster themselves for a final 20-minute rally; they were perhaps the best away fans at OT yet. In contrast, United fans could scarcely bother to acknowledge their presence – during our quarter hour of celebration, our songs were about City and Leeds, not Palace. Occasionally, we did deign to reply when sufficiently provoked: the various 'Barca' chants met with 'Do you know where Europe is?', the amusing 'We'll see you on the motorway' and 'We support our local team' brought forth 'We support the champions' and the Dwayne-hating 'Orwight, orwight'. But in general, we seemed content to let the suburbanites amuse themselves by singing their anthem *Super Palace* (super at what? Letting in three goals?) and pursing their lips for mass 'sshhes'. For a few moments, this vocal surrender irritated me; what were we doing, letting such nobodies outsing us? But it became obvious what was happening when the Newcastle defeat was announced – the explosion of celebration across K stand and below which was the loudest of the day said it all. United fans simply cannot be arsed getting worked up against such nonentities as Palace. They are not, in any sense, our rivals – they are just fortunate enough to share the same division. Fixtures against them and their ilk are precisely the sort we'd all like to avoid in an ideal, Euro-league-dominated world; they have no magic, little history and no real meaning for us. With a team and stadium as great as ours, by all means bring on the Liverpools, Barcas and Geordies – but do we have to keep playing the Palaces and Wimbledons for the rest of eternity? With all due respect to them – ie none at all - it might be the biggest erection of their seasons to come here but I'm afraid the prospect of their visits never dampens our knickers in the slightest.

Team: Schmeichel (Pilkington); Neville, May, Pallister, Irwin, Kanchelskis (Gillespie), McClair, Ince, Davies, Cantona, Hughes

23 November: IFK GOTHENBERG AWAY – UEFA CHAMPS LEAGUE

Final Score: IFK 3 UNITED 1

Scorer: Hughesy 64

Attendance: 36,350

A GOD-FORSAKEN RAILWAY STATION on the Danish coast somewhere around 6 a.m., the ridiculously early morning after the night before. The tightly-knit pack of Reds stuffed into the solitary, unlit train carriage haven't actually been in a bed for 24 hours and it's that time when the prodigious, record-breaking volumes of alcohol intaken before and after the match are beginning to induce near-comatose states in the occupants. You know that stage: you can sleep in virtually any location, in any position, as long as some well-meaning fellow-traveller Swede isn't babbling commiserations and his life story down your lughole. When the hapless buffoon tries to look on the bright side by pointing out the mathematical possibilities of United's qualification, the two semi-slumbering fanzine editors who are listening to their mate and the Swede's discussion make their definitive statements on whether United deserve to proceed. 'No. We're shite' says one, before collapsing back onto the headrest. 'We're f*cking shite,' fine-tunes the other as he disappeared under his fantastically silly IFK ski-hat. As Nutty Norm would say, it was as simple as that. To lose appallingly badly in Europe once can be forgiven – but twice? Twice looks not just like carelessness, as Oscar Wilde might contend, but rank crappiness of an unforgivable order. Deprived of the stimulant buzz of a victory, returning Reds all over northern Europe sank into the depressed drunken stupor of defeat. Wake us up when we're European Champions will you?

'You know what really gets me?' asked Lance rhetorically as we headed back down Ullevistadt, 'I honestly never thought we could lose. Barcelona away, OK, you're half-prepared for it. But here? Here?! This is even worse than the 4-0. I'm just . . . just . . . gutted.' He'd found the *mot juste* all right.

Is there anything in the cosmos that can so devastatingly alter the mood of so many in such a short time as a bad football result? Two hours previously, thousands of multi-national Reds were reaching the apex of drunken, adrenalined pre-match euphoria to which we had been climbing relentlessly since the first arrivals in Scandinavia on

Sunday and Monday. Once again, it had indeed turned out to be better to travel than arrive.

After the Champions League fixture list was announced back in the summer, this particular tie had behaved in advance like its Swedish hosts – shy, self-effacing and huddling almost ignored in the huge shadow cast by the prospects of the much-hyped visits to Barca and Istanbul. Now, thanks to the Catalonian catastrophe and the unexpectedly good showing of IFK themselves, the Ullevi match had been transformed into a quasi-Cup tie, a throwback to the good, the bad and the ugly days of sudden death on foreign fields. Essentially, we needed a win, though a draw could still suffice depending on other teams' results, the conjunction of the Moon and Uranus etc etc. However, one thing was utterly certain and should have been branded on every player's forehead lest his colleagues forget: DO NOT LOSE. Defeat would leave us facing odds against qualification of National Lottery proportions or even instant elimination. But hey, we're the greatest team the world has ever seen, right? A team of hardened, disciplined, sumptuously-paid professionals with Euro-fire in their bellies, *n'est-ce-pas*? Surely defeat against an assortment of herring-chomping journeymen whom we had so recently put four goals past would be incredible even within the confines of a 'Brookside' script? Understand, then, that the thousands of Red Army invaders lurching across the North Sea were buzzing as much on the stimulant of confident anticipation as off the effects of the duty-free. A mini-European Cup Final watched by a proper gathering from Planet United against a team of soft, late-goal-slimers: a mouth-watering menu in Montpellierian style. Ha.

Not that everyone was going to be at the feast, of course. In the run-up to the game, the same sad lament sprang from many Red lips around town: 'Can't go, mate – all spent up in Barca' or occasionally with cruel irony 'I'm starting to save for Paris St Germain in March.' Too many Red wallets were afflicted with fiscal-sexual dysfunction - they'd shot their loads too quickly and it was too soon to get it up again. Pleasingly, this did at least mean that the MUFC Official Tour was having trouble selling seats and was still pleading for customers at the Palace game, which was hardly surprising given the experiences of many on their trip to Barca. For those determined to plough their own furrow, the usual obstacles remained, although tickets were at least slightly easier to come by in advance than those for the Nou Camp had been. Scandinavian Ferries meanwhile were aping their gutless colleagues at Brittany by refusing to take any footie fans anywhere that week; people who'd booked weeks in advance were getting calls from the company cancelling their reservations on the slightest pretext, with 'being from Manchester' apparently condemnation enough.

UF Tours took a full complement on their one-night package, still able to find ample customers despite the reported failings on their Barca trip; others, such as the vanguard from the *Red Issue/United We Stand* elite, took as fiercely independent a line as possible by sorting tickets from IFK and travelling as leisurely and luxuriously as possible via Copenhagen and its fleshpots.

That, of course, is only half the story. Just as in the mass population removal that was the Red expedition to Spain, Gothenberg was the Naked City, full of a thousand stories. Haggard individual Reds, clumped together in little raiding parties, told the usual myriad tales of the bonkers' itineraries, illegal manoeuvres and shameless freeloading that constituted their own voyages. By shared ticketlessness and poverty, somehow the dedicated lumpenproletariat had made it, as they always do. Some Brummie Reds had managed to stowaway on a container ship before blagging tickets by pretending to be the Midlands Branch of the IFK Blue Angels; one Londoner with whom the police are keen to speak in four different countries had sneaked through with the aid of three false passports; a group of particularly wasted Mancs had taken five days to get there, having broken down, crashed or had vans robbed during a journey-total of 15 unforeseen stoppages. Most impressive of all was the Salford lad who claimed to have scored with five different women en route, each of whom then drove him another stage towards Sweden so that he'd got there for free. Those disinclined to believe him were later horrified to see him leave the Bryggeriet with two Andersonian blonde babes . . .

After travelling to Barca with the 'officials' and vowing never to repeat the experience, I took the diametrically opposed route of hitching up with the 'fanzine' tour who were wending their way through Denmark to get to Gothenberg for Tuesday afternoon. Somewhere en route, I picked up a copy of *The Sun* which had a story about the beer consumption of the touring Australian rugby team who had apparently demolished 16,000 tinnies during their stay in Britain. This was supposed to be a gastronomic feat of *Guinness Book* magnitude but a few hours of observation and some quick calculations led me to conclude that the Aussies are virtual teetotallers in comparison to the legendary behemoths who were imbibing entire bars all around. The greatest shock to the system for all those arriving in Scandinavia had, of course, been the price of beer. It's all very well having megastrength Elephant beer on draught wherever you go but when it's six or seven quid a pint, you begin to hanker for your local Boddies emporium. Not that this dissuaded Mick, Chris, Phil and their cohorts from establishing 12-hour sessions across the centres of Copenhagen and Gothenberg during which the amount of wedge passing over the bar must have exceeded the GDP of small African nations. Somebody had indeed remarked beforehand that it would be as well to 'have your drinking legs on' but he'd neglected to mention the large reservoir-cum-septic tank that needed to be affixed to the stomach as well. Monday night in Copenhagen, for those who could remember it amongst the fanzine crew, swag-pedlars and assorted stragglers who were around, was a titanic effort: everybody got completely sunk. With the prescience of the knowledgeable traveller, several revellers also made the most of the red light delights, aware that Gothenberg held little in the way of actual sensual pleasures – not, at least, of those for which you pay. One or two of the luckier lads got close enough to the Danish sex-goddesses who abounded in disconcerting numbers to fall instantly in love; the consensus seemed to be that the Swedish Agnethas would be a much tougher proposition for the budding Casanovas amongst us, so now was the moment to dispense the Ribbed Featherlites.

Let's face it: Gothenberg is not the first city Dionysus would've picked for a weekend of debauched excess. Travelling to the centre from the airport, the place appeared to be something like St Petersburg with money; bleak, uniform, almost grandiose but hardly welcoming. Appallingly, the beer was even more expensive than in Denmark and the women that bit less impressed by leery Mancunian beer-monsters than the Danes. The carnally-obsessed found to their disappointment that the second city of the ultimate porn-exporting nation had a red light district that consisted of two sex shops and a slightly disreputable bar. Everywhere else was clean, polite, proper and passion-less, with a local populace to match; even the most low-rent bars wouldn't have been out of place in the glossiest environs of Manchester's city centre. Inveterate sightseers who had at least found the Little Mermaid and the hippy commune in Copenhagen soon realised that Gothenberg's fish-gutting factories hardly constituted essential visits and joined the rest of the assembling Red clans in the downtown bars, busy spending their life savings. Six quid a pint in a bar, not that much cheaper in the Systembollaget off-licences which are only open till 6 p.m., age restrictions everywhere that can bar even

23-year-olds . . . what is it with Swedes and booze that makes them vote for governments which try to stop them doing what they clearly enjoy as much as the next man? A local smugness claimed 'we use the booze taxes to support our great welfare state, so we pay up happily in bars' but this is clearly bollocks. Sweden used to be a nation of complete alcoholics, like modern Russia but with more suicides, when beer was cheap in the 1930s – the taxes are surely there to prevent them from a) drinking themselves into comas b) littering the roads with smashed–up Volvos and c) getting brewer's droop in the midst of a porn-flick-shoot. All very typically Swedish and sensible but how about cut-price drinks for us improverished tourists? We don't mind the odd lager–coma . . .

Nevertheless, there are 22 decent bars inside one square kilometre in central Gothenberg and by Tuesday evening, Reds could be found in most of them. (I know, because in the interests of research, I toured them all.) The first plane and train loads had arrived mid-afternoon with another consignment to follow at around ten p.m.; the preponderance of Sharp tops marked out the new arrivals from the colour-free hardcore who'd got there early. The first arrests soon followed, police touring the city to pick up a collection of alleged forgers who'd been trying to offload dodgy twenties. If these were the same reprobates who'd been trying to do the same up and down the Warwick Road before the Palace game, good riddance; ripping off fanzine sellers and barrow lads is neither big nor clever. Still, you can't help but reflect that ten years ago, the scene would have been much different, doubtless dominated by bunches of fives rather than rolls of twenties.

Of course, precisely those guys who would have been the ones wielding the fists ten years ago were all there in Gothenberg, despite the efforts of all those security agencies with their 'banned hoolies' lists. Long-serving Cockney Reds paced warily around many a plush hotel lobby, instantly identifiable by the London-smart threats, glinting of gold bracelets and the fact that the more subtly attired Mancs were ignoring them. *Plus ça change.* Quietly intense Northern lads sitting in bar corners would be revealed by companions as 'X, from the Chelsea kick-off' or 'Y, back from a Valencian jail', lads whose troubled lives still had to find time for the Reds in Europe. Amidst the hordes of young lads for whom Dave Sexton is just a name from bedtime horror stories, these older characters whose faces speak of past lives in a very different football universe provided the moment with a sense of historic, if uneasy, continuity.

Sometime during Tuesday night, the 'Auld Dubliner' Irish-style pub off the Kungsportsplats was designated the unofficial HQ of the invading Reds by virtue of the usual subconscious and/or telepathic process that occurs at aways. With the triple-tiered 'Gamle Port' and 'O'Leary's' only yards away, hundreds of Reds were to venture no further than this little corner of a foreign field, forever British. Well, rather more than British actually: as the place began to pack out once more during Wednesday lunch-time, it became clear that the clarion call for Red support had been heeded well beyond our own island borders. Masses of Norwegians and Danes plus a smattering of Germans, Stockholmian Swedes and other assorted foreigners had also made the pilgrimage; it was rumoured that a pub in the north of the city had 500 mad Oslo Reds in it, doing exactly what their emissaries in the 'Dubliner' were: singing our songs in bizarre accents, throwing in their own hurdy-gurdy anthems, getting as pissed as possible and taking their once-in-a-lifetime chance to schmooze with real Manc Reds.

Their motivation was admirable; said a Dane to me, 'I'm here because I love United like I love my mother – and because I f*cking hate the Swedes.' However accustomed you think you are to the phenomenon of the Red Planet, it is still a shock to hear a 20 year-old from Düsseldorf discuss the relative demerits of Paddy Roche and Tommy Jackson in English apparently learned from British football commentaries. There is perhaps something slightly disconcerting about these adherents of United internationalism. Sometimes you feel that foreigners supporting the Reds so fervently is a bit, well, 'cousin-kissing' if you see what I mean – technically legitimate but morally uncertain in a vaguely nauseous way. Perhaps all that City Manc-centrism crap has had its effect and spoiled what should be the unalloyed joy of nations uniting under a Red Flag. Whatever, the lads being offered 100 krone for their United Members' badges by drunken Swedish Reds weren't complaining – although the burly Stockport Red who found himself being repeatedly smothered in slobby kisses by a German shouting 'I love you Manchester' had probably had enough *entente cordiale* for one day.

Wednesday afternoon in the 'Dubliner'. Kick-off is five hours away but both levels are crammed. Downstairs, an impromptu vocal concert is underway, conducted in Pete Boyle's enforced absence by the Cantona lookalike who's now called 'Eric' by all and joined by masses of beered-up celebrants. It seems like the whole of K stand has squeezed itself in although most under-20s have been barred and forced to trot down the Avenyn to find bars to drain dry. Two hours pass by in the flash of an alcoholic daydream but the singers refuse to let up; tables are overturning, the floor is carpeted in glass and the bar is 'doing a week's business in an hour' to quote the delightful pump-maiden. Sporadically, knots of police force their way in to gaze upon the Bacchanalian scene, barely able to supress the huge grins that such gatherings always induce in observers. 'So, where are the English hooligans then?' asks one. 'Back in Leeds, mate,' comes the instant reply. The pig laughs out loud – it was that kind of day. Outside, clutches of bemused Swedes look in through the windows and stand gawping for aeons as the Edgeley Reds put on a show for them; 'Welcome to the EEC' yells one topical wit. And welcome to Nineties away trips: the crack is everything, the beer, strumpets and song – 'among the thugs' is no more.

With a slightly tactless chorus of *No Surrender to the IRA* and a *Rule Britannia* finalé, the 'Dubliner' disgorged its drunken but buzzing masses who headed unsteadily for the Ullevi Stadium a mere ten minutes stagger away. IFK fans materialised as if from nowhere to join the match-bound throng, bantering politely in soft-edged Scandinavian style with the Red-bedecked Danes and Norwegians who were tagging along with us. The Ullevi is only used for the bigger games, IFK being unable to fill it for clashes with the likes of Smorgasbord Athletic; tonight, their own versions of the day-trippers and part-timers had turned up, drawn as much by the lustre of United as by the prospects of qualification. Face-painted 12-year olds are, it seems, a universal currency these days.

The Ullevi works like the Nou Camp in reverse; stunningly impressive in a *Star Trek* kind of way from the outside with its modernistic architecture and roller-coaster roof but mundanely terrestrial within. Cursed by that bane of Euro-stadia, the pitch-side athletics track, part of it looks like Endsleigh league transplants with exits and 'gangways' from a pre-Taylor world of death. Most worryingly, the pitch looked to be about as playable as Fred West's garden, as bad even as Old Trafford's in the winter of '91/'92 – not a good omen at all. And for the first time during our stay, the weather was beginning to live up to its billing i.e. bollock-freezing for us but almost skinny-dipping weather for our hardy hosts. (Shivering up on the top terrace, completely surrounded by IFK, I thought fondly of the body-stocking a lad had displayed under his kit in the pub; 'borrowed it off me bird' he had beamed, although his mate later told me the bloke wore it for kicks whatever the temperature . . .) Sad soothsaying types like me take climate changes seriously. Remember

how weeks of windy weather came to an abrupt end on the day
Hughes scored his Wembley volley and how it didn't really piss down
again until the Final – just as it was raining goals on the pitch? All
right, maybe you don't, but the sudden onset of a soul-biting chill
minutes after kick-off in the Ullevi spoke symbolic volumes to me.

At least United fans could sense they were part of the stadium this
time, unlike in Barca where the dizzy heights of our encampments
made you feel you were celestial observers of the crowd, not
participants in it. The 'officials' had turned up in sufficient numbers
to constitute an impressive-looking presence to the right of the goal
where Hughesy scored; at the other end, three distinct legions had
formed. The UF Tours crowd took the right flank, the massed
Scandinavian Reds had seized the left, whilst the core crew from the
fanzine tour had planted themselves directly behind the goal, shoving
the Swedes in their section behind them. The emblem of 'unofficial'
United abroad, the 'United We Stand' flag, was proudly affixed to the
fence and with the eventual arrival of a certain 'zine editor, fresh from
three days luxury in the Sheraton, all the familiar elements were in
place. Unfortunately, so was David May.

Of course, it would be invidious and cruel to blame one individual
for so clearly a team effort as the subsequent disaster but with Davey
boy, you just can't help yourself. Within a minute, he'd committed his
first blundering foul of the night, causing the free-kick which led to
Hughesy's booking and consequent suspension: within ten minutes, it
was obvious to all that Blomqvist would have enough energy left after
repeatedly savaging May to give Brucey a few duffings-up too. By
half-time – well, by the 20 minute mark actually – Reds in our end
were howling for May to get off the pitch by any means possible.
When it looked as though he was getting a yellow card, one
traumatized Red yelled 'make it red! make it red!'

By this point, we were already a goal down. It was symptomatic of
the night's cruelty that although May had stepped up with the rest of
the line and yet, unbelievably, 'dependable Denis' had played the scorer
on. More portents of doom followed. McClair and Andrei both had
the sort of chances you'd seen them put away a dozen times a season,
but not tonight. Choccy's little looped header found Ravelli's fingers
instead of dribbling across the goal-line as is usual; Andrei chose to flick
at his effort instead of drilling it unstoppably home as he'd been doing
all autumn. Elsewhere, unaccustomed sights abounded – Incey unable
to stamp his authority on midfield, Eric trying desperately to wield an
influence and dropping ever deeper in his forlorn quest, Hughes being

bundled off the ball with depressing regularity et cetera, et bloody cetera. IFK may not be a brilliant side but at least they were showing form, playing like a unit and keeping their cool. By contrast we looked ragged and hot-tempered and Eric in particular seemed as if he was heading for an Istanbulian tantrum. Half-time came as a relief, as some half-expected a Nou Camp-style second just before the break – at least at only 0-1 we had the chance to effect running repairs and save us from yet another continental calamity.

Stunned perhaps by the appalling vista of elimination that was opening up before us, our support had not been at vintage levels with the UFT contingent being especially disappointing after their sterling efforts in Barca. The locals were not much better with only their version of K stand, the 'Blue Angels' to our top left, displaying much vocal talent. Their indecipherable, pause-strewn chants were impressively coherent on the occasions that they did get it together but were met with blank responses from the rest; the OT syndrome of day-tripper-dilution seemed to be at work. We spent half-time plotting May's assassination, laughing at the intoxicated locals falling over and, in big R.'s case, thumping annoying Swedes who insisted on shoving flags in our faces. A collection of Swedish babes fronted a marching band, who stopped in front of the main stand to display their pert little bottoms in a dance for the assembled season-ticket holders; our kind of executive privilege indeed and rather better entertainment than the arse-show we get at OT in Fred the Red. However, the main half-time consolation was that the second half couldn't be worse – and for precisely nineteen minutes, it wasn't. Slowly, deliberately but distinctly, we climbed our way back from the precipice edge in every way. Some semblance of passing began to occur on the pitch and half chances began to materialise; on the terraces, the officials started redeeming themselves for their Nou Camp no-show, inspiring our end to rouse ourselves once more. The stately, drawled 'Yooo-nyyy-tid' that comes so naturally when you're alcoholically challenged was replaced by the urgent, repeated, staccato 'United', a sure sign that life is speeding up to a climax which duly and deservedly arrived in the 64th minute with a goal of pure simplicity. May to Eric's head, down to Hughes and in the net for 1-1 . . . how ridiculously easy it looked after an hour of ham-fisted labouring. Predictably, ecstatic scenes ensued, as you would expect when your entire universe has been transformed in a split-second. Hughes had done for our Euro-season what he had for our double last April; our beloved, heroic leader had saved us all once more. Hadn't he?

Such was the cruelty of that night that even a 'momentary' celebration wasn't allowed to last out the moment itself. I for one barely had time to clear my vision, lift my head out of my neighbour's frenzied embrace and look up to watch the bedlam at the officials' end when I caught sight of May careering towards us in hopeless pursuit of a Swedish winger; the instant he was disgracefully allowed to cross the ball, everything began to go black around the edges of my vision, like the close of some 1930s' movie. The ball was in the net, 'The End' was on the screen and our European dream had become a nightmare from which you can't awaken.

The rest was supremely irrelevant. At the moment when United's performance had sobered up and begun to walk, we had been smashed all over the road by a juggernaut. May, at last, was hauled off to spare him and us further humiliation down the flank but in a typically ironic moment, it was his replacement Neville whose slip led to the penalty which made it 3-1 seven minutes later. Nineteen minutes of hope at the start of the half gave way to a final 19 minutes of hell. We had chances but none were ever going to go in from the moment they were struck, not on a night like this. Nor did we deserve otherwise; Ince's sending off for his introduction to the Italian ref of East End vernacular vocab added an extra, final brush-stroke of shame to the gruesome picture, as if any more were needed. Most of us weren't even aware he'd gone until hours later which tells you something about a) the catatonic state we were in and b) the lack of impact Ince was having on the game anyway. As is apt for such a huge, dramatic club, when we f*ck up we really f*ck it up big-style don't we?

A minute to go. Defeat is now mathematically certain and, as far as we knew for several hours yet, so is elimination. The Swedes are doing – gulp – a Mexican wave, that ultimate symbol that you've been outclassed and are having the piss taken although the locals don't do it with malicious intent. The Swedes have behaved impeccably towards us throughout and there are words of consolation for us that are actually sincere. The players later declare that they want to beat Barca to help United and you believe them. A few local wannabees try to taunt us from the safety of their moving cars but being verbally attacked by a Swede is like being savaged by a dead herring, as Dennis Healey might say. There's no outlet for your disgusted disillusion or your bitter anger here but the bar tap. There is no trouble, no street clamour, no hostility; the scores of circling panda cars are to be obsolete. I pass by the 'Dubliner' to which the beaten have retreated; the songs are still being sung and the glasses drained but the

51

atmosphere has changed from stag night to funeral reception. The f*ck-it-let's-party black humoured *joie de vivre* of Barcelona's aftermath is much harder to summon up now; 'We only lost three-one' doesn't quite have the same ring does it? Those of us who are heading back that night are grateful for the speedy exit – there's no wish to linger at the scene of death, however much we might dread the gleeful reaction of the Bitters & Co. back home. Draining the dregs of the duty-free on the night ferry, we know that notwithstanding the lifeline offered by the Barca result, we are out; no spring trips to Paris, no San Siro showdowns, no Rotterdamesque Final carnivals. As a consequence, we might all be financially better off come May but spiritually, we'll all be unspeakably poorer. Shit.

We meet a Swede on the way back who tells us he is 'quite pleased' by the result. To our suggestion that he's being rather understated about such a momentous victory, he replies that Swedes are a level-headed lot: 'We don't really care that much about winning or losing, we just like to play the game.' Spitting with frustrated incomprehension, Steve B. speaks for us all. 'That's the trouble with you lot; you just don't know how it feels to be gutted. We are totally gutted. See?' That word again – it says it all. Another lad related a story from his aftermatch drinking session. He'd actually come across a few Swedes who were up for a bit of wound-salting and he'd had enough of it. He decided to demonstrate to them what it means to be a United fan, what depth of feeling runs through Red veins. Briefly, he reminded them of the Munich disaster, then stood on a chair and sang the entire version of the unbearably poignant *Flowers of Manchester* with everything he had. 'By the end, they were in total silence. Two of 'em were virtually in tears. That was the end of their piss-taking.' And in that reminder of the stupidity of Shankly's famous maxim, I took the smallest consolation. Football isn't more important than life or death; we'd lost a hugely important game but at least we were all going home relatively unscathed, including the drunk who'd fallen off the back of a Swedish train . . . Thirty-six years ago we'd had no such good fortune. We all use the words 'disaster' and 'catastrophe' to sum up our footballing lowlights but anyone with a feeling for this Club knows that all such terminology is relative. This team will, one day, be back in Europe to fight again – another never had the chance.

The media could not believe their luck – a second feeding-frenzy around United's corpse in the space of three weeks, a chance for every embittered ex-Anfield hack and sad tabloid wordmangler to do his worst. Ince, for months now portrayed as the great English warrior and pre-eminent midfielder of his generation became in Patrick Barclay's words 'the chief standard-bearer for the yob society'. United, we were told, were simply not good enough under any circumstances if we could be beaten by journeymen such as IFK, who were apparently our tactical and technical superiors. (Obviously, it was another unrelated IFK that we trounced 4-2 only eight weeks before.) May was singled out by all, most damningly on *The Sun*'s Faxline ('vote him City's Player of the Year' wrote one wit) whilst the less hysterical pointed out the folly was Fergie's for persevering with the semifit misfit at full back in the first place. Blackpool Red Mick had it exactly right; why not play Neville from the off and if not, why replace May with another full back when you're two down? Other factors were less contentious – the foreigners rule for this particular match had not been as burdensome as usual but the injuries to five habitual first-teamers, overlooked by some observers, had surely been a wound too far?

As for the bigger question as to whether United and English football in general are not up to the European challenge because of fundamental flaws in our game, who can really tell? Is it just that we played badly on two specific nights or is there more to it? Bobby Charlton, who I hope knows what he's talking about, said that it was simply a case of not doing ourselves justice – after all, we did beat IFK and come within a penalty appeal of doing the same to Barca. We can't have become no-hopers overnight – and just because Blackburn, Newcastle and Villa blew out too, it doesn't mean England as a nation is doomed to defeat as Arsenal and ourselves in '91 seemed to demonstrate. Perhaps, as Blackpool's Mick suggested, the Cup Winners Cup doesn't actually prove anything – we won it in the pre-restriction days against less than the best in Europe, some might say. Perhaps we have lulled ourselves into a false sense of Euro-security and that we're just not as good as we think. Certainly, the likes of Rehn, Blomqvist, Bakero and Stoichkov seemed to be on a different plane to Ince, Pally, Bruce *et al* but are they really that ineffably superior for all time or was it just that they had a good day at the wrong time for us?

It is hard to believe that the United that beat Newcastle and City could be said to be so inferior to continentals; it is hard to believe that a defence unbreachable at home could be so devastated in Europe. Can it be true that Pallister, a defensive demi-God who made that tackle in Istanbul and who shines against the best for England, is to be condemned as a sad old English centre-half donkey simply by virtue of the fact that the Catalans had a good night against him? Say it ain't so Joe. Maybe I'm blind to the truth, a hopeless believer in the heroes who've brought us so much domestic glory but I can't accept that on the evidence of two dodgy games. We must dismantle a machine so lovingly assembled and hope that whatever replacements we get do the business next time. Nor can I accept that we must forego all our Euro ambitions and face a decade as also-rans. It's all very well saying 'Buy English' but if there isn't a better English winger than Andrei or a better creator than Eric or a better powerdriver than Keane, what's the point? By all means, make one or two changes and refinements but don't destroy the essence of this still-great side. By all means, let us be less arrogant about our place in the European scheme of things but don't tell me that we can never be Champions. It took Matt Busby four attempts to win that damned trophy; Alex has only had two. If, after two more attempts, a full-strength United is still getting ritually humiliated in Europe, then I'll believe the doom-merchants. Until then, the prosecution case remains unproven and the tabloid jury should keep its mouth shut. United's European war is roughly where Churchill's was in 1940 – there is still all to play for and this is no time to lose our nerve. If these players win the League, give them their chance to make amends – they would deserve that at least.

Team: Walsh; May (Neville), Bruce, Pallister, Irwin, Ince, McClair, Kanchelskis, Cantona, Hughes, Davies (Butt)

26 November: ARSENAL AWAY

Final Score: Arsenal 0 UNITED 0

Attendance: 38,301

THIS WAS TURNING OUT to be some month for the sort of death-obsessed Mozzer-fan Red who likes depression and funereal atmospheres. One week you're administering the last rites to rivals you've just slaughtered like City and the Geordies, the next you're shouldering the coffin that contains your crushed European reputation. En route to an eerily subdued Highbury with belly still bilious from Swedish lager and bitter defeat, the colours of burial were to be seen everywhere. The black United team coach that proceeded hearse-like down Gillespie Road displayed pale grey players' faces through dim charcoal windows, the team inside later to emerge on to the pitch in fitting black mourning garb. A forlorn Bobby Charlton walked alone towards the entrance, exuding the gloom of the beaten – I'd like to think that the plaster covering his nose was necessitated by him smashing his face on a Gothenberg bar in the drunken stupor of defeat but I doubt it. A fellow Red surveying the scene turned to me and said: 'We're gonna get hammered today. Three-nil. A Wright hat-trick and May to blame for 'em all.' He had a manic, intense gleam in his eye and spoke with the doomed certainty of a criminal facing a firing squad. Mentally, I prepared the day's obituary.

Fortunately, Paul Merson had picked up the week's Grobbelaar Award by announcing his coke addiction in the *Daily Mirror* the previous day ('Well, we knew it couldn't have been speed,' quipped a Gooner) thus causing the home club and their fans to appear as preoccupied by events elsewhere as we were. The pre-match atmosphere in the bar below United's half of the South Stand was both anti-climactic and unreal; those who'd managed to grab what was one of the hottest away tickets so far – and thus many familiar faces were absent – still seemed to have their heads filled with hellish Ullevi flashbacks. Or perhaps they were having *déjà vu* from Villa Park; once again, having only just staggered back from Euro-disaster, we were simply going to have to get our heads down, battle through somehow and get back to Manc to tend the wounds to our bodies and psyches.

Not that the assembled Gooners were going to play nurse for us, naturally. 'There's only one team in Europe' might not yet have been technically correct but it was the obvious favourite to be stuck on repeat on the Arsenal vocal jukebox which was situated right next to us in the South Stand. Now Highbury is a nice ground; any footie purist can appreciate the way it nestles seductively within the bosom of the local community's terraced streets, how you can almost lean over from a front row seat and finger the touchline (fetish tip) and how the video screens give you an instant replay of all the fabulously vicious fouls, minute-by-minute offside decisions and referee-abuse that are Highbury's usual currency. The redevelopment has been almost tasteful, despite the fact that 2,000 away fans are expected to piss inside a cupboard; the way that the South Stand is designated as the singing area for home and away to lock antlers is creditable. Such a pity, then, that all this is so wasted on the Arsenal fans themselves. Perhaps they are all on coke down there and it has addled their synapses so much that their brain functions have sludged down to Little & Large standards of witlessness; what else can explain their choice of choral rendition? Chanting 'Stoichkov and Romario' whilst waving the odd Barca shirt might have been vaguely amusing three weeks ago but by now was as stale as a Paul Hince joke. Veg introduced the Gooners to the concept of topical terrace repartee at this point by instantly launching into 'Merson – and a line of coke . . .' Sadly, his instructional example of telling terrace point-scoring was lost on them. Singing 'Do you come from Manchester?' when most of your support commutes from the home counties is laughably pathetic, the equivalent of an Adams' own goal. Such too was their attempt to rag Ince and Eric for their disciplinary shortcomings which was a little rich coming from a club currently undergoing mass dope-testing. (Isn't that what they do to horses? I suppose given the amount of donkeys in the Arsenal team, that's wholly appropriate.) Boring, boring Arsenal – boring, boring fans. Reds contented themselves with a medley of 'Who the f*ck do you support?', 'One Leicester City' and, of course, 'Campiones', the only song to which there can be no effective reply.

In truth, the Red Army, diluted by the lack of Boyle & Co and the surfeit of Club Classers, were only at half-strength all afternoon but at least mounted the odd telling attack. The team, in contrast, showed their strength only too obviously – unfortunately, this was reflected in studmarks on Arsenal limbs rather than chances on the Seaman goal. For some reason, Arsenal and United bring out the howling, hacking beast in each other, like two sets of werewolves who always meet at full moon. For the Red fan, this is entirely understandable – in a Pavlovian process, you see an Arsenal shirt, you think Wembley '79 and you're immediately ready to chew jugulars. What gets the players going, however, is a mystery – it just seems to be a virus that's transmitted down the generations. At Highbury, it's probably passed on through the sharing of needles . . .

The referee, as is so wearingly habitual these days, was little help. Booking sweet, innocent Gillespie after 20 seconds with a macho swagger, then proceeding to ignore assaults by Morrow and Bould within minutes boded ill for all who recalled our last visit here. The ref's name was Kelvin, which says everything about his gene-pool; show me a man called Kelvin and I'll show you a set of parents who can't spell 'Kevin'. A tiresome, fraught and bad-tempered encounter unfolded untidily between two teams who'd had a crappy week – imagine a grumpy Sunday park game with two hungover sides who've been nagged by the wife all week and who are likely to gob the next bastard who goes through them and you have it in a nutshell. What attacking play there was came from the Gunners who nevertheless

found Pally virtually impassable; when they did break through, Smith
ballooned over whilst Pally saved another on the line late on. We were
all fight but no fluidity; if the players' hearts were certainly in it, their
heads were elsewhere as we showed virtually none of our usual
creative powers. On the day, our wings were clipped by efficient
Arsenal backs but in a larger sense, our wings had been savagely
burned flying too close, Icarus-like, to the European sun. In the
circumstances, we were going to do well to draw – our defence, at
least, was demonstrating their continued capacity to hold any domestic
attack with even May at centre back refusing to give any goals away.
Be thankful for minor miracles.

Oh, we had our moments: Denis and Hughsey did at least trouble
Seaman; Choccy, playing surprisingly well in both covering May and
getting forward, was robbed by Dixon at the fateful moment. Even
Pally almost turned goal-provider for Eric at one point before the
game descended into madness. For the second time in four days, it was
becoming increasingly obvious to nerve-ridden Reds that someone
was going to be sent off but like West Midlands Police fitting up the
innocent suspect, we'd fingered the wrong villain. On Wednesday,
they closed the book at half-time – surely Eric was about to do a
Galatasaray? Instead, it was Ince who went; similarly now, as Incey
himself carved up Jensen and Dickov, his dismissal appeared imminent.
Yet with 12 minutes left, having won a free-kick a split-second
previously, Hughes went through and tickled Morrow ever-so-gently.
The brittle-boned boy span like a Catherine Wheel and Hughes,
unjustly booked earlier, was on his way with a cheery 'f*ck off'
parting shot to the ref. Even the Reverend Trevor, patron saint of
fence-sitting non-confrontation on *Match of the Day*, bludgeoned the
ref for booking Hughes in the first place and for allowing anyone who
fancied it to pile through the back of his legs throughout the game. To
hear Brooking repeat what we have always said about Hughesy's lack
of protection was amazing enough but for him to slag the ref like that
was akin to seeing Mother Theresa do a porn flick – respect is due, as
another ex-Hammer would say.

Incredibly enough, Arsenal refused even to attempt a final sword
thrust. We watched in wonder as the team and their fans turned their
attention to securing a nil-nil draw, this being the one art form at
which Gooners excel unless you include snorting drugs, molesting
strippers and drunkenly crashing cars. The habits of history are clearly
hard to break. The right side of the South stand was subsumed in
silence, leaving us to mock their wretched timidity, sing *We shall not*

be moved and watch the lads rescue a result. Gooners queuing outside Arsenal tube station actually seemed quite content afterwards but then this game had been well down to the normal Highbury standards they expect; it is remarkable that a team tipped for the title pre-season by the southern-based hacks had declined to such an extent that they thought a 0-0 against ten off-form men was a good result. Poor, ugly Arsenal – once they were boring but good, now they're just boring and mediocre. If Merson is to be punished, there can be no stiffer sentence than having to watch his team from the stands for the rest of the season. Though that's enough to drive a man to heroin . . .

As for the travelling Reds filing back into Manchester towards midnight, we may have seen the worse game of football since, ooh, last Wednesday but at least we had returned from the fray unbowed. Instead of rolling around in muddy self-pity, we should reflect on the triumph of recovery that getting a point with ten men at Highbury truly represents. Admittedly the best entertainment of the day was provided by the half-time computer game on the vid screens but there are times when all you can do is fight and that we surely did. We have had to come back from stunning, atrocious Euro-defeats twice in a month to face immediate tricky away games and have come through unscathed: twice, a defence shredded by foreign invaders has miraculously repaired itself to repel domestic boarders. The Highbury game provided further evidence of the unmistakable parallels with the 'Ides of March' crisis, especially with the repetition of a red card, but we came through that and we can come through this. As long as the fight is still there, the flair will surely follow.

Team: Walsh; Neville, May, Pallister, Irwin, Kanchelskis (Butt), McClair, Ince, Gillespie (Davies), Cantona, Hughes

NB: Two days later, the injured Schmeichel was ruled out for a further six weeks.

PS: After the match, an enraged Martin Edwards burst into the ref's room and yelled at him for several minutes, at one point telling the hapless official, 'You are the worst referee I've seen in 20 years of watching United.' The ref's response was to tell Edwards, 'I don't think you should be in here', and to report the matter to the FA. Top stuff, Martin – what's next? Would you like to come down to Chelsea with us and kick a few heads in?

3 December: NORWICH CITY AT HOME

Final Score: UNITED 1 Norwich 0

Scorer: Eric 36

Attendance: 43,789

SO UNITED RETURN TO Old Trafford for the first time since our humiliating appearance in that Swedish S&M farrago, now only second in the League and in the throes of a dual injury and confidence crisis, and what is the pre-match hype? Forget football, folks: today saw the opening of the new United megastore behind the Strettie, to which you were all directed by the programme supplement, Man U Radio, Uncle Tom Tyrell and all. What timing – there's clearly a great ironist at work somewhere behind the scenes. Forgive me for using the word symbolism yet again but who could fail to see the significance of what now lies behind the grave of the hallowed Stretford End: a temple to day-tripping commercialism facing multiple entrances to various lounges, suites and classes of 'superior' stand? What was once 'our' piece of the stadium has been comprehensively gutted, reformed and christened fit for family habitation; the entire area has indeed 'gone west'.

We are left with the east end nowadays, the last redoubt of football's working classes, just as the east ends of Glasgow and London remained the proletarian heartlands whilst the rest of those cities underwent gentrification. Not that this means everyone in the east stand is a horny-handed son of toil; the football working class is something non-economic, more a state of mind if anything. It consists of those who still remember what the work of a true supporter is and are still prepared to do it: it's not just a matter of turning up and coughing a tenner, it's recognition of your duty to sing, chant, create atmosphere and get behind the lads. (In an ideal world, stewards should be chucking punters out for *not* singing – after all, the non-singer is virtually aiding and abetting the enemy, isn't he?) Sadly, it seems that the majority at OT these days have abandoned the traditional ways and rushed to embrace the new era of Thatcherite modernisation. To them, football is merely an entertainment solely confined to the pitch and on a par with a theatre or cinema trip. The public are there to consume, not participate – we're all 'customers' now. Like the miners taking a final stand against the forces of 'progress', the working minority seem to be losing the class struggle.

Market forces, under a sympathetic Edwards government, are apparently winning as much at Old Trafford as elsewhere. How long before we noisy, swearing, singing 'yobboes' become the officially condemned 'enemy within'?

Actually, I don't know why I was so generous as to include the East Lower in the paen to that end of the ground. Out of necessity and choice, I get to sit in virtually every part of the ground during the season and therein sample the different levels of atmosphere – or the lack of it. Against Norwich, most sections of this stand were a disgrace, despite the encouragement they were receiving from a K stand hardcore. I did a headcount in my block: of around 150 'Reds' that were visible to me, only 18 were singing at every opportunity. At least 70 never opened their mouths save for inserting bits of dog pie, this despite being situated right next to the away fans, a prime location for those who need a bit of incitement to sing. Across the pitch, the West Stand Boys were too true to their name - like children, they were seen but never heard. Some have been saying that the atmos had been improving this season; perhaps they spoke too soon.

Fortunately, the Norwich farmboys who'd tractored up the motorway did little to add to our embarrassment. For the first five minutes, they sang some incomprehensible songs at decent volume in the strangest foreign accents imaginable - the IFK fans sounded more English than these outlandish Canaries. Presumably exhausted by their efforts, they collapsed into G-standish silence for most of the duration, content to suck on their hayseeds and discuss combine harvester parts until the Norwich rally late on.

Alex said afterwards that we were 'fabulous' in the first half, hyerbole that was perhaps excusable after the drek of United's last three hours' football. The relief in discovering that the team's forward play could still work effectively was tangible, like having successful sex again after a couple of impotence attacks. Most gratifying of all was the return of Eric to something at least on nodding terms with his best, imposing himself on the game and setting up a succession of chances wasted by lesser mortals. Choccy, remarkably, was playing with a verve we'd forgotten he once had, seizing his chance to play while the big cats were away in the treatment room. He deserved a goal but hit a post after the move of the match; soon afterwards, he repaid Eric for the opportunity by precisely setting up the French god who slotted home with *élan*. The ten minutes left before the break were enlivened by a complete run through the Cantona songbook, conducted from K stand – the King was back in his castle and all was well with the world once more.

All the other alleged failures, the 'Euroflops', the English donkeys and hotheads, quietly dominated with total assurance: Ince was master of all the midfield he surveyed, Pallister so towering that he made Norwich's forwards look like geriatric midgets. It may have been as cold and wet as Gothenberg out there but this time the performance was tropically smooth and glistening.

And then, inexplicably, just as even David May was beginning to impress after making six good touches in a row for the first time ever, United suddenly switched to autopilot during the second half and came as close as possible to throwing away the points. Admittedly, it felt like a Palace game *déjà vu* out there but the difference was this time we were only one up with 30 minutes to go, ie not normally the stage at which you start playing for time. Only Ince seemed to be fully alert as the rest padded around in metaphorical pyjamas; Norwich sensed their moment had come, added bite to their tackles and drove forward relentlessly. The haystack-dwellers in the corner woke up to the possibilities and opened their throats at last; Robins had the ball in the net but had been marginally offside and later appealed for a penalty after Neville's brusque challenge.

Eric snapped out of his reverie to lead the counter-charge, forcing the slap-headed Gunn to save superbly and setting up the sub Gillespie only to see the Ulsterman's first touch fail him. If not quite in the same class as last season's 2-2 classic, this had at least developed into a thundering, quintessentially English end-to-ender. As cigarette consumption in the stands soared and Alex gesticulated wildly on the bench, Reds had the novel experience of whistling frantically for full-time – this had been the first time this season that we'd been forced on to the back foot to hold out for the points. And you know, as unforgivable as it was for United to slip into slumber before finishing the game off, it was kind of satisfying in a perverse way to come out of Old Trafford with the feeling you had witnessed a contest instead of a procession. Not that we want them making a habit of it, mind . . .

As we streamed out, news came through that Newcastle had lost again but Blackburn had won. Now, surely, the landscape of the season had been properly formed. We were back in an eyeball-to-eyeball confrontation with Dalglish, Shearer and their band of worthy dullards. Familiar territory at last after the uncharted killing fields of Europe; make mine another double please, barman.

Team: Walsh; Neville, May, Pallister, Irwin, Kanchelskis (Butt), McClair, Ince, Davies (Gillespie), Cantona, Hughes

7 December: GALATASARAY AT HOME – CHAMPS LEAGUE

Final Score: UNITED 4 Turks 0

Scorers: Davies 3, Beckham 37, Keane 49, Bulent o.g. 88

Attendance: 39,220

I DUNNO, YOU WAIT in vain for a tabloid headline for bloody ages and then half-a-dozen turn up all at once . . . Over a year since it should have appeared on back pages, 'Stuffed Turkey' and all its predictable variations were finally printed in the wake of the richly-deserved kebabbing we inflicted on the Ottoman onanists. For adult readers, here's a particularly disgusting metaphorical twist that didn't get into *The Sun*. There's a popular bestial practice in the east that involves taking a plump turkey, shoving your pork truncheon up its rear and sticking your fingers down its throat so it vomits, thus resulting in a fabulously pleasurable muscular constriction spasm on your member. The turkey, incidentally, often croaks its last at this point. Now that is the sort of turkey-stuffing we enjoyed tonight – not just the routine ejaculation of victory but a tremendous sperm-spurting knee-trembling orgasmatron. Had we actually qualified, knobs all round Old Trafford would have simply exploded.

Before kick-off however, and switching poultry for a moment, the team sheet had borne witness to the amount of chickens that had come home to roost. Injuries and suspensions had reached such pandemic proportions that we were left with both a midfield and attack that had never played together before. Four lads from what we still call our Youth team together with Choccy, their 'teacher' from Vale Park, were drafted in to face a battle which would have daunted our toughest war-veterans. But if two of our hard men were out, the surprise return of our third, Keane, gave us hope – in true Robsonian fashion, the semi-injured Irishman was to fulfil every possible expectation as the 'older brother' figure in a teenybop midfield. Following his inspirational lead, boys became men that night; in doing so, they restored both our pride and our faith that this Club does still have a European future.

Context is everything of course; whatever we achieved in absolute terms within the confines of Old Trafford had a rather different relative value when compared to events in the Nou Camp. Most of us, especially those who were at the Ullevi, agreed with Fergie that

United had to proceed on the assumption that we were out of Europe – you couldn't hold any realistic hope that IFK, their passage already secured, were going to beat the mighty Barca in their own cauldron. If this game didn't actually constitute a 'dead rubber' in the technical sense, it had certainly already had the last rites administered to it. And yet, of course, a corner of the Red heart remained devoted to the impossible dream and, like those Saturday saddoes I'd mocked so often, an orifice of my body spent the game stuffed with a radio ear-piece transmitting Catalonian events. Later, I was to wish I could stuff the entire radio set up another orifice - the arsehole belonging to the rectum-head who spread the rumour that IFK had taken the lead. That moment in the 56th minute was the cruellest of all we'd suffered in six Champs league games; 40,000 celebrating souls given a glimpse of salvation, only for it to disappear amidst confusion as reality crowded back in. It would have been so much better if those hidden hopes of a miracle had remained buried: all the better to concentrate on a night that, on its own terms, provided a different kind of deliverance – and one that might endure.

So I'm taking my seat in the freezing East Lower, still following the toilet's orders to adjust my dress with frostbitten fingers and – shit, what's that noise? The roof is rattling in unprecedented fashion . . . well, well, at last the East Lower has done what it could have been designed for and decided to join in unity with K stand to form one, whole, singing throng. Banished, it seems, are the Saturday shoppers; a majority have actually come to support the boys, not the Superstore. There's something in the air reminiscent of that last Spurs game in '92 when, in the teeth of the bitterest disappointment imaginable, resolute Reds still determined to show their passion and pride in our lads' efforts. After all, player and supporter can be bound together just as much by terrible defeat as wonderful victory and this vibrant atmosphere provided further proof.

There was, of course, something else in the air – the stench of the infidel Turk. For all bar 150, this was our first sight of 'massed' Turk-meat since the barbarous criminality of Istanbul '93 and even the passage of time mixed with the night's Barcelonian preoccupations had done nothing to assuage the utter contempt Reds felt for them. To be honest, they looked a weedy, timorous bunch; 250 marooned in the middle of L-stand, surrounded by police, waving the odd moth-bitten flag and keeping very, very quiet. Moreover, most of them were probably kebab-house owners from Stoke Newington whose only connection with Istanbul was that their mothers spread syphilis there as young girls on the game. Nevertheless, the knowledge that amongst their number must have been someone who was in Istanbul and up to no good that nefarious night was enough for most of us. When, five minutes in, they attempted to make some sort of noise, they received a deafening volley of abuse from the entire East Stand – there was to be no repeat attempt. As special tokens of disgust, the usual anti-Leeds songs which are *de rigeur* at all televised games were tonight adapted for the Turks; the concerted booing that we usually reserve for John Barnes and his ilk was reprised for every Turk who dared either to linger on the ball or venture into our half. Of course, there is something vaguely absurd in all this given that 95 per cent of both them and us had no connection with what happened last year save for our tribal allegiances. But then, that's enough in football isn't it? Hurt one of us and you hurt us all; stay silent and indolent when your countrymen are kicking shit out of innocent visitors and you're as morally guilty as the perpetrators. Mass hatred is the result. (And hey, with so many sad-mustachioed, Cyprus-invading, anal-rape fiends amongst them, these Turks aren't easy to like in the first place . . .)

This Champions League has, at least, made Reds experience the whole gamut of emotions – from the nightmare of Gothenberg to the ever-expanding delights of tonight's fairy-tale performance, you have had your life-enhancing money's worth. Within 150 seconds, a starburst of skill from Simon Davies ripped the game apart as the kid finished with the complete self-confidence of Giggs at his prime; indeed, squinting from the East Stand, the shimmering figure of the teenager looked, mirage-like, as if the Ryan of '93 vintage had stepped onto the pitch. It was a devastating strike but it became rapidly obvious that Simon would not be claiming the Boy Wonder tag alone tonight. David Beckham, Nicky Butt and Gary Neville were, given the context of the game, astonishingly accomplished. Neville demonstrated once and for all why David May should never be allowed near the full-back berth again and must have given Paul Parker the most sleepless of nights; Butt buzzed and sparked all night like a terrier on 'E'; Beckham, perhaps above all, displayed the touch, bite and confidence of a future international mainstay. 'Where've you been all my life?' shouted one completely enamoured Red; in the schoolyard, obviously, but surely destined for the highest footballing degrees.

United's midfield – oldest player 23 – seized hold of the game by the throat and squeezed till the Turks' eyes splattered out of their sockets. By half-time, Galatasaray looked totally dejected, humiliated even; they must have had pre-match hopes that they could pull off their own particular mission impossible to qualify, faced with such a motley crew of kids and oldies, but instead had been outclassed and outfought. After the Ullevi experience, how gratifying to see Red shirts fighting to be first to every ball, closing down every space, tackling back for every lost possession. This hastily assembled midfield machine had already provided golden chances for Eric, Roy and Nicky - denied goals only by woodwork, glove and bad bounce – when David Beckham took advantage of more tireless McClair foraging to drill home the second after 37 minutes. His face – which has happy echoes of Gordon Hill about it – was a picture to savour as the Red shirts clamoured around him: a girl watching it on TV later told me, quite seriously, that she'd burst into tears when she saw him like that, a personification of joyous innocence.

If Keane was our Man of the Match in his favourite role of the complete, all-field performer, and Cantona a close second by virtue of his constant, creative vision, it was the collective showing of the youngsters that had the greatest emotional impact. There's nothing the true, genetically-programmed Red likes more than to watch thrilling, fresh young boys do their stuff . . . er, as a Liverpool midfielder might say. This might just be our conceit but there is no Club who desires to see youth break through more than ours. That, of course, is hugely ironic given our propensity to spend our multi-millioned way to success but anyone who saw either Busby's Babes or the Docherty Kids will display alarming homo-erotic tendencies when faced with a collection of talented 18-year olds in shorts. If the Fergie Fledglings Mark One of '88/'89 ended up going rather limp, the modern incarnations are threatening to stand firm and erect together for the rest of their footballing lives. Oh, for a sight of the future – what might these boys be achieving in, say, '98/'99? Their finest hour might, of course, arrive much sooner than that – are they going to be the solution to our Euro/Anglo problems, even as soon as next year? Fergie is about to face the greatest balancing act of his manager-as-juggler career - buying enough new English players to succeed in the short term without damaging the potential of our youth. We can only pray that this time he gets the balance right.

Fittingly, the game as a contest was terminated by the Predator Roy Keane himself, four minutes after the restart. Deliciously, he suddenly gave an almost balletic demonstration of touch and technique to score the goal of the game as if to contrast purposely with his normal Wagnerian *sturm und drang*. The newly-forged

Cantona-McClair one-two put Roy through; agonizingly, teasingly, he danced around both defenders, almost feinting as if to cock it up, before applying a God-like touch. I was right behind the line of fire and even with only six inches left to travel, I swore the ball was going wide. As if by remote control, the ball curled gorgeously at the last moment before nestling sweetly in the back of the net. Roy smiled the coy smile of one who knows he's been touched by genius. 'Keano, Keano' rang out, for only the second time of the night – a rather miserly ration of approbation considering his contribution. Or is it that we're embarrassed to voice such an inadequate song? Isn't it time we came up with something better for the lad?

With the game won, minds drifted to the Nou Camp both on and off the pitch, or so it seemed. Sporadic outbreaks of bad temper and Neanderthal marauding from the Turks enlivened proceedings, though not as spectacularly as in the 43rd minute when Bulent had flared up with Beckham and almost incited a players' retribution for Istanbul '93. How pleasing it was to see the *esprit de corps* of the youngsters, Neville haring 60 yards to get amongst the ruck to defend his mate. It was just desserts for the belligerent Bulent that he was the buffoon to hook Eric's cross into the net for our fourth with moments to go. Four-nil, the second slaughter of hated rivals in four weeks and a sort of reckoning-up for the Nou Camp disaster – we simply could not have expected or asked for more. Sadly, once the 56th minute eruption had dissipated, nothing so satisfying had been forthcoming from IFK. Heroically as the Swedes had performed, Bakero's goal had crushed the last remnants of hope – Rehn's equalizer caused no more than a frisson amongst the OT crowd for we knew that particular game was up. Instead, we paid due homage to our own heroes – the boys who, one day, might be the sort of men from whom European Champions are fashioned.

So, as is usual for United in Europe, we go out on the slimmest accounting method possible. In recent times we've been ko'd on away goals, penalties and now on goal difference. Amidst all the talk of humiliation and disaster, it should be remembered that had we been given that penalty against Barca, it would have been us rather than the Catalans enjoying a Paris awayday in March. We remain unbeaten at home in Europe – a record that Blackburn lost at the first attempt, incidentally – and scored ten at home, one of the Champs' League's best such tallies. How quickly the press labelled us as inferior to IFK and Barca, how soon they forgot that we smacked one and almost beat the other at Fortress Old Trafford. A European Cup 'disaster', surely, is something along the lines of getting knocked out in a preliminary round – hello, City – not coming within a goal of a quarter-final. However low we felt in the Ullevi, let's bear that in mind.

The question remains, what do we need to do in Europe? Eric Cantona, speaking on *The Bootroom*, provided the answer. It is not, as I also suggested earlier, that our individuals are technically inferior. Scoring, certainly, seems to be no problem at least when we're playing decently. It is more a question of tactics, the use of space when not in possession and adaptability, according to Cantona. Playing strung-out-in-a-line 4-4-2 with two orthodox wingers in an away leg is naive, at least, and stupid at best. Ferguson has presumably learned that much; perhaps he could borrow Eric's AC videos to illustrate the lesson about controlling space and working as a midfield unit. There may have been defensive mistakes that led to the conceding of goals but the games as a whole were lost in the geometry of midfield play. As for adaptability, in particular the ability to cover other midfield and defensive positions as the units become more mobile, that is clearly a job for Kidd and the players. If they can't adapt, they should go. Fortunately, all but May could probably be taught to do so. And they should all remember Eric's expert opinion: 'The English are not inferior to the Continentals as players: they just need better tactics and systems.' Our time *will* come.

Team: Walsh; Neville, Irwin, Bruce, Pallister, Keane, Butt, Cantona, McClair, Beckham, Davies

10 December: QUEEN'S PARK RANGERS AWAY

Final Score: Queen's Park Rangers 2 UNITED 3

Scorers: Scholes 34 & 47, Keane 44

Attendance: 18,948

IS THE COMPUTER THAT schedules fixtures as infected by the anti-Red virus *rubrophobia virulens* as the rest of the football world is? With Christmas coming up and Reds needing to find festive cabbage for Yuletide booze (and the odd present), where do we get sent to play away? Three consecutive trips to malodorous Big Wen, with voyages to Sweden and Southampton thrown in (The Dell being almost as inaccessible on New Year's Eve as the Ullevi was). What's that smokey smell: the yulelogs burning in the hearth? Marshmallows gently toasting? No – it's a thousand Red bank statements and credit cards combusting from over-extension.

Remember when the Premiership started and we were told that the fans' interests would be paramount? Even the old Football League managed to avoid sending us to the far corners of the earth during holiday periods. Would it be too much to expect that one day, fixtures might be arranged to minimise inconvenience to travelling fans at all times? Don't the hypocrites at Lancaster Gate understand what a complete shag it is also going to be for us to travel to Norwich and Wimbledon midweek? Are they even aware that these are the sorts of issues that matter to fans? How did these blazered buffoons ever get to be in charge of our game anyway?

Still, let us say this for the besieged Thompson regime at Loftus Road: at least they provide us with a decent allocation. Twenty-two per cent of their capacity goes to the away fans, the best ratio in the Premiership, which allowed us to annex the entire School End and then some. Not that this goes down too well with the Rangers loyalists; their 'zine *In The Loft*, which is entirely devoted to expressions of howling rage against their owner and his chairman stooge, still found space to decry this generosity to away support and call for some seasonal spirit – that of Scrooge. As the underlying reason for this was not so much the difficulty for home fans in obtaining tickets, sellouts being as rare as weeks without a crime at Highbury, but because they were embarrassed at being outsung every week 'even by Man City fans', you can't have much sympathy for them. What it meant for us is that more than 4,000 Reds could get in, often by that most miraculous of means, the face-value ticket. Even those in on the bargain bin £6 tickets had to laugh at the innocent honesty of the QPR club-stamped across them was the legend 'diabolical view', a unique touch of plain-speaking in these days when 'standard accommodation' and 'economy class' actually mean 'shithole'.

Whether it was the sense of well-being induced from not being fleeced at a match for once, or the light-headed feeling you get when a weight such as the Euro-Cup burden-of-expectation is lifted from your shoulders, I dunno; but didn't everyone at QPR seem, well, 'happier' than massed Reds have seemed for weeks? Perhaps it was just the Christmas spirit, with Santa hats and ear-rings (!) much in evidence and *Jingle Bells* later to get its first full airing of the season. Outside the Springbok pub, the Boyle Chorus had taken up its now traditional position, regaling passers-by, inspiring the massed Reds knocking back £2 cans inside and hailing the heroes on the team coach as they passed down South Africa Road. Pete himself had now reached the stage where he'd virtually become the equivalent of a working pop group, issuing new 'singles' on songsheets every couple of weeks and preparing to release his follow-up album to *United We Sing* in the New Year. (Can we also expect a nude promo video *à la* Kylie from the man who resurrected streaking?)

Once inside the quaintly ancient, double-tiered garden shed that is the School End, Reds revelled in the barrelling acoustics of the claustrophobic surroundings to outsing the blue-hooped Cinderellas of London football at the other end. Those up top took the opportunity afforded by the Bronze Age construction to engage in some concerted Hillsborough-style foot-stamping; together, our audio-supremacy was sealed, with the 'celebrated' Loft going unheard until the bedlam of the last 20 minutes. On-pitch supremacy, however, was another matter altogether – for half-an-hour our teen-stuffed makeshift outfit received a drubbing of almost European proportions. Sluggish, second to every ball and distributing woefully badly, United appeared to be heading for a melt-down to rival that of New Year's Day '92. Rangers, to their credit always try to play rather than contain against us, even if they have a tendency to chuck some Wimbledonian physicality into the mix. In the past few meetings this admirable attitude had cost them dear as they were repeatedly caught by Red counter-thrusts; today it looked as though the only Red thrusting would be of their dicks into the metaphorical blender. Somehow we escaped until the 23rd minute, even seeing the ball hit our wood twice within the second, when Ferdinand turned Ince to score simply the greatest goal we've conceded for months. It happened right in front of us, yet some around could scarcely believe the speed and power we'd just witnessed. The morning press had said that we were bidding for Collymore – had we picked the wrong black English centre-forward after all?

Moments later, Walsh saved one-handedly, quite brilliantly, from Impey's sly header which had seemed assuredly goal-bound to us lot behind the goal; it proved to be the turning point. Had it gone in, few would dispute that QPR would have walked it.

Instead, United's forwards began to move and find space at last; the midfield began to compete and some of the fire went out of QPR's attacks. Scholes was denied by the bar after a stunningly executed overhead attempt; with his next chance he found the net in hugely improbable fashion. The guy is five-foot-six, he looks like he should still be behind playground bikesheds smoking Embassy No 1 and he has the Premiership experience of a cocker spaniel – so you have no right to expect that he should soar into the air, beat hardened, hulking centre-backs and power home crushing headers from miles out. The boy is blessed, and so are we: one-all meant deliverance from potential humiliation.

Not that we cared too much that it should be QPR in particular to whom we might lose; of all the London clubs, they are surely the least likely to provoke any animosity amongst Reds. We have a 'history' with most of the rest, of course, often dating back to the Seventies and beyond but QPR have always been a bit 'girlie', haven't they? The name itself is suspect enough: 'Queen's Park Rangers' conjures up images of mascara'd Quentin Crisps mincing their way across Shepherd's Bush Green. Their image has never had a trace of the cool you might detect in Chelsea or Spurs; sure, the almost iconic Westway thoroughfare, namechecked in many a song, might traverse their patch to the east of the ground but QPR were never The Clash of London football – more the Big Audio Dynamite II. Consequently, not a single song was directed at QPR or their monastic following all day as we contented ourselves with the usual terrace classics. Steve Hodge, QPR's ex-sheepshagger, came in for more scum-related abuse than he probably deserves simply because we had no-one else to be vitriolic at; this was a game entirely about the three points with nothing else at stake or of importance. Not that Rs in the Loft felt the same; enough were sufficiently venomous to turn on a few isolated Reds up in the top left corner when we equalized, necessitating the tiresomely habitual steward invasion. Has there been any away game yet when all Reds have gone home unthumped?

Reds these days seem to prefer the violence to be allegorical and on the pitch. When are the best times to sucker-punch an aggravating bloke in a pub? One, when he's preoccupied with a bursting bladder on the way to the bog, the other, when he's still putting his squirrel back in the tree on the way out. Such were United's tactics before and after QPR's half-time trip to the toilet. Keane completed the greatest post-injury come-back since Robson's heydays by scoring his second classic in four days, legging down towards the Loft, all pistons pumping, before finishing with the coolest aplomb. Within 200 seconds of the restart, Scholes used his head again to squeeze the ball into the top corner right in front of us before saluting the adoring masses; how sweet to see the ball leave ex-sheep Hodge flailing as it passed through the exact spot where Ferdinand's rocket had blazed.

Purring with pleasure at the remarkable turnaround in fortune, we sat back to enjoy what should have followed - QPR pouring forward in desperation, United scoring a hatful on the break. For about ten minutes, all went to plan. The Reds looking increasingly bloodthirsty at every breakaway as a fourth seemed inevitable. Instead, the Loft were the ones to burst into life at last as young Gallen, who'd bothered Brucey all day, got in a killer cross for Ferdinand to head home. The parade we had expected was now to become 25 minutes of increasingly frantic and unpleasant scrabbling along the edge of a precipice. Blackburn and Newcastle were winning; two dropped points could not be afforded. Walsh, having his best game yet, made a smart save from a deflected shot; Impey and Gallen continued to buzz whilst Ince was forced to get down into the trenches and slug it out in midfield, abandoning his creative role. Even amidst the growing maelstrom, McClair still had perhaps the best chance of the half until the final nerve-grating moment arrived. The mounting tension and aggression of the half exploded into what could have been the best punch-up since the infamous Arsenal game after a spat between Barker and Nicky Butt turned promisingly nasty. The referee, who minutes before had given a foul against Ince which he could not possibly have seen (OK, so Ince did boot the Ranger in the bollocks but it was right behind the ref's back), this time saw everything but astonishingly refused to book anyone. We were left to face the final trauma of a well-placed free kick, which some Reds couldn't bear to watch; QPR duly cocked it up, deservedly so after picking on young Nicky like that – we were home and slightly damp. For the third year in a row, Loftus Road had produced a minor classic – for the third time, we'd scored three and won. Jingle bells, jingle bells. . .

Walking back down towards Westway, having joined in the abuse of Dani Behr who had been spotted sitting rather unwisely in the School End, I eavesdropped on a couple of typically reasonable Rangers fans resignedly discussing the game. 'Could've gone either way . . . Suppose those kids are pretty good, considering . . . at least their lot didn't keep invading the bloody pitch like City's did.' So far, so fair. Then one remarked how you'd never see a game like that on *Football Italia*. Now I don't know whether he meant that as a compliment to or condemnation of the players but, in conjunction with the way our kids restored our pride against the Turks, didn't this game make you feel good to be British? After the endless sirening of the media Cassandras in recent weeks, these three hours of football constituted some sort of answer to the critics, on behalf of both

United and British football as a whole. Where else would you see such a thrilling, fast, passionate and pugilistic match as this one? Nowhere but Britain. Of course, we may not be quite as technically perfect as the rest and our games might feature more mistakes but then, as Jurgen Klinsmann put it so simply and rightly, what else can you expect from such a fantastically speedy and powerful national style? In the space of four days, our boys had done more than just win two games well; they had proved that we still have much to be proud about, we still have a future, and that as a spectator sport our football is the best. Life is short. Get your thrills where you can, while you can: United remain the most prodigious source of visceral excitement outside Bangkok.

Team: Walsh; Neville (Gillespie), Bruce, Pallister, Irwin, Kanchelskis, Keane, Ince, Davies (Butt) Scholes, McClair

17 December: NOTTINGHAM FOREST AT HOME

Final Score: UNITED 1 Forest 2

Scorer: Eric 68

Attendance: 43,744

USUALLY, EVERYONE LOVES A bit of nostalgia at Christmas but there are certain festive traditions from yesteryear that you'd rather did not repeat themselves like some curry-stench belch. One such is the Tricky Tree Holiday Hex (not to be confused with the Cloughie Transfer Curse) in which Forest sides down the ages decided to celebrate the onsets of Yuletide or Easter by mounting awayday ramraids on Old Trafford, robbing the rich to feed their poor yokel supporters as if they were some demented descendants of Robin Hood. Perhaps we tend to over-exaggerate the frequency with which this actually happened but the shadows cast, for example, by the 0-4 Xmas defeat in the late Seventies and the 1-2 of Easter '92 darkened our spirits for many a month. The oddest thing is that Forest and United have never really been crunching rivals; despite all the wounds they have seemed to inflict on us since their '77 promotion, there are plenty of Reds who maintain a grudging respect for their hitherto traditional style, good sportsmanship and half decent fans. In fact, Nottingham is all right as parochial provinces go: a kinda 'nice' city, some nationally renowned top crumpet and a working class whose vanguard had the good sense not to jump lemming-like over the Scargillian precipice in '84. All that, combined with the fact that they gave Liverpool some crucial kickings in the Seventies, made them a hard club to hate. All the more remarkable, then, that by the end of this match a typical expression of Red feeling was exhibited by the Southport Red who clambered frenziedly across the length of the Scoreboard End in a futile attempt to get his hands on one of them. It wasn't so much that we lost, more the manner in which Forest bad-mouthed, bad-tackled and generally bad-assed their way to the points.

Back in August, after the draw at the City Ground, you might have looked ahead to this fixture as one home game we might well lose, such was the form of Collymore and Roy and the way Forest were racking up the early goals and points. But ironically, by the time this return came around you could be forgiven for taking a victory for granted. Forest were seemingly a spent force, suffering a decline of Newcastlian proportions. Surely Forest were no more likely to score the first opposition league goal at OT than Liverpool or the Geordies had been? With United now getting back to something approaching full-strength, our seasonal optimism seemed well-founded. Instead of worrying about the result, we focused on the individuals. Giggs was making his post-Dani return, the *wunderkind* having turned 21 and presumably keen to demonstrate that the tabloid obituaries had been a tad premature; the gossip-mongers had it that Miss Behr had been at Loftus Road to support her alleged new beau Les Ferdinand. The young girls, who had no doubt been responsible for much of the £100,000 spent in four hours in the Megastore, were to be in for an afternoon of anti-climax from the once-orgasmic Ryan. For those with more strategic concerns, the spotlight was to be firmly trained on the respective performances of line-leaders Hughes and Collymore, with the press confidently predicting the latter was about to replace the former. Just as at Loftus Road, a Great Black Hope was about to get his once-in-a-lifetime chance to do a live audition for the biggest Scottish impresario since Cameron Mackintosh. And once again the old Lion King of Old Trafford, Hughsey, would suffer in comparison, his grip on the throne looking decidedly shaky in the face of the challenge from yet another young pretender.

The first five minutes were as grim as the last five were exhilarating. Not only were the Forest contingent outsinging us easily but Collymore was already playing Stoichkov to Bruce 'n' Pally's Two Stooges show, forcing Ince to hare back for a goal-saving tackle.

Although the Forest fans, like mouthy blokes entering a pub, soon shut up once they'd registered their presence amongst us, their subsequent silence had no dampening effect on Stanley's ardour. Every Kan-Kan crossed arrow found dull outer-rim green instead of red bullseye (gratuitous Robin Hood archery allusion) whilst Giggs was more Robin Reliant than Hood, being unable to get past anything at all. Scrooge-like, the Ghost of Cloughie Christmasses Past haunted us as Forest counter-attacked swiftly like Robertson and O'Hare of old. It was no surprise, in truth, when Collymore added a million to his price-tag by scoring a blinder at the East Stand end. 'Anything Ferdie can do, I can do better' seemed to be the subtext of that strike. Or perhaps it was 'Please buy me, Fergie'. Whatever, the shock of seeing domestic opposition score at Old Trafford was tempered by the teasing subconscious thought that one day we might be watching Stan do that in a devil-badged shirt. I saw some Reds furtively applauding, *sotto voce*: the Forest fans might well chant 'Who needs Cantona when we've got Collymore' but some of us were contemplating the olde worlde charm of having players called Stan and Eric up front . . .

By the time Forest scored their second, the spawniest of deflected shots seeming to spin off a Red heel at a time when we'd just begun to threaten, the character of the game had been transformed. As early as the half-hour mark, Forest players had astonishingly started time-wasting, possibly setting some sort of record. At goal-kicks Crossley sauntered about scratching his arse, picking his nose and generally malingering; Forest outfield players traipsed over for throws and kicks as unwillingly as one would head for the scaffold. When defending, Forest's laudably tight pressing and closing down became something more insidiously vicious, scattering late challenges, shirt-tugging and wrestling holds around the pitch as if a reincarnation of 1970 Leeds. Given our own track-record for hot-temperedness, it was equally miraculous that Ince, Hughes and Keane were keeping so calm under such provocation, as if they too could not believe there could be any malicious intent from such nicely brought-up Cloughie Boys. By the end of the game more than half the Forest team were in the book, Brian Roy had Incey's handprints embedded in his neck and Lyttle was lucky not to have had Giggsy's forehead spot burst all over his face after their confrontation almost ended in a head-butt-fest. Most notorious of all was Stuart Pearce's alleged racial abuse of Paul Ince which momentarily promised to combust into a conflagration that would have befitted Red Lion Square in the Seventies (a cultural reference for our friends at *Red Attitude* there). The PFA later stood

74

by Ince and asked Pearce to apologise but nothing more was said and libel laws prevent me from saying any more publicly.

Around the hour mark, Forest fans chanted for three minutes; I'd like to think that their 'You're so shit it's unbelievable' was directed at the appalling McClair, who was managing to erase all memory of his previous decent performances that month. At least this terrace chant's cheek seemed to help rouse both us and the players: on 68 minutes Eric rose to head home a corner and the game was afoot at last. For a good ten minutes Old Trafford was as raucously vibrant as it had been all season, reminding us that the roar created by 40,000 Red throats can still be one of the most spine-tingling sounds in Christendom. Forest fans shrank in their seats and their players back-pedalled frantically as United assaults rained down upon the Scoreboard goal. How the ball failed to go in remains a mystery; the match simply failed to follow the Barcelonian script and no gorgeous equalizer was forthcoming. When Ince let fly with his now customary 20-yard vaporizer, a Forest boot at the foot of the post was there to save their awayday when a goal seemed screamingly certain. As the last five minutes ticked inexorably away, Reds increasingly resigned themselves to fate – 'It's just one of those days': one of those almost forgotten days that were once so common in the darker months of the Seventies and Eighties when luck was as telling a factor as skill, when home victories were never taken for granted and when doomed last-gasp cavalry charges were a frequent occurrence. And at the risk of sounding masochistic, days like these are good for the true Red soul. A parade of untrammelled supremacy can dull the senses; victories are all the balmier when the memory of stinging defeat is still so fresh. It's obvious that this season, compared to last, is more of a bitter-sweet roller-coaster ride than the slightly detoured, arrogant promenade that was '93/'94. Any trophy that we might yet pluck from it will be all the worthier to have won. (Keep this up – I've almost convinced myself . . .)

Team: Walsh; Keane, Bruce, Pallister, Irwin, Kanchelskis (Neville), Ince, McClair, Giggs (Butt), Cantona, Hughes

26 December: CHELSEA AWAY

Final Score: Chelsea 2 UNITED 3

Scorers: Hughesy 22, Eric 46 (*pen*), Choccy 78

Attendance: 31,161

AT FIRST GLANCE OF the fixture list, there was not much to fill the Mancunian Red with festive cheer in the prospect of Christmas week visits to London and The Dell. Short of whacking in an extra trip to East Anglia, the computer could not have been more spiteful. A Boxing Day start of six am after a weekend of Yuletide excess was hardly what any Red wanted from Santa's sack; the sheer impractability of a 12 o'clock kick-off at The Bridge meant that many familiar faces were missing from the usual Manchester posse, their places snapped up by fortunate Cockney Reds who made up the majority of our lower East Stand allocation. Not that they had any sympathy for us; as one Manc-exile from Brixton responded to my moans, 'Now you know what it's like for us virtually every week.' Only the most *ultra* of Manc regional supremacists would begrudge the southern tribes their 'week off' and besides, by Boxing Day you usually feel grateful for the opportunity to put 200 miles between yourself and the odious relatives who've been drinking all your Jack Daniels. The Mancs who had made it were readily identifiable due to their patently wasted condition, many having foregone the night's kip and looking the worse for their yearly reacquaintance with sweet sherry and assorted post-prandial liqueurs. When your belly is filled with a greater selection of exotic drinks than is available in any standard pub, five hours of churning about in a charabanc is not exactly what the doctor ordered. Thankfully there is no tight Loftus Road-style roof on that East Lower Stand, otherwise the evil pungency of the day's Christmas farts would have surely claimed a victim or two.

About a week before the game, I'm sure I heard Alan Hansen on TV extolling the virtues of the 'new' Stamford Bridge, to whit the smart facilities, improved atmosphere and excellent architecture. Perhaps I dreamed it because the Chelsea he was describing clearly belongs to a parallel universe. The Bridge that *we* saw still bore all the traits of a particularly grotty graveyard as run by the hoodlums of Westminster Council. If anything, the place seems to have been given yet another charisma by-pass; how on earth did this club ever get the reputation of being the capital's 'glamour side'?

The new North Stand manages, like most of this part of London, to be both big yet unimpressively characterless; the East and West spent 88 minutes of the game in silence. In place of the old Shed end there stands a bizarre temporary construction that looks as though it's been built up from those bench-things you stand on in school photos. It appeared to be about as safe as the rhythm method and its occupants behaved accordingly, avoiding any sudden noise lest the edifice collapse around them. You could tell which of them were remnants from the old psycho Shed – they were the ones who tried to start foot-stampings, oblivious in their lobotomised way to the grimaces of fear around them. Back off in the distance you could see the old stone terracing and marvel at Chelsea's bravery in bringing the stand so far forward. You would think they'd want to carry on keeping Shed-types as far away from the pitch as possible in the interests of the safety of the civilised (Southend would be close enough, for example). As we were to witness later on, the temptation to invade the pitch is just too great to resist for these Parklife boys.

Once Reds had battled through the one double-turnstile to get in and disgustedly digested the 'facilities' – £1.50 for 12 wet chips in a beaker? Piss-drenched bogs from the Bronze Age? Gangways built for midgets/Chelsea forwards? – we endured 20 minutes of semi-drunken stumbling about on the pitch that boded ill. Andrei was on the bench, Chelsea's pitch being thought by Alex to be too small to accommodate two wingers.(?) Ryan consequently looked a touch confused. Suddenly, like drinkers snapping awake at the sound of an opening can, United found their bearings and came to life. Giggs bunged over two cracking crosses and Hughes found the second to stab home right in front of us. The Christmas party was back on track.

By now it was clear that the redevelopment had indeed drained the last dregs of atmosphere out of the home 'support'. Even though Reds were hardly in vintage vocal form with so many cheer-leaders back in Manc – 'Eric' doing his best to fill the role vacated by the expectant Boyle - our fairly feeble efforts were still the only sounds resounding around the ground. As our goal celebrations died down, the scoreboard flashed up one of the most pathetic messages we'd seen since 'United 0 Barca 4': 'We can't hear you in The Shed', it wailed electronically. Sadder still was the response from the erstwhile vanguard – total silence. Just after the half hour, the home fans did manage one run-through of *Mow A Meadow* ('One of football's greatest sounds,' says 90 Minutes!!) which collapsed in disco-ordination and virtually concluded their afternoon's efforts. With only a couple of concerted renditions of *The Twelve Days of Cantona* and *Jingle Bells*, we had won the vocal competition almost by default.

We cruised to half-time virtually unmolested, save for an assault on Ince that Keano later avenged but which was to lead to serious consequences. At half-time, Keane was mandated to pick up the Ince mantle with Neville taking over at right back; the Irishman proceeded to give a display of gubernatorial dominance good enough to win any Guvnor's election. We had barely returned from the half-time struggle to eat and leak, clutching those ridiculous 'half-time passes', when Keane charged all pistons pumping through their entire half to win a penalty which Eric, of course, converted. The fouler, naturally, was Sinclair. Is this man a United fan or something? He seems to insist on doing all he can to help anyone he sees in a Red shirt. He gift-wraps two goals for us at Wembley, gives us the perfect half-start here and later shows great presence of mind to deflect the ball to Choccy for our winner. Alex should give him the win bonus: he's deserved it.

During the 32 minutes between the penalty and the Keane-inspired winner came the small matter of a couple of Chelsea goals that, momentarily, turned a seasonal saunter into a Christmas crisis. Admittedly, Chelsea deserved *one* goal for their attacking efforts but the manner of their first tested Red seasonal goodwill. Stein's frail little body toppled over under the weight of his weird knobbly head somewhere between the penalty area and centre circle; the fact that Gary Pallister was lingering innocently behind him was enough for the ref to give a penalty. David Meek later gave Mike Reed eight out of ten for a generally abject display which suggests the *Evening News* had been overdoing it at the office party again. Yet, even at 2-1, it always looked more likely that we would score a third, with Keane rampant and Neville outstanding; Brucey even found time for some Romarian ball-skill display right in front of us, eliciting the warmest if most ironic applause of the day. But somehow a speculative effort looped ever so slowly into our net and bedlam briefly descended. Sheddites staged an impromptu Nuremberg rally on the pitch; the North Stand even made a faint noise and Fergie's face turned as purple as a Christmas pud. Instead, another pudding saved the day as Choccy found the target with unbelievable accuracy within the minute. Chelsea fans looked as mortified as kids whose presents consist entirely of socks; for us, it was *Jingle Bells* all the way to the whistle thanks to the Power Ranger in the Number 16 shirt. Not even the incredibly pedantic Scroogeian booking of Eric for his wonderfully finished 'goal' after an offside whistle could take the gloss off a minor classic of an awayday. Give us six o'clock starts every holiday if thrillers like this are guaranteed. (Incidentally, whatever the aim was of the half-time announcer who played *Barcelona* over the tannoy, how amusing an effect it had on our moral – a goal in 60 seconds . . .)

We were top of the table for a few hours until City's second-rate but typical performance against Blackburn. Of more pressing concern was Ince's hamstring injury which was looking likely to keep him out for a month. Cometh the hour, cometh the Irishman – for Roy Keane the moment of truth was now at hand, for it would be to him that the task of midfield leadership now fell.

Team: Walsh; Keane, Bruce, Pallister, Irwin, McClair, Ince (Neville), Butt (Kanchelskis), Giggs, Cantona, Hughes

28 December: LEICESTER CITY AT HOME

Final Score: UNITED 1 Leicester 1

Scorer: Kanchelskis 60

Attendance: 43,789

NOSTALGIA USUALLY INVOLVES HARKING back to some often-mythical golden age in an attempt to tell the youngsters of today that there's 'nowt like the ancient ways' or some such dewy-eyed bollocks. At United in the winter of '94, we put a slightly different spin on it; time-served OT regulars had got into the habit of reminiscing not about the Sixties or Seventies but the 'good old bad old days' of Fergie's F*ckwits. In typically Mancunian fashion, those 20- and 30-somethings who'd suffered the ravages of the late Eighties could be heard in pub corners surrounded by like-minded souls bemoaning modern United with its easy success, band-wagoners and glory-hunters and instead celebrating with mordant wit the grimmest days of Wallace, Milne and Phelan. We even had our own catchphrase that recurred regularly in both fanzine columns and conversation – 'Wimbledon '89'. That was our shorthand for the whole appalling yet fondly remembered vista of crapola that passed for football in those days. It was a strange kind of glory indeed, those years of embarrassing home defeats, five-at-the-back long ball tactics, dreadful journeymen players and so on, but there was something in that vision of a few hundred die-hard Reds shivering in the rain on a wet midweek night at Wimbledon, watching atrocious football with no hope of a trophy at the season's end that plucked the Red heart-strings. Of course to summon up such spirits that you'd think were best forgotten had a 'political' purpose. Those who were there could justifiably feel that they were the Red Guard, the élite, the hard-core; it was a way of emphasising their superior status over the *parvenus* and *arrivistes* who now flooded Old Trafford. And I dare say that for the most twisted amongst us who are prone to such a curmudgeonly mentality, the games against Forest, and Leicester in particular, bore a bizarre silver lining amidst the clouding of lost points. Against Leicester, above all, you could close your eyes and almost be transported back to 1990. By 'eck, deathly depression and misery – I luv it, me.

The game had all the requisites for a late Eighties revivalist meeting. Firstly, a proper night-game atmosphere. Who knows why tonight should have felt so charged and vibrant but for the first 40 minutes at least, Old Trafford felt like part of the National Grid once more, just like it used to for every evening kick-off. Secondly, a decent Manchester downpour. Whether this is due to global warming or not, it never rains enough at Old Trafford any more. By contrast, it feels in retrospect that scarcely a game passed in those late Eighties nights without everyone getting a good soaking, although I'd concede this recollection is more metaphorical and psychological than meteorological. Thirdly, as was *de rigeur* back then, our most in-form player MUST be injured at the season's most crucial point. Back then, it was usually Robson's role of course; now, it was the hitherto indestructible Ince who played the fallen guy. Admittedly, for more than an hour, he was barely missed but who could have failed to spot how crucial his absence was in those last 25 minutes? No disrespect to Keano, who was as awesome as ever, but no-one is better than the Guvnor at smashing those break-outs from defence that Leicester lived off in the closing stages.

The case for this fanciful simile is sealed conclusively by the way we played for most of the first 60 minutes. The midfield was dictatorially dominant, the defence barely needing to touch the ball; Leicester's anonymous players - would anyone in the world even notice if they were all abducted by aliens from the *X-files*? – appeared in our box four times in the entire first half. And yet this grinding, relentless, unending pressure produced barely a handful of chances, so poor was the final ball, so clumsy the hopeful cross; it was like shoving ten pounds of beef into a sausage machine to produce one weedy lowfat chipolata. Those chances that did arise were blown with

McClairesque abandon, Hughes miscueing horrendously and Giggs finding the side net as the goal gaped like a Scouse mother's pussy. Eric at least found the target, only for his header to be cleared off the line; in the rain-induced shimmer, Leicester began to resemble the Ipswich of last season but with ten defenders instead of nine. They had come for the nil-nil and were looking likely to get it.

It was a pattern familiar to any who saw United in the late Eighties but in the second half, as the Scoreboard roused itself once more, Kanchelskis at last did what no-one else had seemed willing to do – shoot at the target with venom. His gorgeous goal lifted the weight from every shoulder and we sat back to enjoy what should have been a rout. Instead, within five minutes, a rare Fox incursion had produced a corner from which the scrattiest, scruffiest goal imaginable was scored and United promptly fell apart. The frantic, hacking long balls, wayward passes and limp-wristed finishing that followed were vintage '89; less excusable was the lack of fight and grit as Blue shirts reached every 50-50 ball first. Even so, we still should have won it; how Keane and Eric conspired to miss a far post chance eluded most of us whilst sub Scholes, having battled hard to secure a chance, prodded his into the goalie's grateful arms. Travelling Leicester fans, who had spent most of the game in silence, finally broke into the excremental 'Who the f*ck are Man United', to which United fans, who'd earlier given the longest and loudest rendition of 'Red and White Army' of the season, did not bother to reply. We were too preoccupied; faces looked far gloomier than they had been after the Forest defeat. It wasn't so much that we'd missed the opportunity to go top after the Rovers-Leeds postponement – hey, really tough break there, travelling scum – but that so much of what we'd seen was strange and troubling. Andrei, despite his goal, was not crossing as he once was. Giggs was barely crossing at all but had done his best work playing a couple of killer balls from midfield. Hughes was leading the line well but looking less likely to score, *pace* Stamford Bridge, than ever. McClair was back to lumpy, pie-ridden mediocrity but was good for the team's balance and so on and so on . . . in short, nothing quite added up. We seemed disjointed, malfunctioning, lopsided; no element was wholly good or wholly bad either. And with Ince and Sharpe missing and Keane likely to follow after the next card, the immediate future looked as murky as an Arsenal bank statement. Even in such injury and suspension-addled times, the ingredients to make magic were still there and available – but which spell to use? And with Fergie's Tinkerbell record, would he know which to pick?

Team: Walsh; Neville, Bruce, Pallister, Irwin, Kanchelskis, Keane, McClair, Giggs, Hughes (Scholes), Cantona

31 December: SOUTHAMPTON AWAY

Final Score: Saints 2 UNITED 2

Scorers: Butt 51, Pallister 78

Attendance: 15,204

'NO ONE LOOKS FORWARD to a trip to the Dell . . . the police take a special country bumpkin delight in annoying Northern urbanites.' Thus opens the book *United We Stood* and there was good cause to remember that line on New Year's Eve. As the Red Army Expeditionary Force gathered outside 'The Mission' on Archer's Road, the traditional routine got underway, *viz* Pete Boyle and acolytes standing on tables in the beer garden to lead a hundred or so Reds through the terrace songbook. Within seconds of a rendition of the line '18 Years and won f*ck all', hayseed-chewing pigs trotted over to hand out warnings about our 'offensive language' – the aforementioned chant was sarcastically doctored to run '. . . and won Donald Duck all'. Jokingly, I remarked to a strangely sober Boyle that with police like these about, he'd be lucky to get into the ground: 'They probably think a song counts as an offensive weapon.'

Sadly, I had underestimated the local constabulary's potential to impersonate total arseholes. Pete was arrested as he tried to get into our end, the police shouting 'We've got him!' as they pounced. He was accused of being 'dangerously drunk', was held in the cells until 5.15 and forced to sign a caution without legal advice under the threat that he'd be held overnight, thus missing both his train and perhaps his baby's delivery. The irony was that, unlike at Loftus Road where a similar fate had befallen him, Pete was virtually sober, having decided to concentrate on the game rather than the drink 'n' sing session.

I mention this episode not just because Pete is a mate but because it illustrates a wider truth; the travelling fan is still treated as a second-class citizen at the mercy of local policing peculiarities and subject more than most to arm-twisting threats of overnight detention, blacklisting and the like. Pete was never charged, nor was any attempt made to 'prove' his alleged drunkenness, for such a trial would have failed. It was simply a case of arbitrary detention under the arbitrary rules of a corrupted system. The sad fact remains that the football fan who chooses to travel away also, *de facto*, chooses to jettison his rights as a citizen equal under the law. This incident may have been a relatively 'trivial' one but the principle is what counts: we are all seemingly guilty until proved innocent. So much for the Brave New World of post-Taylor football.

The local radio station was playing the Madness classic *Embarrassment* as our coach pulled in, which was rather a fitting theme for the first-half as a whole. Before kick-off, it was the Saints whose blushes were as red as their shirt chevrons as United fans, nicely positioned directly adjacent to the Saints' Archers Road End hardcore, chorused mockingly, 'This is the worst f*cking ground we've ever seen.' And indeed it was, as the Saints who stared glumly at their shoes in shame would admit. The most amusing 'stand' is the Milton Road End; as my neighbour remarked, 'That's not a stand – it's a wall with some seats stuck on it.' Our own accommodation resembled the Loftus Road School End, but as constructed by a blind architect and penniless builder with 'facilities' to match – a toilet built for three and one sad excuse for a food bar. No wonder the club is desperate to move, even if it means sharing with Portsmouth; in the eyes of visitors, the ground brings more shame to the club than Bruce Grobbelaar.

Within minutes, however, the embarrassment was all ours. as United took the field, we clapped eyes on the design abomination that is the new away kit. Can there truly be any merchandise-victims out there who would stoop so low as to fork out for a strip that looks like a misprinted deckchair? Saints fans promptly recovered from their ground-shame to yell, 'What the f*ckin' hell is that?!', and several Reds had a hard time restraining themselves from joining in. Doubtless, the usual litany of pseudo-outrage from United-haters about commercial exploitation will pollute the airwaves once more – a caller on *606* later duly got in there first – but surely there could not have been any design more calculated to wean the shirt-collecting train-spotters off their expensive addiction than this tasteless polyester abortion?

Nobody performs well in bad threads, which might explain why the rest of the first-half embarrassment belonged to United's team; their birthday present for Alex was a wingless, witless, wankers' performance of unprecedented awfulness. Southampton looked like a unified, organised team and dominated in Barcelonian proportion. By contrast, United looked like eleven semi-acquainted individuals who had no idea what their positions, roles or even names were. It took 20 minutes for us to create the slightest opening; we managed one more before Magilton scored Southampton's thoroughly deserved opener on the stroke of half-time after they'd spurned several glittering opportunities. What was happening to us? At the risk of incurring a *fatwah* from Fergie zealots, let me suggest that two points were needlessly lost because the chickens of doubt many have expressed all season about Alex's selection skills all came home to roost that day.

Apparently, the CBE Alex got that morning stands for Commander of the British Empire but when we saw the team sheet we could be forgiven for thinking that the 'C' stood for a rather more vulgar word. Clearly, the losses of Denis and Andrei to hospital and treatment rooms combined with the absence of Ince made for a three-pipe problem, as Holmes would say. But just how many defensive disasters must ensue before Alex understands that David May CANNOT be allowed on the pitch until Brucey retires? There are plankton-brained amoeba on planets beyond Alpha Centurai who are scarcely aware of their own existence who nevertheless know for a fact that May is not and never will be a full back. Why does Ferguson persist with the hapless liability in that position at every opportunity? Can he not admit he's either wasted his cash or that May must stay in the reserves until his centre-half time comes? May at right back also meant Neville, unhappily, had to play on the left. No wonder, then, that we looked so uncomfortable at the back, with a reserve goalie and two out-of-position defenders. We are not the 1970s Dutch playing total football; only megatalents like Keane can switch around and play anywhere. Wouldn't it have been so much better to leave Gary at right back and bring in any other reserve at left back? We would rather see even someone from the youth or schoolboy teams at number two if it would spare us the groan-inducing sight of May's ginger head spinning around in confusion as yet another move leaves him for dead. As the Magilton goal demonstrated, May is the Skoda of right backs: everyone else can pass it with ease, no-one else wants to own one and the only person who likes it is its owner.

Similarly, further forward, what was the point of playing Giggs as the lone semi-winger and keeping McClair in the team for no specific purpose? United have a system: it is built on having two wingers. The mathematical logic is that by playing one – and one who is off-form at that – you cut in half the number of chances we can create as well as leaving a flank gap which Southampton so readily exploited. The folly of the selection that left the team as badly balanced as City's accounts was illuminated perfectly by the impact Gillespie made when he came on, transforming us into a team that looked as if it might take all three points. Later, Fergie made noises suggesting he knew he 'should have brought Gillespie on sooner'. Well bugger that – why wasn't he on the pitch from the start? The treatment of McClair as 'Fergie's lovechild' has got beyond a joke; Choccy in '94/'95 makes an excellent supersub but as a 90-minute integral part of the team he is Yesterday's Man. Gillespie is not only the future, but the present too. And without TWO wingers on the pitch at all times we are not really United, just another bunch of through-the-middle trundlers.

Thankfully, Nicky Butt and King Eric responded manfully to what must have been a vintage teacup-chucking session from Fergie at half-time. Or perhaps, just as at Stamford Bridge, it was the talismanic effect of the scrotum DJ playing *Barcelona* at half-time, whose chorus the Archers End bellowed amidst our jeers of 'Do you know where Europe is?' Whatever, within six minutes we were level, Eric taking it upon himself to fill the gap on the wing to centre for Butt's debut senior goal with the sexiest of volleys. United at last took a grip of the midfield and began to string together some chances, with the Saints resorting to the occasional break. Butt controlled Le Tissier superbly, whilst Eric increasingly succeeded in wangling himself out of Benali's hitherto suffocating attention, thus in tandem making rather a mockery of the Saints' chant, 'Who needs Cantona when we've got Matt le Tiss?' Reds, who'd spent much of the first half brooding pessimistically, came alive at last; although one must admit we were often out-volumed by the home support for the first time in months, at least we displayed some variety in song-choice – by the time of its 20th rendition, the Archers' *When the Saints* was getting tiresome to say the least. In denying the Saints the accolade of best home fans of the season so far, the judges remind them that size of vocal support isn't everything – it's what you do with it that counts . . .

As United continued to rack up the chances – with McClair and Butt going close – and unfortunately the yellow cards too, a winner seemed inevitable. Horrifically, however, it appeared to be the Saints who'd got it as our defence abandoned all pretence at marking to let in Hughes for their second. That David May should be loitering without intent once again was no surprise; that three Red shirts were left helpless in the box was more worrying. Reds turned their attention from baiting *You've Been Framed* star Brucie at the Archers End goal to exhorting Nicky and Eric to fashion the salvation which our second-half deserved and, within five minutes, Eric delivered. Benali, who'd tried to bisect Eric as he crossed for the first, was left floundering this time as the French god found Pally's head with celestial vision and precision. As the rest of the team galloped back for the restart and final assault, Eric strutted in front of the foaming-mouthed Saints fans, struck a poise of purest Gallic arrogance and *savoir-faire* and sneered. Two pies were launched at him and missed; the *Empereur* smiled gently, with that *de haut en bas* smirk that so enrages our enemies, before trotting coolly away, his point made: Le Tissier may be half-French but he is only quarter the man that our Eric is. *N'est-ce-pas, mes amis?*

We could have won it too, thanks to Gillespie, who had three runs at their frantic defence in his eleven-minute appearance, almost creating two goals before being denied a blatant penalty. Later, I was told Radio Five had accused him of diving, which from their vantage point on the other side of the pitch behind Keith's back was hardly a well-founded observation, you sheepskin-coated tossers. Butt was booked for complaining that the challenge had left Gillespie injured, completing another afternoon of refereeing excellence; they talk of premiership refs being put in green or in black but personally I'd like to see several of them in coffins and dole queues. Not that we should make this into another case of result-robbery – the officials had missed a staggeringly obvious handball by Neville in the box early on, so I guess these things even out. That doesn't excuse the officials' incompetence, of course: forget Merson, bungs and Brucey – the greatest scandal in football is the uniform awfulness of the men in green and their bastard siblings on the lines. Forget the parlour game 'Name six famous Belgians', how about 'Pick five good refs'? That would keep you going for hours . . .

During the long hours of the journey back north, having got over the post-match paradox of feeling both relieved to have got a draw and aggrieved not to have won it at the death, the implications of the day's results sank in. So how was the ride for you, darling? On my coach there was much complaining about Fergie's selection of course but this was soon replaced by calculations of points and goals comparing Rovers and us. Three points and a game in hand was ominous indeed: their goal difference superiority meant that we now needed two wins and a draw over and above whatever Rovers achieved, assuming they beat Leeds. The feeling of the title trophy slipping out of our grasp was tangible – and weird, after what seemed like an eternity of being able to call ourselves champions. Ignoring the fact that the Scousers themselves were now also sat on our shoulders, four points behind, Blackburn's progress was indeed reminiscent of the old Liverpool –

steady, drab, efficient away wins matching home impregnability. Meanwhile, we were engaged in a series of four- and five-goal thrillers but losing a furlong at every step. Maybe Rovers will win the title, which would be a minor disaster for us all – no hat-trick and no European Cup revenge mission – but doubtless they will 'deserve' it and, after all, better them than the Dirties or Scum. But when I reflect on how they have fared recently compared to us, I still say style is all, even if it doesn't bring success. Rovers' wins in both recent Selhurst Park games were the worst reviewed I can remember for a winning, title-chasing side. The manner of their play and victories, even in the 3-0 against Wimbledon, has been reviled by most neutral observers; if it wasn't for the fact that they might stop United, they would garner no public support at all and be as unpopular as 1970 Leeds. They are the epitome of the adjective 'workmanlike' which is something United must never be – and I for one would rather sacrifice a trophy than our style. Of course, I would rather not see Rovers become the Liverpool of the late Nineties and United revert back to their early Eighties status of being the nation's entertainers instead but if it *does* come to that my love of United would not diminish. I watch them for the thrill, the sensual pleasure – you don't necessarily need silver to validate that. And if such slippage in our position were to rid Old Trafford of the superstore-groupies, glory-hunters and part-timers, it might almost become a prospect to be welcomed. As you can see, I'm getting in my end-of-season rationalisation nice and early - it's best to be prepared. . .

Team: Walsh; May, Bruce, Pallister, Neville, Butt, Keane, McClair (Gillespie), Cantona, Giggs, Hughes

3 January: COVENTRY CITY AT HOME

Final Score: UNITED 2 Coventry 0

Scorers: Scholes 29, Eric 49 (*pen*)

Attendance: 43,130

I ALMOST FORGOT THAT this was the first game of a New Year. Like taxmen and teachers, football fans tend to divide life up into seasons rather than calendar years; I for one always find an August eve-of-new-season more exciting than the desperate revelry of 31

December. Still, contrived references to the latest milestone to the grave are *de rigeur* for all. Numerologically speaking, postwar years with a '5' on the end have traditionally been rather excellent for United: '45 saw Matt arrive; '55 the Birth Of The Babes; '65 brought Bestie's Boys the title; '75 witnessed the rebirth of the modern United; and '85 was to be the Year of the Norm. How can we possibly fail? And rather strangely, United's players have always seemed rather susceptible to the cosmic consequences of Janus' arrival. We tend to have good and bad *years* rather than seasons; thus 1985 was wholly excellent yet 1986 uniformly crap, a trend followed for example by 1991 and 1992 amongst many other examples. So, in spite of our season-by-season mindset, perhaps that first game of a New Year does indeed have some talismanic significance. It certainly did in '92 . . .

For those who inhabit the world of the rational rather than that of the omen and starsign, the night's importance was rather more prosaic. Blackburn's spawny comeback against the Hammers on the Monday had put them six points ahead and victory was simply essential if our forthcoming showdown with Rovers was to have any real worth. Sky TV, doubtless slavering rabidly at the chance to show a Red-hating nation another home slip-up, gratefully seized the opportunity afforded by the Loftus Road postponement to show the game live. That meant that a minimum of four consecutive United matches would be live on Sky in January – why don't they just hand over their sad new Sky Sports 2 to United and be done with it?

This was not a night that would find favour with your genitals, if they could give an opinion. The freezing temperature, down to Gothenberg levels, shrunk many a Red trouser-packet; further scrote damage ensued as tensed-up Reds clutched themselves frantically during the hugely worrying first 20 minutes. The mild unease caused by the sight of our makeshift team – half under 21 – scrabbling about on a tricky surface without the option of the boot-up to Hughes was replaced at the Scoreboard End by mild panic in the 11th and 15th minutes; Pally appeared to handle in the box, then Wegerle just failed to connect for what would have been a disastrous opener. With ten behind the ball but more pace on the break, sky-blue Coventry resembled Leicester-lite; and we were threatening to make heavy weather of them. Despite Pally redeeming himself with the narrowest of headed misses after 20 minutes, we looked uncomfortable, in desperate need of the security blanket of a goal.

On half an hour, with perfect appropriateness, the kids to whom Alex has turned repaid his faith. Like lads doing schoolyard impressions, Butt and Scholes performed their sketch 'If Sharpe And Law Had Played Together', Nicky attempting to reproduce Lee's Barcelonian trickery before Paul roared in to score like the Old King himself. The Middleton urchin had buzzed, harried and probed relentlessly and, with Eric, was to be the key to our success. To step into the boots of Hughes is a task that has defeated and destroyed many before him; moreover, it's not as though he's even a faintly similar player. For the tactically minded, there was much to muse upon in considering the Uniteds with Hughes or Scholes; the suspicion must be that Alex is still in deep thought over the matter of Eric's future partner too. Tonight, Eric was often to drop back and play the Hughesy pivot role, with Scholes foraging right up front – is this the shape of '95 to come? Or is Scholes already marked as the new Mark Robins, a short-term supernova that leaves no permanent trace in the Old Trafford galaxy? At the moment, the entire area around the Number Ten position is an unfathomable black hole – let us hope Alex sorts it before it undoes us.

The cheers that greeted the goal were rather strange – the sound of relief rather than joy, since a win was all that was expected or permissible. Jenkinson did his best to animate the Scoreboard End by getting in on the impressionist game, performing a sublime Klinsmannism right in front of us to provoke a storm of crowd obscenities around his head. He was duly punished by missing a 32nd minute chance and Coventry never really threatened again. United spent the rest of the half creating ever-increasing circles of passing movements, before emerging after the break to finish them off with a classic one-two-three. Keith Gillespie went close, Keane closer still, until Scholes caught Pressley fannying about with a smart piece of Law-like poaching to win a penalty. If the decision was borderline, the finish certainly wasn't, Eric continuing to prove his almost Papal infallibility from the spot. That Pressley was ordered off as a result of a second yellow for the penalty offence made it all the sweeter; in his former incarnation as a filthy Hun he had caused Eric to receive his marching orders at Ibrox. At two down with ten men, Coventry were beaten. The honour, won back in the mists of pre-history, to be the last Coventry scorer against United remained safe in the gloved hands of Cyrille Regis.

For a while, United sought a third with some passion, with even Brucey snuffling in the box for chances like some waddling Dordogne truffle-pig (a creature soon to be extinct, allegory-fans). Gillespie was blatantly brought down in the box on 57 minutes, failing to get the penalty he deserved for the second time in four days – perhaps Keith should study some old vids of Mickey Thomas to acquire the knack of convincing dives. United, unjustly knocked-back, appeared to sulk for the best part of quarter of an hour until the game and stadium bizarrely exploded into life on 75 minutes. Coventry's support had been odd to say the least. From about the 40th minute they had maintained an almost constant vocal presence, even throughout half-time, which was an OT first this season. Yet they'd done so at a volume that would rarely trouble the most sensitive of decibel meters; their low murmuring made you wonder if they'd all contracted laryngitis on the cold coach journey north. Presumably fed up of being unable to provoke us even to acknowledge their presence, and with the match clearly lost, they resorted to Barca songs which promptly had the entire Scoreboard End on their feet. 'Sutton United' is not a chant you hear very often from K stand but it kept us warm for ten minutes. The team responded with a flurry of bombing raids over ten minutes, Keith, Scholes and Butt all seeming set to make it 3-0. Butt's effort would have made a Goal of the Month contender as a partially rejuvenated Giggs inspired the first rendition of *Running Down The Wing* for aeons to set Nicky up delightfully. Choccy, in his best role as supersub, gave a typical and vintage McClair cameo. One minute he'd be treading on the ball, getting caught dozing fatly in possession and fluffing the simplest of passes, the next he'd be playing demon through-balls, chasing down over 70 yards or bending blinders just wide, as twice attempted within two minutes.

In contrast to our domination, Coventry's second-half efforts produced but one on-target attempt from Dion, who received a tremendous reception from us as befitting his former cult-hero status. Of course, each Red chant of 'Dion, Dion' carried the fervent subtext 'Play well, old son – but don't score, you bastard', and the great man duly obliged us.

Shuffling home past the stalls who'd done a frenzied trade in daft woolly hats, some might have muttered disappointedly about our failure to put four or five past ten very average men but most were surely grateful that three taken-for-granted points had indeed been safely secured. Nicky Butt and Paul Scholes had continued to paint themselves into the picture of United's future and King Eric, as at Southampton, had re-emerged at his flamboyant, string-pulling best. To win against a team so desperate for points without Hughes, Ince, Parker, Sharpe, Schmeichel and Andrei – half our Double team – constitutes an achievement that might go unsung but should not be ignored. We now faced three games that would shape the rest of 1995: if we were no longer as arrogant as we were back in New Year 1994, it could still be argued that our prospects were just as bright.

Team: Walsh; Neville, Irwin, Bruce, Gillespie, Pallister, Cantona, Keane (McClair), Scholes, Butt, Giggs

9 January: SHEFFIELD UNITED AWAY – FA CUP ROUND THREE

Final Score: Sheff United 0 UNITED 2

Scorers: Hughes 79, Eric 82

Attendance: 22,322

MY O-LEVEL MATHS TELLS me that the odds against United drawing the Blades three years running were something like 65,000 to 1 which, funnily enough, are approximately City's chances of winning the League sometime before the Sun explodes and Time ends. The self-satisfied smirk on Bert Millichip's face after his ball-bag fondling had produced this dreaded tie made you want to torch Lancaster Gate. Thanks to Sky's intervention, the game was switched to a Monday night just to add to the fixture's lack of appeal; thus it was that thousands of Reds braved the howling gales to fill the Bramall Lane End, expecting no more than the god-awful 'entertainment' served up last January. The gaping chasm left by the John Street Stand, which was not so much under construction as completely non-existent, merely added to the swirling maelstrom within the ground; this would not be a matter of having the wind behind or ahead of you but of 80mph gusts going up your keks, down your neck and spinning madly around your head. The one consolation provided by the appalling conditions was that the Blades would surely have to forego their habitual up-and-under long-ball bollocks version of football; anything going above six feet was likely to be swept straight off to the Pennines to startle the indigenous sheep and their Elland Road lovers on the hills. Unfortunately, it appeared that the home side were all too capable of reverting to proper football – for much of the first half, they threatened to ruin both ours and Wrexham's night.

For Sheffield, back in their customary position as the Yorkie town's Man City, tonight was the highlight of their season. Posters outside the ground trumpeted 'Up For The Cup!' in quaint 1930s' fashion whilst inside they sought to make the most of their Sky at night with frenzied PA announcements and balloon releases. Poor Blades – the cameras and opposition gave them a teasing reminder of the Premiership world to which they will never return.

Reds who filled both tiers at our end were meanwhile enjoying the largest tribal gathering since Loftus Road; if this was not quite a vintage singing display, there was at least a tangible Cup buzz even though the FA Cup no longer holds quite the same magic for United as it did in the Eighties. Whatever, our vocal power was quite sufficient to smother the Kop End's rather puny efforts which nevertheless still outdecibelled their Wednesdayite neighbours' tawdry showing back in October. The Blades also had an answer to Hillsborough's *Aida* march song, a bizarre, drum-intro'd, grunting apelike medley that deserved a rather better performance than it got – in Blade throats, it sounded like a hundred narcoleptic gibbons getting moderately worked up. Highly amused by this, Reds took it up with a gusto after they heard its one Blade rendition on 30 minutes, transforming it into an urgent mass chimpfest as both a pisstake and a demonstration of vocal supremacy which kept us grinning for the next 20 minutes.

Such self-entertainment was entirely necessary as United, dressed in the deckchairs once more, produced but one shot in the first half. Sheffield attacked with admirable verve, with the wind vaguely behind them as far as one could tell, against a United team who clearly felt discomforted by the conditions and the brashness of the opposition. Schmeichel, back from injury and forced straight into the fray after Walsh's flu attack, saved us twice whilst Blake obviously felt most aggrieved not to have got a penalty when Brucey collided with him. Fortunately, the excellent ref – possibly the best we've had this season – understood our Stevie very well. Everything Bruce does looks far worse than it is: the players call him Mr Ugly, and that probably refers to his style as well as his distorted features. This is a player whose running resembles that of a fat ten-year-old girl in the playground trying desperately to get caught in a game of 'Chase 'n' Kiss': a player whose best headers at goal look like the leaps of a destitute drunk hallucinating that he's pirouetting in *Swan Lake*. Naturally, even his cleanest penalty box tackles consequently resemble the savage, premeditated assaults of a Souness. So thank you, Mr Hart of Darlington, for your understanding; step up on to the podium to join David Elleray in the Semi-Decent Refs Club.

Of course his other great service to the Red cause was to send off Hartfield after 14 minutes when many a ref, spotting Cantona within 50 feet, would have automatically red-carded the Red hero out of instinct.

The effect on the game was anything but instantaneous however. The Blades continued to play with spirit and unexpected skill, although they grew blunter as the game wore on. Giggs threatened sporadically and provided a cross from which Hughes hit a post right in front of us, but it was Hodges who was looking the star man at this point. Thankfully, the oldest cliché in football was about to be applied once more – 'It's a game of two halves, Brian' (or, indeed, Andy). After a nervy half-time break, not improved by the local police swooping about with dogs, fully tensed up as if a 'kick-off' were imminent, United took control. Roy Keane took over about three positions at once to dominate quite superbly; Giggs, perhaps gingered up by the presence of ready-made replacement Sharpe on the bench, began both to run and cross with some definable purpose. With both Eric and Hughes flowering on a sodden surface, Blade incursions up to our end became increasingly infrequent and ineffective. And yet, with our wall of monkey sound and the wind behind them, with Sheffield's ten men stretched on the rack and with chances being created by the minute, United simply refused to score with almost wilful wastefulness. When Butt missed and Eric's easy sidefoot from a yard was saved, my neighbour Bert moaned softly, a sound easily translated as 'This isn't going to be our night'. A wallet-draining replay – or something worse – loomed large.

The wall of noise at our end took on a strained, frantic quality as if it might collapse at any moment until, with about ten minutes to go, Giggs and Hughes combined to score a goal of almost stupid simplicity. As our two tiers relievedly revelled uproariously and *Que Sera* rang confidently out, the Blades came forward with the final flailing effort of drowning men. Within seconds a piece of sublime, divine control and two precision passes had found Eric at the corner of the other end's box. As Reds stood poised on the brink of ejaculation, the King floated home the most delicious chip imaginable; as the net billowed gently, he stood transfixed momentarily, as if even he was stunned by his own brilliance. The juices of ecstasy flowed freely in our stand; God had fashioned yet another minor miracle but with two feet and a ball instead of loaves and fishes. The Double Double was on.

Suddenly, Red life seemed sweet once more. Sharpe was back, Giggs was improving with every game, Schmeichel was back home in goal and Ince would be returning within the week. With Eric and Keane at the peak of their game, the future looked so much more safely familiar. As I shuffled out, someone nearby said 'Did you see Keegan on the touchline? What was he up to, then?' Within 12 hours the comforting vision of our Double team's reassembly was about to be shattered, and our world turned completely upside down.

Team: Schmeichel; O'Kane (Sharpe), Bruce, Pallister, Irwin, Keane, McClair (Scholes), Butt, Giggs, Cantona, Hughes

15 January: NEWCASTLE UNITED AWAY

Final Score: Newcastle 1 UNITED 1

Scorer: Hughes 12

Attendance: 34,471

AS ANY CHILD OF the seventies will confirm, the most celebrated 'phone calls were once those made on radio by the loathsome Noel Edmonds. Not any more though: Alex Ferguson has supplanted Noel's 'Funny Phone Calls' (*sic*) with his own Trunk Tariff Terrorism. Once upon a time, the hapless victim was Sergeant Wilkinson and, by extension, thousands of heart-broken Tykes. Barely two years later, as Sky Sport Text astonishingly confirmed the morning after Bramall Lane, we discovered he'd been at it again – this time it would be the Geordies' turn to suffer death by seven million cuts. Andy Cole, the greatest Tyneside cult hero since Supermac, the record-breaking goal-scorer, was coming to Old Trafford, almost incidentally breaking the UK transfer record in the process.

Staring bleary-eyed and in shock at the bald, flickering text on-screen, I recognised that shivering sensation throughout my nervous system at once. It was 'that Cantona moment' once more. Such instances used to be called 'JFK moments', of course – where were you when you heard? . . . etc. Not that anything as trivial as the death of a philandering, overrated US Prez could be compared to the seismic shock of the Cantona deal, I hasten to add. That the Cole deal announcement was on roughly the same plane became unquestionably evident within hours.

It soon transpired that Fergie's fingers had done the epochal walking the previous Wednesday. Just as in '92, he'd been knocked back yet again for a much-hyped target – then it was Hirst, this time it had been Collymore – whose manager had refused to answer the 'phone. On an inspired hunch befitting a man whose resemblance to Taggart is so remarkable, he called Keegan to try once more, routinely, for Cole. In place of the point-blank refusal Alex had received in September came an astonishing, though qualified, 'maybe'. By Thursday afternoon Hughesy had turned down the chance of being part of a swap; Gillespie, apparently adored by Keegan, became the deal's linchpin. By Monday evening the transfer was sealed, ready to be announced at a one pm press conference to a disbelieving world. Fergie remarked casually how satisfying it had been to prise a jewel from the heart of enemy territory; in fact, he had plunged his hand into the chest of the Toon Army and ripped out its heart. Blood-spattered Geordies looked on, transfixed with horror – the past nightmares of selling Supermac, Waddle, Gazza and Co had returned to haunt them. How very sad indeed . . .

The time for serious implications comes later. The primary pleasure is to revel in the misery of others, of course. The tabloids are terrific at moments like these and unearthed every type of wretched creature on the Tyne to illustrate the locals' devastation. One found a particularly dense specimen who'd come home, fresh from submitting to a massive Cole tattoo on his thigh, to find that his eternal hero had been stolen. Several removal sessions at the cost of a grand would now be needed, fitting punishment for any cretin who believes any decent player would want to spend his entire life marooned in the North-East amidst white-stilletoed slappers and hair-bleached, real-life *Viz* stereotypes. Even better, another reported on the local primary school assembly being awash with tears as eight-year-old mini-Toons were told the news by a grieving headmaster. Geordie kids traumatised for life – brilliant work, Fergie! (As if being Geordie wasn't handicap enough on anyone's existence.) The souvenir shop's main trade became a steady stream of red-eyed, bawling Geordies – and that's just the adults – bringing back their Cole shirts and mugs for refunds, the transfer having wiped out the pleasure of many a Christmas present collection. Enjoyment doesn't come much richer than this, does it, fellow misanthropes?

In interesting contrast to their Sunday show of defiance, few Newcastle fans seemed keen to stick up for Keegan at first. Press quotes of Tony Garretty, David Craggs and other leading Toon fans hardly displayed the rampant Keegan-kissing frenzy that later followed. Instinct is the best guide – whatever Toons pretended to feel subsequently, let there be no doubt that this deal hurt them every bit as much as the Cantona sale emotionally wrecked the sheepshaggers. They just had the self-awareness to cover it up as soon as possible instead of bleeding over it for the next two years à la Elland Road.

As for Reds, most that I know simply wanted to ride the megabuzz for as long as possible before, in true Mancunian style, looking at the worst possible outcome. As all girlies know, there's nothing like the hit of a spending spree, and few Reds are immune to the sensual sensation of being part of a club that's just wadded £6 million on the counter and said 'Wrap him up – we'll 'ave 'im.' The blissful schadenfreude of having 'done a Cantona' on the Geordies simply prolonged the buzz, as did the epic nervous breakdown suffered by the media who spent the next week collapsing in heaps of newsprint all over the story. For sensation-starved journos, bored by yet another United-Rovers title race and without a megabuck transfer tale after weeks of speculative foreplay, the collective mass orgasm over Cole must have been some relief. How perfect, too, that it wasn't Collymore but instead the complete surprise of Cole – 'Stan the Man at OT' would have been so predictable an outcome that it would hardly have generated any excitement at all. This, however, could have no peer in the surprise-stakes, save for Shearer going to Burnley: this viscerally thrillsome Tuesday, whose ramifications you could feel spreading trepidation throughout the Premiership, may yet be seen to be one of the keystone dates in United's modern era. The first BC Era - Before Cantona – ended on 26 November 1992. Will 10 January 1995 go down as the end of the Second BC epoch – Before Cole?

Naturally, this enormous silver lining had a small cloud attached to it. Keith Gillespie, to whom I previously referred as both the present and future of United, has turned out to be no such phenomenon. Faced with the prospect of three 'superior' wingers ahead of the queue for first team places, his decision to agree to leave was understandable. Fergie's willingness to let him be the bargaining chip was equally intelligible, given the manager's Eurozeal. To be Irish in the current climate is akin to being a plague-carrier – with UEFA insisting on English teams being stuffed with blond Aryans if they wish to be Euro Champs, only those foreigners of the Keane and Cantona class can feel safe. With the memory of his wonder goal against the Toons still fresh in the mind, we bade him a fond farewell and trust that he will be the only 'second generation fledgling' to be let go.

Furthermore, behind this small passing cloud rumbled a brewing thunderstorm. What would all this mean for the contract-negotiating

Bert, as ever, captures the Zeitgeist perfectly (© Bert for Red Issue)

© *Drastic for* Red Issue

UF Productions tell you all you need to know about the first three days of tabloid coverage

(© UF Productions for Red Issue)

Man United Anti-Fascists

City BNP Supporter meets
Man United Anti-Fascists
28.1.95

In Action

Red Attitude *does its bit for inter-ideological harmony* (© Red Attitude)

Bert spells out the worst case scenario for the New Old Trafford (© Bert for Red Issue)

Contempt of Court (© Red Issue)

Mid way through the first half against A[...] the junta in charge of this great football club dec[...] war against [...] true United supporter. In the middle of play, a tannoy announcement repeated the new instruction printed in the program: if you [...] up from your seat at any point during the game, the [...] club [...] allow you to be thrown out of the match, or arrested, or [...] club membership or LMTB revoked.

The message could not [...] clearer. Supporting your team in the way we have all done for gene[...]ns past is now [...] "anti-social activity". The timing of this announcement should tell y[...] at is going on, coming days after the unveiling of t[...] development pla[...] he club does not want you, the genuine hard-core [...] at the NEW Old [...] rd. They are going to take this once-in-a-lifetime opportunity to create a new kind of audience at U[...]al footb[...] are ou[...] eek, mil[...] annered [...] seat [...] ers are [...] This announcement is the first s[...] of the y[...] ar [...] it is tim[...] stood and fought.

To p[...] a RED from standing and singing strik[...] at the very essence of being a United fan. If they ca[...] conform to this, there [...] nothing they won't [...] able to [...] o in the future. [...]oug[...] has h[...]ped i[...] the past a[...] [...]s Club i[...] the face [...] fans' [...]position; [...] is t[...]e for [...] nd [...] unite a[...] le[...] [...]t of the stadium.

Thirty minutes into today's second half, genuine United fans all over K Stand will rise to sing "Fergie's Red And White Army." They will stay on their feet until the end of the game. We urge everyone in K. Stand to join with them. The media have been alerted that a campaign is underway. This might be the last chance we get to fight for the club we love. STAND UP AND FIGHT AND BE COUNTED.

The IMUSA take their first public action

HOW TO BECOME A WEST HAM FAN

A NORMAL HUMAN

GROW A PONY TAIL AND WEAR AN EAR RING

CALL YOURSELF RODERICK, TRISTIAN OR SOME GIRLY NAME

DEVELOP A NAUSEATING ACCENT

BECOME A RACIST BIGOT

LAUGH AT ALF GARNET

GO TO WEMBLEY ONCE EVERY 30 YEARS

PRETEND YOUR HARD

IF YOU CAN BE ALL THESE THINGS -

WELL DONE BONZO!

now why don't you piss off to Upton Park with 18,000 of your other <u>buddies</u> !!!!!

© *Drastic for* Red Issue

Hughes? There was no escaping the implications: unless a complete change in the team system was about to be wrought, there would be no room for Eric, Cole and Sparky in a United eleven. Hughes, surely, would be too proud a man to accept the role of twelfth man, too enamoured with Eric to be willing to play gooseberry whilst Cantona and Cole got it together up front. Everton, Leeds and City flew straight over to our overflowing honeypot of forward talent like the pestilential flies that they are - it soon became clear that Joe Royle had arrived first and was offering £2.5 million to lead Hughes down the path that the last OT warrior, Norman Whiteside, had heartbreakingly trodden. We had an embarrassment of riches that was threatening to cause as much pain as joy.

Wiser, pessimistic heads pointed out further pitfalls. If Cole was to be a straight replacement for Hughes, how could it work? Who could fill Hughesy's holding-up role that has always been so vital for the counter-attacking United? How could Cole and Cantona be expected to gel instantly and rescue our season before Rovers disappeared over the horizon? Indeed, how could the team adapt as a whole, and do so at least to some degree before the arrival of the league leaders in ten days time? And if we were still intending seriously to defend the Double, how could we switch back and forth between systems, given that Cole would be Cup-tied?

As rumours emanated from Tyneside about the reality behind the PR façade of the Cole deal, they brought further grist to the doom merchant mill. Brian Woolnough on Sky was the first to say publicly what many suspected – something smelled a bit fishy, and he didn't mean the Geordie fat slags. The MEN talked of Cole's 'social withdrawal' from his team-mates, of his lonely lifestyle in Crook and hinted at 'personality problems'. Others argued baldly that he remained homesick for his London mates like Wrighty and for his family in Nottingham – and not least his girl living alone in North London. There was certainly talk of Cole's disgust at the continued racist behaviour of some Geordie crowd elements towards his family, suggesting by extension that he might find the 'Northern mentality' as a whole somewhat problematic. *The Guardian* reprinted a recent mysterious quote from Keegan which ran: 'I've heard a lot of nasty things said about him in the last few weeks but he's never been any trouble to me.' Ignoring the fact that the last bit of that quote is not strictly true, Mr Keegan, what does all this mean? Just what have United bought? Is there something to be concerned about more than his mere failure to score for two months?

The man himself gave few pointers, not even of his true feelings about the move. In good PR-speak he was anxious to clear himself with the Newcastle fans but also, as is usual at OT post-transfer press gigs, made all the right noises about the hugeness of our Club, his boyhood desires for the Red shirt and so on. He looked uncomfortable, shell-shocked even, but that's to be expected. The truth is that we all stepped into the unknown. Peter Corrigan, in that day's *Indie on Sunday*, remarked that the steely look in the eyes of both Keegan and Fergie as they shook on the deal spoke of a common realisation that one man would, eventually, emerge as the winner of the bargain, the other to regret forever his mistake. Actually that was not strictly true – the deal wasn't necessarily a zero-sum game. It is quite conceivable that both could lose or both win, depending on how Cole fares and how Keegan spends the money. Still, you can't help feeling that this was a last-hand poker showdown; our entire season, and the next too, hung on the draw.

The Sunday-for-Sky fixture itself was transformed in character by the epochal events of the week. What was once to be an occasion for football connoisseurs instead became a mediafest, an opportunity for symbolism, the match a mere peg on which journos could hang articles of every conceivable variety. The oppressive atmosphere inside the stadium was a testament to the pendulous weight of unanswered questions about the future of both clubs that hung low over St James' Park. Outside, Geordies exhibited levels of self-consciousness not usually seen anywhere else but Anfield. Packs of earnest, post-traumatic-stress-disordered Toons waylaid the dozens of wandering media types to rattle off the new 'Castle mantra: 'Keegan's our hero – it's a good deal – we're a buying club you know' etc etc *ad nauseam*. They spoke with the 'protesteth too much' zealotry and consistency of men who haven't yet fully convinced themselves, let alone anyone else. Some, fresh from declaring that they were 'as big a club as Man U', nevertheless reacted to the sight of Reds with the small-time vocal venom you only get from adherents of clubs with inferiority complexes. For the 800 or so Reds who had made it, it promised to be an uncomfortable afternoon, as you would expect when visiting a delinquent family in the throes of a domestic. Even before the Cole announcement, this had proved to be the hottest ticket of the season so far. Old Trafford touts were actually to be seen empty-handed; scores of home and awayers would miss their first game for months as the box holders rushed to seize advantage of their privileges. Sods.

Cole himself had been ordered not to attend, a decision by the home club that had caused the erstwhile hero some distress. Despite his corporeal absence, Cole's ghostly shadow was the dominant figure on the pitch. Newcastle fans, of course, had their own ramifications to work out; for Reds, there was the dizzying realisation that this could be not only Hughesy's last game but this team's last display of what might soon be called 'the old style'. Little did we realise that within minutes we would be getting the perfect comparatory illustrations of Life With and Without Hughes.

The Toons had clearly decided that this was a chance to demonstrate to the nation that they were NOT undergoing the same revulsion and trauma as had Leeds fans in November '92. They opened vocally with a ten-minute medley of Keegan support, almost as if they had one eye on the pitch and the other on the cameras; after a strangely quiescent rest of the first half, they supported their team's second-half offensive with admirable, gusto. The Red contingent, packed into a block opposite the terraces that had held such a party on our last visit, carried too many sleeping partners to be able to put up that much of a fight. Once Hughes had gone off, the event took on an overwhelmingly black and white hue and not only in terms of the play – this was an afternoon about Newcastle, their fans, their manager, their future. The fact that they were playing us seemed almost incidental. It felt like we were the villains in a poor pantomime, under constant audience-pleasing assault from the plucky young upstarts who, despite the losses of their leading boys Cole and Beardsley, were nevertheless going to triumph before the final curtain.

As it turned out, our hopes were both raised and thwarted in the same instant. With our first serious chance, after ten minutes of Geordie headless chicken impressions, Hughes encapsulated everything that is great about him to score. From Eric's dummy, Sparky executed a shot of supreme technique, power and intelligence to beat the racing Srnicek. But above all, the attempt testified to Hughesy's bravery and passion – and for once he lost the gamble that he takes every time he goes in where it can hurt. As he was carted off, curtailing all celebration, he reminded me of the scene in *Animal Farm* when the heroic workhorse Boxer is injured. It is always a shock to see something you thought indestructible felled, like a son seeing his dad beaten up. Yet, in the maelstrom of the moment, I am ashamed to admit I felt a twinge of secret glee; perhaps, unlike Boxer, Hughesy would now be spared a knacker's yard destiny at Goodison. Any such feelings were soon extinguished when it became rapidly obvious that without Hughes to hold the ball up and distribute, United's attacking blade had been shattered. Eighty minutes of football's equivalent of the defence of Leningrad followed.

I can't recall the last time I saw United get such a relentless pummelling. We were fortunate that for most of it Kitson and Clark were showing themselves to be singularly incapable of stepping into Cole's scoring boots. Howey missed an absolute sitter almost on half-time but for the previous 30 minutes, neither our midfield nor attack had seemed to have spent more than five seconds at a time in possession, let alone created a chance. Their five-man midfield swamped our Ince-less and toothless opposite numbers and half-time was a blessed relief. Surely it could not get worse? Naturally, it did. Our defence began to crumble, Fergie from the bench metaphorically having to rush around plunging digits into dyke holes (oo-er) before switching to three centre-backs to stem the flooding. Stevie Bruce should have gone off but couldn't as Butt's double-vision necessitated immediate substitution; despite all the frantic re-organisation and the strange-but-true apparition of a decently performing May, Kitson's equalizer was no surprise and fully deserved. The remaining hour-like minutes passed agonisingly slowly for every anguished Red.

The final irony, however, was that the very thing that so inspired the Geordies to batter us – the Cole deal - remained the one reason why they failed to finish us off. Without his lethal touch the on-target chances didn't materialise for them – in a sense the pre-match timing of the deal may have cost us victory but it also saved us the point. In the last eight minutes, Keane and Eric both had platinum-plated opportunities to win it for us but justice prevailed, it has to be said. If anything, you might wish they hadn't had those chances, for they meant that the overwhelming sense of relief that we all felt at escaping unbeaten was tinged with the gnawing regret that we hadn't stolen the points at the last. I daresay some in the Red enclosure felt the extra secret relief of not having to emerge onto the St James' concourses to face a beaten Geordie horde – as it stood, you could see in Toon faces that they felt their honour had been salvaged. And, after all, so had ours. Pre-season, you'd have settled for a point up there; it was just unfortunate that we now languished five points and a game behind Rovers. Fergie looked entirely miserable afterwards, for it had truly been a shitty, inglorious day all round. The Hughes injury had, it appeared, genuinely upset him but in brutal *realpolitik* terms, it made the manager's immediate task somewhat simpler. We had to beat Rovers on Sunday, and do so with a new forward playing within what must be a new system. What a time to have to engage in such a dramatic footballing experiment; for an apparently sober-living Glaswegian Protestant, Fergie can be one hell of a gambler – this was the equivalent of staking your house on the turn of a card. Let us pray that the Black King comes up trumps.

Team: Schmeichel; Irwin, Bruce, Pallister, Sharpe, Keane, McClair, Butt (May), Giggs, Cantona, Hughes (Scholes)

22 January: BLACKBURN ROVERS AT HOME

Final Score: UNITED 1 Blackburn 0

Scorer: Eric 80

Attendance: 43,742

IT MAY WELL HAVE been hypemaster bollocks of the first order for the tabloids to dub a January fixture 'the title showdown' but in the circumstances you have to admit they had a point. Never has the Western movie cliché 'We'll head 'em off at the pass' been more appropriate for a footie match. At five points behind, having played a game more than Rovers, the simplicity of the task was agonisingly acute – if our troops failed to trample all over the opposition at this vital junction, Rovers would be off into the distance and halfway up the title summit, leaving us to eat their dust in the foothills of the Also-Rans.

Moreover, United being United, we had to make it that little bit harder by having to overcome the division's meanest defence with a new boy upfront. To say that the poor lad was under the spotlight was an understatement of some scale: the glare of a thousand flashbulbs and TV cameras beamed straight into his mournful eyes from point-blank range. His was probably the most media-drenched debut in British football history, a baptism fiery enough without the additional burden of it being the biggest Premiership fixture since the new League began. If he'd legged straight back to Crook howling in terror at this point, you'd have sympathised.

Of course Old Trafford is subtly different on days like these. On the face of it the scenes outside are 'normal' but the atmospheric change is tangible. You talk to some Reds and they reply in a clipped, slightly strained manner; you catch intense gleams in the eyes from passers-by; even the way people walk changes. Everywhere you can feel Reds experiencing the same mixture of excited anticipation, pessimistic worry and grim, determined intent on victory. Everything *looks* no different than it would for, say, the visit of Norwich, but the air is so charged as to make you feel you're on another planet.

The touts are buzzing, mainlining on the day's profit forecasts as you hear snatched snippets of dealing everywhere: 'Two together mate? £180'; 'Give me your watch and it's yours, pal'. On the stalls, the T-shirts bear witness to the latest epic developments as new Cole designs mingle in with merchandising varieties carrying the legend 'Hughesy must stay'.

Those of us who enjoy commercial exploitation are gratified to see the hideous new kit everywhere, the more optimistic having already taken the plunge to affix 'COLE – 17' on the back; and even on a day when you'd think the prospect of 90 crucial minutes would drown out every other mental consideration, the Megastore remains crammed with those who can still find the motivation to shop.

Once inside – and once Keith Fane has desisted from inflicting his dreaded record collection on us – the real business can begin. The great thing about fixtures like this, especially when live on Sky, is that you can translate all those months of pub grumblings and fanzine complaints into direct verbal assaults on the targets themselves sat in L stand, and their inbred brethren back in Blackburn. Not all the chants have the wit of the song *Shearer's a Greedy Bastard* or the incision of the questioning 'Where were you when you were shit?' but when the enemy and the cameras are there, few clamourous chants are as satisfying as a simple 'F*ck Off, Shearer' repeated ten times at top volume by 15,000 Reds. For once, it seemed to me at least in the Scoreboard, the stewards had wisely decided to leave off the usual nanny-State interference, perhaps appreciating that on days like this it's important for the Club that we are let off the leash to play our part of intimidating the opposition. Before the game, a veteran K stander, having congratulated me on *United We Stood*, scolded me gently for daring to tweak the tail of the mighty beast that is K stand in print. 'We may sit back quietly a bit too much these days,' he remarked, 'but when we're needed, we're always there. We're like the big guns in reserve – we can still blow anyone away.' Indeed they can – and did. Like an opening artillery barrage from the Great War, the 15-minute cavalcade of abuse, singing and venom which K stand led from kick-off softened up the enemy trenches brilliantly. The travelling Rovers were cowed into near silence until almost half-time, whilst the mercenaries on the pitch took flight.

Had Cole taken his tricky, bobbling chance after two minutes, the ensuing bedlam would have threatened the stadium's construction. It was quite clear that all Reds had put aside any misgivings about the deal to get behind the lad, virtually swamping him with goodwill. Terrace opinion had perfectly expressed itself at the start with three chants in quick succession – for Eric, still the King; for Cole, cheekily swiping the Geordies' own Andy anthem; and for Hughes, the unforgotten hero. Schizophrenic and illogical we may be, for all three cannot co-exist here, but emotional loyalty is never a logical subject.

United dominated the first half to such an embarrassing extent that Rovers' half-time shot tally stood at two - neither on target. With an abjectly negative display reminiscent of Leeds last New Year's Day, you had to conclude that they'd come for the nil-nil draw rather than engage us in a true test of footballing ability. Typical Rovers, of course: all prose with none of United's poetry. Minutes after his initial miss, Cole was doing an unexpected Hughes impression to hold up the ball and set up McClair's predictable miss; on 22 minutes, Giggs and Eric doubled up in failing to score the opener. Best of all, on the stroke of half-time, was Incey's trademark longranger which twice forced itself out of Flowers' clutches before trickling to safety. However, most of our dominance wasn't reflected so much in clear-cut opportunities wasted but in perfect positions that were never quite realised as connections begging to be made went unmatched, particularly after the break: McClair just failing to find Giggs on 52; Keane's archetypal cross on 53; Sharpe falling milli-metrically short on 45 . . . all pauses pregnant with potential that narrowly failed to give birth to goals.

Blackburn's efforts had been risible. On a rare excursion to our end's goal-line, Sutton collapsed sackishly into hoardings – as the corner-taking Wilcox could have told him, that piece of the pitch was not an area in which to linger alone. With the howls of pisstaking merriment ringing around his ears, he staggered off to spend much of the remainder of the game looking grumpy, confused and clumsy, feeling parts of his body for imaginary injuries and being generally as effective as a chocolate condom. Rovers' greatest first-half moment, an edge of the area free-kick, elicited derision as their 'expert' deadballers found only Andy Cole's face. Good defensive work, fella! Brcuey would be proud of you.

Their fans, too, were hardly being adroit. Summoning up the courage to squeak near half-time, when admittedly we had gone a little quiet due to our gobsmackedness at failing to score, Rovers tried a chorus of 'You're supposed to be at home'. About half of the

Scoreboard appeared to have difficulty in not bursting out laughing at this point, as anyone who's ever been to Ewood Mausoleum would comprehend. It was as if Scousers had started to chant 'Get a Job'. Still, you have to excuse the Rovers rabble; most have only had two years' experience of football fandom and have clearly yet to learn the art of terrace point-scoring.

For about 15 minutes after Keane's cross had whizzed wide Rovers at last mounted one or two attacks, having presumably realised that United were bound to score sometime and that their one-point target would necessitate a goal from them too. Such ambition! Fortunately Shearer displayed the same shooting form as he had in the FA Cup replay by missing two golden chances at the Strettie End. That was to be the sum of his contribution, beyond that last-gasp slyness that cost his team-mates the result they wanted. So much, then, for the SAS – as my neighbour remarked, the initials would seem to stand for 'Shit and Shite'.

Even during this period of Rovers' alleged supremacy, Eric almost went through for a solo goal on 57 before Cole was brought down a minute later in the game's strangest incident. Nobody but Andy appealed for a penalty, yet TV replays later demonstrated that indeed should have been the result. In his post-match anti-ref diatribe, the myopic Dalglish missed that one, it seems. Nevertheless, by the time Andrei replaced Sharpe to cacophonous crowd approval, the game had swung back to the Reds. The patience of the team contrasted sharply with the increasingly rabid impatience of us lot chainsmoking and nailbiting in the seats.

Unflummoxed and unflustered, Eric and the rampantly resurgent Giggs continued to probe, pass and play as if we had hours left in which to get the winner. With Le Saux going to pieces at his side – and getting most pleasingly booked on 77 – the Herculean Hendry could hold up the Rovers defence no more. With ten to go, Giggs tackled back quite brilliantly and, bursting with refound confidence, curled the ball superbly to the far post for Eric to find the only six-inch square of the net that Flowers couldn't cover. Clutching his Club badge as if it were the very heart of him, Eric raced to the corner, cocked his fingers in a gunlike pose and 'fired' at the stricken Rovers masses. The original Lone Gunman, the Sheriff of Old Trafford, had saved us again and had, indeed, headed 'em off at the pass. Yee-haa, pardner.

As Blackburn flapped about, struggling to make any headway with their neo-Route One rubbish, three minutes of fervent Cantona worship occupied the stands' attention as we revelled in the most joyous goal since the fifth against City. The sheer vital centrality of the goal in League terms caused the sense of relief but the guttural roar of 40,000 also held something else. It wasn't just the sense of justice being done over 90 minutes or the satisfaction of a climax after such patient building, like finally bedding a cracker after three weeks hard chasing. It was the feeling that, at last, we had demonstrated United's supremacy over Rovers and with it the superiority of traditional power and classic style over nouveau riche arrivism and percentage-play bollocks. For if we concede to Rovers that October's was not a 'fair' trial of true strength, then the only match that has ever featured two full-strength sides was last December's 1-1 draw at OT. Their 2-0 win in April and our two previous wins this season all lack legitimacy because so many key players were missing. Now, by shutting out the SAS, dominating the game and winning it, we finally had the proof of the superiority we all knew was ours; now the rest of the world could see it too. This might not be much consolation if we lose the title but it still matters to us, doesn't it?

Naturally, Rovers will cling to the dramatic postscript that Sherwood and Shearer combined to write, just as they were still vilifying poor Gerald Ashby as recently as the latest edition of 'Loadsamoney', three months after the 4-2 drubbing. The long-haired, bug-eyed Rovers captain, who resembles any one of a thousand sad, dildonic indie-group bassists, headed home after an early whistle indicated Shearer had fouled Keane to win the assisting knock-on. This was a nice touch, giving Rovers five seconds of ecstasy (such as Ince had given us last December) before bludgeoning their celebrations to create a wake. Dalglish, whose deathly grimace as he trooped off the pitch would make the perfect bedroom poster for any Red, needed little encouragement to go nuclear afterwards. 'It's a disgrace,' he whined in vintage Liverpool fashion, before going on to claim that TV replays cleared Shearer of any wrongdoing. *The Guardian* drily noted, however, that 'television appeared to bear the referee out'; the fact was that just for once a referee had been sharp enough to spot what most either miss or ignore *viz* the traditional, barging English centre-forward using his bulk to mask the slyest, deftest of nudges. As Fergie noted rather splendidly, it showed the courage of the ref to give what most in the stadium, save the cameras, failed to see: 'Kenny wanted a strong official. He got one.'

Dalglish, prompting some observers to wonder whether he was heading for an Anfield-style crack-up, also added that he 'thought

Blackburn deserved to get something from the game'. What they deserved, of course, was a right good stuffing in every orifice. As Fergie spoke for us all, 'It would have been a travesty if we had not won today.' And win we did, to rejuvenate the season; those heading for Selhurst on Wednesday night could now do so with a real sense of purpose and the hope that Cole, back on home turf, could dispel those images of Gary Birtles that are flickering in the mind's nightmare production department.

As jubilant Reds swarmed out on to the concourses, the rare sound of singing down the Warwick Road could be heard, always a sign of especially good days at OT. A hapless pack of beaten Rovers were encircled by Reds and taunted vocally all the way down the road, but in good-humoured, Nineties PC-style. You can't be too hard on sad small-towners who still have outside lavs and think a bidet is what you mix black puddings in, can you? Elsewhere on the concourse, the less acceptable side to inbreeding – a couple of demented Rovers, out to prove that their parents were brother and sister, struck up a 'Munich 58' in the midst of hundreds of Reds. What did I say about these bandwagon-jumpers not knowing the ropes? Or perhaps they were euthanasia enthusiasts – fancy doing what even the most sheepsex-addled Tyke would shy from! A Red promptly stepped forward to remind them of their Ps and Qs with a swift right to the jaw. Regrettable, but then Seventies mentalities sometimes require Seventies correctional methods. I trust Rovers will bring some properly educated fans with them next time.

Team: Schmeichel; Keane, Bruce, Pallister, Irwin, Giggs, Ince, McClair, Sharpe (Kanchelskis), Cantona, Cole

25 January: CRYSTAL PALACE AWAY

Final Score: Palace 1 UNITED 1

Scorer: May 56

Attendance: 18,224

AS I SAT CHAINSMOKING at half-time, a couple of mates turned up, having been delayed by court appearances and traffic snarl-ups. Panting breathlessly after sprinting across Thornton Heath, one asked if he'd missed anything. 'Bugger all,' I replied. 'It's been the most tedious match of the season. You could've stayed at home and had no regrets.' Four minutes later, football's equivalent of the A-bomb had exploded before us, threatening to devastate one man's career and his club's future. Picking up his dropped jaw from the floor, my neighbour murmured, 'I think you might've made a slight misjudgment there.' Indeed: the most innocuous of midweek tussles had, in a split second, been transformed into the most infamous match of the decade.

Eric wasn't supposed to be the top-of-the-bill main bout of course. This should have been Andy Cole's night, or so we hoped. The script was written in our minds – Cole scores, kickstarting a glorious OT striking career, and thus leads United back to the table summit to round off an epic four days of title assault. Selhurst Park, despite being a dustbin that can't decide whether it's a sporting complex, shopping village or rabbit warren, had until recently been a centre of Red epiphany. The title-clincher in '93, the second championship party two weeks later and the Cup dream-performance last February had all been staged at this ugly suburban outpost. Sadly, it appears that the ground's lucky charm status really did turn sour for good last April. For Eric in particular, who had marked the beginning of his third year in English football with that celestial volley versus Wimbledon, Selhurst Park was about to cause the annulment of the Year Four commemorations.

The Red tribes, swelled by the habitual Cockney influx, annexed the entire left half of the Arthur Wait stand, which is truly a throwback to the *ancien régime*. A cavernous, vaguely Kippaxish old-timer, stuffed with decrepit wooden seats built for those with the backside of Kate Moss, smelling suspiciously of urine – luvverly. Much was later made of the allegedly aggressive, intimidating atmosphere generated by Palace but, bar one 'We support a local team' (who else would support Palace?), all I could hear were the Reds down the left flank. On an Endsleigh-bog pitch against an overtly physical bunch of local journeymen, we did little that I can now recall in the first half. Somebody remarked upon the appalling lack of protection given to the leg-studded Cantona – *plus ça change* – but we thought nothing much of it at the time. All eyes darted nervously towards Cole whenever the ball approached him, Reds fighting furiously to prevent images of Gary Birtles settling in the mind, as we did our best vocally to keep the lad's spirits up. (You could groan *sotto voce* to yourself when he blundered but on no account was this to be expressed publicly.) Nil-nil at the break and the game was lucky to reach that.

The sole excitement in our stand had been provided by two ejections, carried out in the most mob-handed manner imaginable by the local sty's plod, as punishment for the most heinous crime of singing a song with a swear word in it. How remarkable that such a small-time, no-mark club should play host to the sort of hardline crowd control tactics that would befit Belfast. As we soon discovered, Palace decline to impose such a policy throughout *every* stand. . .

And so to the moment of madness, the resurrection of Bruce Lee, the defining image of the season or whatever other label you like. Reds were still taking their post-lavatorial seats when a ball from our left looped limply over the heads of Eric and his 'marker' Richard Shaw. Seconds earlier, Shaw had fouled Eric for the third time and gone unpunished once more. As the ball passed by, Eric extended a mildly petulant leg which, if it actually caught Shaw, could have done no more harm than a breath of summer breeze. His gymnastic roll prompted Geordie Alan Wilkie to flash the most unwarranted red card Eric has ever received. Perhaps 'wor Alan' has a Toon shirt at home with 'Cole' on the back? Safe to say he won't be on Fergie's Christmas card list.

Our stand was imbued with resignation rather than shock. After all, it had been six months since Eric's last dismissal and our knowledge of English refs is such that we knew one was well overdue. We watched from a position directly opposite as Eric traipsed down the touchline with Norm 'Munster' Davies in half-hearted pursuit. If only he'd set off alongside him . . .

Everyone I've spoken to since had their eyes fixed on Eric. We saw what the TV cameras missed and what few cameras captured. Some lone lout, hardly the type that's supposed to be in a Family Stand, hurtles several rows down to the front. His nastily naff leather-jacket is unmistakable from even 70 yards. He crosses 'the line' – not necessarily a physical mark on the ground but that boundary that we all recognise, the one that separates the players' universe from ours. He's in the 'no-man's-land' behind the hoardings, as close to the pitch as is possible without actually invading it, yet still a location in which a fan's presence would guarantee official intervention at any other ground. From our vantage point, he appears to be leaning over, inches from Cantona's face – he could be carrying a knife or bottle but a steward feet away does nothing. Someone shouts near me, 'What's he throwing?' (The better papers duly note that he appears to throw something, whether an object or a fist.) To us, it looks as though some sort of attempted assault is in preparation – but by the lout, not Eric. Norm chugs up at last, pulling Eric away and we think, 'It's all over'

... Then something snaps within the mind of the genius and a hundred front pages are born. You've seen the rest.

It could have been so much worse – or better, depending on your point of view. For about five seconds as the pitch-side mêlée developed, a fan-player brawl seemed imminent. Despite the anchoring presence of the seats below us, you could feel a surging undercurrent throughout the Wait stand. Suddenly, we're in Red Army timewarp: it's 1975 and we're about to stage an *en masse* pitch invasion. I turn and see that look in Red eyes all around, that manic gleam I'd almost forgotten, and hear the time-honoured phrase, 'It's kickin' off.' Had any other Palace-head attempted to lamp a Red-shirted hero, the consequences could have been apocalyptic.

With hindsight, it's hard to credit, but once Eric had been led off by a tea-drenched Schmeichel, Reds seemed to put all thoughts of the long-term consequences of Eric's action out of their minds. Instead, we focused completely on the struggle in hand – we were simply down to ten men and there were points to be won. Everything else could wait its turn. To say we were fired up would be an understatement - you could almost hear the adrenalin pumping through Red veins all around the stand. For 15 minutes we were at our best, a spell of passion both on and off the pitch that reminded you of why you love United. Every man, woman and child in that stand remained on their feet throughout; every Red was, as requested, singing his or her heart out for the lads. Driven forward by the greatest concerted awayday support for months, the improbable happened – just as my neighbour gasped that 'even May's got more chance of scoring than Cole', the Ginger One obliged with a header from Sharpe's cross. Needless to say, he put it straight into the keeper's arms with the goal at his mercy but it squirmed into the net nevertheless. 'Oo-ah, Cantona' for the moment, was replaced by the first non-ironic 'Oo-ay, David May' of the season.

As we roared, 'We've only got ten men', and, 'You're so shit . . .', the Reds pressed home the advantage. Sharpe hit the woodwork and Cole, through on goal at last, scooped it embarrassingly wide. Their scruffy, scrabbled, mud-drenched equaliser ten minutes from time took the edge off our righteous fervour momentarily but at the whistle, even though we were a man short, Reds were begging for more time to finish the job. It had been a performance built on passion and pride rather than skill and talent, but it deserved all three points.

For someone who's supposed to be an historian with a sense of the importance of events, it's a poor do to have to admit that I didn't really grasp the implication of Eric's actions until leaving the stand. Brooding on the lost points, pausing only to watch the pack of Reds who hared down the hill to sort out a Palace mob, I was startled to hear a pair of Dwaynes discussing Eric's prospects using phrases such as 'life ban'. Only then, as police horses in the background clattered towards the warring fans yards away, did it strike me what the world would make of Eric's pugilistics. With battling Reds scarpering from the police in all directions, I reflected that the time for fighting had passed. Somewhere out there under the London night-sky, the media would be preparing a gallows.

Team: Schmeichel; Keane, May, Pallister, Irwin, Giggs, Ince, McClair, Sharpe (Kanchelskis), Cantona, Cole

UNITED HAVE CREATED SOME big stories in their time, stories good enough to hog both front and back pages. We've led more than our fair share of news bulletins and dominated many a radio show. Yet nothing since 1958, not even that first English European Cup or our worst '70s hoolie excesses, has come close to securing the sort of media melt-down that Cantona's kick achieved. If you could, as a Red, temporarily detach yourself from those subjective feelings of hurt, anger, shock and sorrow, you had to marvel at the sheer acreage and intensity of the coverage. Clearly, however shocking and unprecedented the televisual image was, the scale of the public response was entirely unpredictable. Those momentary kicks and punches had unleashed something deep not only in football's psyche but also the nation's.

More predictable, however, were the identities of those queuing up to slam gleeful kicks into Eric's prostrate reputation. The monstrous regiments of sanctimony-pedlars, who had all Reds choking back the vomit for weeks, contained all the usual suspects: the tabloid footie 'writers', the FA hierarchy, ex-pros like Mullery, Crooks and Lineker as well as every right-wing 'yob culture' expert commentator in the land. Lined up behind them, the foot soldiers filling the letters pages and faxlines – the Anyone But United brigades – unable to resist the greatest anti-Red open goal they'd had since our return to pre-eminence. Let us not give their contribution any further oxygen of publicity.

We know what the world thought; there's no need to rehash every agonizing day of *l'affaire Cantona*, watching the swirl of public opinion eddying for and against our King. What matters here is what we, Eric's

Red subjects, thought – and in discovering that, we might get an explanation as to what English nerve Eric's kick had exposed to such media-exploding effect.

Forget the contributions of the first so-called Reds to appear in the media on the Wednesday who talked of sacking Eric or banning him for life. Whoever these Megastore-designed cretins were, they were soon seen to represent no-one but a twisted, tiny minority. Once real Reds seized the agenda on Thursday, a United front behind Eric was forged for the duration. Whether expressed through the fanzines, the media or in the stands, our opinion was clear to the world – and, thankfully as it turned out, to Eric.

Still, for public consumption, every Red justification and mitigation was still preceded by the phrase 'We can't condone what Eric did but . . .' In private, however, we could reveal the truth to our Red-blooded brothers. Hours after the incident, I spoke to two fanzine editors to get their real views. One said simply, 'He's the King. He can do what he likes. He can do no wrong.' Subjectivity run riot, perhaps; an encapsulation of what most of us felt, certainly. The other editor put the kick into a wider context that goes some way to explaining why Eric has since become deified by us and demonized by others.

It's all about respect. When we used to go to places like that in the Seventies and Eighties, the fact that we were United was a status to be respected, even feared. These suburban nobodies had to watch themselves: they knew they couldn't just say or do what they liked because if we got the hump over it, they got the kicking. And generally, we got respect and admiration when we deserved it, whether it be for the style with which we tried to play or for the devotion and power of our support. Now what do we get? We go to shit-holes like Swindon who used to dream about the privilege of receiving United and what happens? They show no respect; they take the piss, they assault our players at the touchline, they attack our coaches and sing 'Munich' songs at us. Who the f*ck do they think they are? Because they're in the safe, molly-coddled world of Nineties football, they think they can get away with it. Ten years ago, if they'd behaved like that, we'd have beaten them to shit and pulled their crappy ground to pieces. At Selhurst Park, they thought they could come down to the touchline and call our players 'motherfuckers' from the safety of a family stand. Ten years back, they wouldn't have dared; that stand would've been full of handy

Reds who'd have stopped him opening his gob or getting anywhere near Eric. What Eric did was strike a blow for, not against, our self-respect. He just did what many of us would've done if we'd been near Simmons. Simmons didn't show Eric the respect he deserves; he thought he could act with impunity and he was wrong. You see, in that moment, Eric stood for Manchester United – and Simmons for the rest of the Red-hating world. We might say we can't condone it but of course we can. It was a great last punch too.

Exactly. On a superficial level, of course many Reds loved those ten seconds of videotape. What typically Gallic flair to do the posey and unexpected, a flying kick instead of a simple opening jab. What a thrilling sight to see Eric's final, bout-winning punch, forcing Simmons into shocked retreat, arms up in surrender. We may have been shocked but we certainly weren't horrified. Far from it.

Away from the visceral momentary pleasure, however, it was the emblematic nature of what Eric did and how he behaved afterwards that mattered long-term. The reason why Eric's status in Red eyes moved within weeks from merely regal to divine – and why the response from the wider public was so impassioned - is that Eric is the personification of the extraordinary nature of United. It is United's uniqueness that draws such devotion from us and such jealous suspicion from others. We are not as other typically English clubs. We have always seen style as important as function; we have always exalted the individual; we have always been typified by the multi-national nature of both players and fans. Moreover, we rejoice in the very qualities that the English are supposed to disdain – we are glamorous, sexy, arrogant, hot-tempered and exhibitionist. Not for us the dogged, humble and dourly understated Protestant work ethic of the rest. Long before our European stars arrived, we were already not of this world – we were a Continental club stuck in a downbeat English league.

So we haven't just rallied to Eric because he's our best player or even just because our own siege mentality produces an empathy with his own personal ordeal. Surely, it is because we see in Eric a distillation of everything that we are. When others attack his 'Gallic' faults, they are actually citing the very 'faults' that are the characteristics of Manchester United. All those qualities I listed above are common to both us and Eric. Sadly, the rest of football and most of the nation cannot come to terms with this. They have exhibited one of the worst English traits - the suspicion of, and hostility to, arrogant excellence. England prefers humble mediocrity. Their virulent reaction to *l'affaire Cantona* was that of people disturbed by their own inferiority complexes. By all means, let those of us Reds who are be proud of being English but let's also be grateful that we don't suffer that particular English neurosis. Truly, to be a Red is to be a better breed of Englander.

Allow me a Hornbyism at this point. I spent all Friday morning dashing about Manchester to appear on various breakfast shows, defending Eric wherever I could to whomever would listen. Getting home at 11 o'clock, feeling pathetically pleased with myself, I slammed on Sky News to get the latest on the Cantona saga, ready to overdose on it just as I had the previous day. Instead, however, I found Sky were showing live coverage of the Auschwitz Memorial ceremony. Twenty minutes was enough to bring me to my senses. I had seen Eric's actions described as those of 'an animal', 'an evil maniac', 'a madman' and 'an uncivilised savage beast'. How inappropriate those adjectives now appeared – if Eric is all those things, what words could possibly describe the SS? And for a few hours, I actually forgot about Eric altogether. Real life has a funny habit of reminding you what is truly historically tragic. Of course, by tomorrow I'd be back treating United as the be-all-and-end-all, and Eric's suspension as unparalleled personal catastrophe. But you should appreciate the odd, jarring reminders that there are bigger things in life – and death.

28 January: WREXHAM AT HOME – FA CUP ROUND FOUR

Final Score: UNITED 5 Wrexham 2

Scorers: Irwin 17 & 73 (*pen*), Giggs 26, McClair 67, Humes 80 (*o.g.*)

Attendance: 43,222

WHEN THE DRAW WAS made for the fourth round of the Cup, the momentary elation of emerging first from the velvet scrotum was immediately tempered by the groan-inducing anti-climax that the name 'Wrexham' engenders. Until the seismic events at Selhurst transformed our world, many Reds had been looking forward to this tie as much as they would a holiday in Istanbul. For clubs of our magnitude, the so-called 'magic' of the FA Cup is confined to the very latest stages of the competition. Invariably, the early rounds are about as magical as a Paul Daniels wig when we are forced to play a succession of pantomime-villain roles, all variations on the 'tottering Giant waiting to be slain by plucky minnows'. There's no credit in victory by whatever margin, unless it reaches cricket-score proportions – you either fulfil the tiresome formality or, if beaten, make the front page of every English-language publication from here to Alpha Centurai.

If anything, it's worse to be at home. Then, the Club is forced to play 'mine host' to the daytrip of a lifetime for thousands of small-town cretins, lugging their hideous, inbred families along too for their first-ever match. As the balloon–wielding invaders (behaving like people who wear 'I'm mad, me' T-shirts at an office party) take over your precious Scoreboard End seats, the United hard-core are dispensed to the four corners of the earth from where they must endure a grim 90 minutes. Six thousand hyperactive dolts, possibly in fancy-dress and certainly leaving all sorts of rural disease-bacteria on your LMTB seat, will then proceed to outsing you for the entire game, taunting Reds as you sit in mouldering indifference, whilst their team give a spirited performance before going down 2-0 to an off-form United.

Pace Leicester and Charlton in '93/'94, that's how it's always seemed to be. This time, of course, was quite different. Although Wrexhamites stuck with tradition to give the perfect demonstration of 'Village Idiot Convention Awayday', the Cantona Crisis had now made this a game that Reds HAD to attend. I found myself racing to get to Old Trafford as quickly as possible, the bizarrest of situations given the opposition but wholly consistent with what was almost a surrealistic afternoon. How ironic that the Red psychological state now resembled that of Newcastle's a fortnight before; then, we had been the perpetrators of the trauma, now we were victims. Just as the Toons had attempted to do, both our team and support were duty-bound to rally publicly behind the Fallen Idol whilst simultaneously demonstrating that we could survive without him for this forthcoming six months of extended emotional winter.

They say a week is a long time in politics but what of six days in football? From the apex of Eric's goal on Sunday that put us back on Title track to the nadir of his suspension, gift-wrapped for Rovers: that's some distance to plummet. Almost a year to the day since we mourned Sir Matt, Old Trafford was metaphorically dressed in black once more – but black laced with silver lining of hope for a promised

Resurrection. So it is written in the Books of Edwards, pending confirmation from Graham 'Pontius Pilate' Kelly: the Number Seven 'Dieu' may have been crucified but will rise again after the Solstice. Pity he couldn't do it in three days flat like the last fella.

For the media, as for the rest of us, the spiritual presence of the absent Cantona suffused every moment of the day. As Reds congregated early on the concourses, the cameras and mikes were still everywhere, picking up every last ramification of *l'affaire Cantona*, grilling every Red in range. The first T-shirts had remarkably appeared in time for kick-off, testament to three days midnight-oil work by the barrow-boy artistic fraternity – the one of Eric as 'The Wild One' on his Harley, roaring 'I'll be back' struck the right defiantly Brando-esque note. Over at Maine Road, Rosler tops were being outsold by one depicting two kick-imprints above the line: 'I've met Cantona'. As ever, the Bluenose Red-obsession outstrips their own City-love. A couple of local anti-racist organisations infiltrated the Warwick Road crowd, rather distastefully using the Selhurst Incident to drum up new memberships but also introducing the rather excellent Eric-justification that he'd merely been taking wholly moral 'direct action' against a neo-Nazi mouthpiece. Whilst I can't see Kelly & Co. signing up for that one, it remains the most original excuse yet.

Inside the stadium, the on-pitch work of 25 players and officials remained in danger of being overshadowed by the memory of the absent 26th – the Cantona Context defined the content of everything. A saddo behind me had tuned his ear-piece to Radio 2 before kick-off, from which I was jolted to hear emit the strains of *Les Misérables'* 'Empty Chairs at Empty Tables', a Red revolutionary's lament for missing heroes. Too subtle for Keith Smasheronee Fane perhaps but utterly apt for me and, it soon transpired, the crowd. If Eric was at the forefront of our minds, and the subject of the majority of the singing that mixed mournfulness for his absence with celebration of his past heroics, Hughes and Cole were in there too. 'Hughesy must stay' and the Andy Cole song were aired as if to demonstrate the Mancunian realism with which we had grasped the truth: for now, Eric was the past – the rest of the season depended on the combustion of Sparks igniting Cole.

For ten minutes or so, you could be excused for wondering whether our vocal lionisation of absent heroes had been to the chagrin of our eleven on the pitch. They looked resentfully slothful in comparison to the buzzing assortment of Welshmen and Scousers who pressed frenziedly, as though as coke-addled as their fans appeared to be. Somebody called Durkan nutmegged Schmeichel for the opener and immortality fleetingly beckoned. You could almost hear the blood-curdling scratching as a thousand media scribes scrawled some provisional Sunday headlines. Win or lose, United were bound to provide a great story today: we are essentially a tabloid page-filling machine aren't we? To think that a fair proportion of these lowlifes' jobs is entirely maintained by the sheer volume of United column-inch acreage – how aggravating that the Cantona Crisis should have illustrated that they have absolutely no compunction about snapping off the hand that feeds them. Asquith's aphorism about harlots and the press was far too kind . . .

Whatever back-page visions were materialising in front of K-stand's Wrexham eyes, we had no doubts that the day would be ours – that was foresight then, not hindsight now. They had, as the phrase has it, climaxed too soon to last the course. Within minutes, it was obvious that class would prevail; it was equally obvious that the Reds were rising above the treacherously difficult circumstances to show the professional control and attitude that the tabloids so vociferously accused them of lacking. Wrexhamites paid for their eager cheek as, within seconds of 'Are you Chester in disguise?' dying out, Irwin cracked home the 'in yer face' equaliser. Symbolism ahoy – the personification of level-headed calm diligence rescuing us after a week of hot-tempered histrionics.

Wrexham, to their credit, at least did what few Premiership sides are prepared to try at OT – play some proper football. They had their share of sweet moves and Bennett almost rounded one off before our stand-in kids provided an object lesson in penetration, Scholes and Neville combining to set up Giggs for the lead. Incredibly, it was Ryan's first since September and the clearest sign yet that his rehabilitation was virtually complete.

That helped subdue the daffodil-merchants behind the goal somewhat, although their team stubbornly refused to roll over for another 40 minutes yet, with their number seven being particularly annoying both by virtue of his talent and his rabid petulance. Scoreboard Enders, clumps of whom found themselves marooned in unfamiliar patches all over the stadium, inspired those around them to join the leading packs in the West Upper and J-stand who were busy mounting a vocal Cantona Defence Campaign. Even if Eric wasn't there to hear it for himself, surely he would now know what real Reds thought, as opposed to what some of the pondlife the media had trawled up on Thursday reckoned.

By the time Choccy curled home the third, killer goal on 66, he, Neville and Pally had all already hit the woodwork as Red domination approached overwhelming scale. Nobody let down the name of United this day, and certainly not young Phil Neville who was making the most assured of debuts. The ginger creature Scholes may not have scored for once but beavered and ferreted about superbly, garnering many a Wrexham accolade afterwards. As a team, as men, as colleagues, they made the point to the rest of the world on behalf of us all. There is still no greater pride than that which the Red Shirt inspires.

Wrexham still pushed forward enough to force Peter into a classic pair of saves, one of Banksian single-handedness, but they were dead in the water. J-standers struck up the chorus of *Swing Low Sweet Chariot*, a one-off exception to the no-rugger-bugger-song rule, which delightfully aggrieved the beaten hordes to their left. Considering this was the game of their meagre lives and that they had 6,000 there, it was odd to reflect that Port Vale had hit higher decibel levels with only several hundred. Perhaps they were expending too much energy on their sly, sporadic 'Munich waves' which happily resulted in some of their daytrippers getting a free tour of the OT cells. Or was it that they were too concerned in executing their utterly mystifying 'boating' movements, swaying to and fro like a bunch of schoolgirls on a charabanc. Maybe this is some sort of sheep-attracting mating signal from the North Wales hills, I dunno. In any event, it was a relief from their grating accents when they were silenced by Ince – at last! – winning a penalty. As 35,000 realised this should've been Eric's cue to step forward, Denis rode the bellows of 'Cantona' to slot it home in the French fashion.

The fifth, deflected from Giggsy's shot, did spur a last-gasp reply which the Wrexham team – if not some of their support – deserved. No sooner had the Wrexham side performed a final whistle genuflection to their fans, my grumbling words of 'Welsh wan. . .' stuck in my throat as the men in gold trotted over to the Strettie to pay homage to *us*. Gulp – how sweet! Better omit the joke about Wrexham farmers, a flock of sheep, and being a pimp.

So the storm, temporarily, had abated. But a few miles out of town, almost unnoticed by the United-fixated media, Rovers were thrashing Ipswich 4-1. The Title Summit, so clearly visible only six days before, had vanished again amidst a swirl of the blackest clouds imaginable. And the alternative path to glory, the one to Wembley, currently has the slavering, pustulous beast that is Leeds sat squatly in the way. February promises to be some month.

As one departs, another arrives: with Eric on his way to a family reunion in Marseilles, away from the doorstepping English press, Mark Hughes announced that he was healing fast and would possibly return for the derby. The man on the verge of being discarded onto the Goodison scrapheap may yet return to play his favourite role of season-saver. This time, however, it will surely take rather more than one well-timed Wembley volley to pull Red nuts out of the fire.

Team: Schmeichel; Irwin, May, Pallister, P. Neville, Sharpe, Keane (Kanchelskis), Ince, Giggs, McClair (Beckham), Scholes

4 February: ASTON VILLA AT HOME

Final Score: UNITED 1 Villa 0

Scorer: Cole 18

Attendance: 43,795

AS BLACKBURN STRUGGLE PITIFULLY to fulfil the role of a 'big club' – and continue to prove that money alone does not buy class or status – they seem to be slavishly aping United a tad too much these days. Witness their own carbon-copy the previous Wednesday to our Selhurst débâcle: two dropped points, a red card and some headline-grabbing argy-bargy involving a home season-ticket holder. Imitation may be flattering – and the way the Rovers turn up their collars in Cantonesque style is almost touching – but they've been following our script a little too closely. For Reds, the bizarre and rather embarrassing experience of having to root for the Tyke sheepshaggers had all been worthwhile – now, a capitalizing win over the Midlands combination of pensioners and psychotics would throw the title race wide open once more.

As ever during this increasingly remarkable season, every United match carries a sub-plot to run alongside the title narrative. It's becoming harder to recall the last time nothing else was at stake but the three Championship points. The intertwining fates of our three loner gun-men (Cole, Cantona and Hughes) continued to dominate the theatre's stage. Rumours swept through town on Friday night that Hughes, on his way to Goodison only two weeks ago, was now on the brink of pledging the rest of his life to the Reds. Those who revel in life's ironies must have enjoyed the new *realpolitik*: United's season now rests at the feet of a man saved from the Merseybin and the would-be nemesis Cole who put him there in the first place.

As for Cole himself, those with long memories darkened by the ghost of Gary Birtles had pointed out the similarities of the Birtles and Cole introductions. Both men had missed 'sitters' in their opening two games; Birtles then had a terrible third and never recovered. In these circumstances, pressure multiplies as a geometric progression, maths-fans, doubling with every scoreless game until the striker is crushed. Irrational though it might have been to say, you felt that the Cole goal had to come today or a soul-destroying barren spell of Choccy proportions would ensue, the cost of which would be the Title.

Eric, however, remained the dominant vision in Red frontal lobes. *L'affaire Cantona* had now had another week to ferment in the media bottle. Like any home brew, the earlier noxious condition of the contents had settled down to produce something almost drinkable. The hysterics, harpies and hate-merchants had by now exhausted themselves and more reflective, mature, *simpatico* voices had emerged. The sense of loss had now permeated beyond Old Trafford to all parts of the football world where genius is cherished. At Old Trafford, we had made the most of the week to get organised and give our sense of grievance a focus. *Red Issue* had a well-timed new edition out which expressed the full range of emotional and rational responses. Condemnations of the media, the FA and Simmons himself nestled alongside sorrow, regret and criticisms of those Reds who'd abandoned Eric in the media. The 'zine also launched two write-in campaigns, one to Eric himself, printed in French, appealing for him to stay, another in vitriolic English to Graham Kelly which ran through the complete Cantona defence, m'lud.

The T-shirts, always an accurate barometer of the *zeitgeist*, continued to multiply. One, rather inaccurately, trumpeted 'Eric Is Innocent!', understandable shorthand given the unwieldiness of 'Eric Is A Bit Guilty With Loads Of Mitigating Circumstances'. Another, taking a lead from the 'FATWA(T)' on Simmons from *Red Issue's* pages, announced that Simmons was 'Wanted for Treason' and handily printed his address on the reverse for the benefit of Reds going down to Wimbledon away on 7 March who fancied a spot of manhunting. As *The Guardian* reported later, Simmons had already got the message and gone into hiding, hopefully for good. Meanwhile, Pete Boyle and his K-Stand Chorus made preparations to rush out a pro-Cantona record, with the Great Man's blessing, whilst various Red learned friends began collating evidence for the defence should Eric have to face a court. If there was any anti-Cantona sentiment about that day, it was being very carefully secreted.

Inside the stadium as kick-off approached, we got a couple of reminders of how crass this Club can be. A tumultuous reception greeted Hughesy as he came onto the pitch to the announcement that he'd 'signed' a two-year deal. But Edwards' comments that morning left a bitter taste – they confirmed what we suspected, that Hughes had been on his way despite the official denials, with the prime concern appearing to be the potential recouping of £2m to set against the Cole fee, this despite the fact that he'd have been needed for the FA Cup and in case of injuries or loss of form upfront. Or, indeed, in case of an Eric brainstorm, which was precisely what happened. What if Eric had kicked off a week later, with Hughes already ensconced at Everton?

It was lucky for us that Hughes is so in love with United; a man of his immense and justifiable pride would have been well within his rights to tell the Club to get stuffed – if they didn't want him two weeks ago, why should he stay after such an insult? Lucky for the Board too that their parsimonious financial short-termism hadn't lost us Hughesy's services and left us humiliatingly exposed. Scholes may be good, potentially brilliant even, but surely was not ready to step into the Cantona breach and shoulder the burden just yet.

Moments after came further cringing embarrassment. One might have expected some sort of crowd commemoration for the Munich dead at some point, with the anniversary two days away. Instead, the crowd were entreated to sing *Happy Birthday* for Norman Wisdom in an attempt to get into the *Guinness Book* for the loudest something or other. The looks of incomprehension and disgust on fans as they heard this absurd request said it all. Someone at the Club must have thought this was a 'groovy' idea. Truly, the Red Army are lions led by donkeys.

This was to be the team's first top-flight experience of Life Without Eric; if, for 25 minutes or so, it appeared that we might actually prosper, let alone merely survive, the remainder of the 90 brought the doubts crowding back. Fergie later noted that most of the team simply stopped playing for an hour – and in Lee Sharpe's case, never actually started. When he missed an early open goal, Villa fans sang 'Lee Sharpe is a Villa fan' and you felt the former Boy Wonder was in for a stinker reminiscent of his shambolic display at Hillsborough. À *propos* of nothing in particular, did anyone notice that there was some especially heavy weed about that week?

Salvation came from the quarter we had all most fervently hoped to find it. Cole's pace won a corner – later questioned by the Fault-Finder-General, LSC's Alan Hansen from which he eventually received the trickiest of loose balls. His swivelling turn and crackshot finish were pure penalty-box lightning of Denis Law vintage; the stadium erupted in joyous relief for one of the highest decibel counts of the season to acclaim the new, if temporary, King. Cole disappeared under a Red scrum of genuinely delighted colleagues – the goodwill that flowed from all quarters towards Cole was almost touching.

For me, Cole was one of the few performers to emerge with any credit from that game. He looked sharper, faster and more aware although there were plenty around me who saw his apparently lazy gait and nonchalance as an unhappy reminder of Mr Davenport.

For some reason, United eschewed their trademark wingplay and resorted to battering through the middle, leaving Cole non-plussed. Without Hughes, such tactics are useless. Cole was often forced to play winger himself in the absence of others, only to be left with no-one in the middle to find. We were disjointed, ill-at-ease, and losing possession in the most dis-United way; today would be a game for the defence, in which Pally excelled, to 'grind out a result' as Fergie later put it.

The one shaft of unpredictable light on the pitch was Giggs; once he was injured and off, our game became as murky and ill-defined as the Manchester afternoon sky. For a moment, when Fashanu's trailing leg had 'accidentally' felled our boy and a stretcher was called, disaster loomed. Happily, Giggs pulled off yet another footballing first – he got up whilst the Gladiator stayed down. Some of us at the East End hadn't sussed which of Villa's black lads was departing; when the tannoy announced that it was indeed Fash the Bash, few could resist a cheer. Somewhere out yonder, Gary Mabbutt must've been laughing till his eye fell out. It seems, as I write, that Fashanu is out for the season. That's a pity: we were hoping it would be for life.

Minutes after that clash, Saunders hit the woodwork as a prelude to Villa's second half dominance. As an attacking force, we scarcely existed; hard to admit it, but the introduction of aged Scouse reject Houghton made all the difference. So did the behaviour of David Elleray, apparently doing his best to make amends for his alleged pro-United favouritism at Wembley, missing more handballs and fouls than you thought possible. For much of the half, we watched in near silence, rousing only to abuse the Kraut-assaulter Bosnich and ginge-minge Staunton as Villa piled forward. Villa fans, who'd earlier disgraced themselves with Munich waves resulting in ejections, responded to our chants of 'Yer gonna win fuck all' with a chorus of 'We're going to be together'. Doctor, stitch up me sides, quick. . .

Into the last fifteen minutes, as Villa hit wood again (although Cole had done likewise from Scholes' cross-shot) and Schmeichel performed heroics, something odd happened. The crowd began to roar and growl in that particular way that was once so common in the BC Era. I'd almost forgotten this terrifying sound that combines feverish support for the lads with angry resentment at the atrocious performance on the pitch. It was a monthly occurrence before Cantona arrived: let us hope the team give no further cause for its frequent return.

As the ref greeted our whistles with his own at last, there was predictable grumbling about what had been perhaps our worst home showing of the season. But amidst the groans 'n' moans, and the worries about the post-Cantona future, we still had much to celebrate: Cole's goal, Hughesy's 'signing' and, above all, three gorgeous points. It may well have been our least-deserved and most unconvincing win of the campaign but, with Rovers meeting class opposition and thus losing again on Sunday, it might yet prove to be one of the most timely. Level on games and only two points behind: 'I'm terrified,' sneered Dalglish sarcastically when asked about United's hot pursuit – but one Rovers slip and we can pounce.

Team: Schmeichel; Irwin, Pallister, Bruce, Neville, Giggs (Kanchelskis), McClair, Ince, Sharpe, Scholes, Cole

11 February: MANCHESTER CITY AWAY

Final Score: Bitters 0 UNITED 3

Scorers: Ince 58, Andrei 74, Cole 77

Attendance: 26,368

PITY THE POOR, BITTER Bluenoses; they never learn from even the simplest of lessons do they? Before every derby match in recent years, the soundtrack of the run-up is always the same: Blue players and officials mouthing off to the media, hyping up their prospects and cruelly building up the hopes of every Magoo, ready to be mercilessly crushed by the Reds. It's as ritualistic as a Greek tragi-comedy, only funnier and without the skirts. Franny 'Bogroll' Lee set the stage nicely with his talk of a 'top six place for City' and the Blues beating us 'for the sake of the kids in the schoolyard' before Brian Horton – whose first name appears to be 'beleaguered' – provided the main turn. 'Cantona's goal (in '94s 2-0) was offside'; 'We are, after all, the city's club'; 'We can beat United and turn our season around' . . . stop! stop! I can't take any more merriment. The man's ironic comedy would be worthy of Steve Coogan.

United, of course, kept their mouths shut as per usual in anticipation of the feet doing all the talking on Saturday. As with old money, sheer class does not require grotesque media-megaphoning. It is simply apparent in the way that you move. City would be receiving their fourth reminder in a row of that life verity in the second half. Until then, United publicly ignored City and instead concentrated on rivals who *are* vaguely in our class. Paul Ince rather smartly rattled Dalglish's cage with some comments pertaining to Blackburn's potential lack of bottle, in reply to which Kenny protested too much, methinks. When a man who once said 'I can't handle the matchday pressure anymore – my head feels like it'll explode' claims to be unconcerned by our pursuit, the smell of pork pies is distinctly discernible.

If United were appearing to treat this fixture as just another opportunity for three away points, City seemed to be busy preparing for the Battle of Maine Road. With Horton and his motley collection of second-rate Krauts, cast-offs and closet Reds talking all week of 'fight', 'struggle' and 'revenge', it was no surprise to witness Bluenoses picking up on the vibes and preparing to turn Saturday into a 24-hour Blitzkreig. Were bookies to take such bets, the odds on violence occurring would have been even shorter than those for a United win.

City's hooligan element had been thriving for some time, sheltering virtually undetected by the media under the cover of the Cole and Cantona affairs. In recent weeks they'd kicked off at Palace, even to the extent of fighting amongst themselves, before going on to incite a punch-up with Villa fans at the Kippax-North corner after the Cup tie. Their general Bitterness Index level must, by now, have reached the top of the scale as United continued to dominate English football, despite all our injuries and suspensions, whilst City's promised rebirth seemed to be stillborn. (Even City's brief moment of glory – provided by someone else, naturally – had been obliterated by Reds when the Moss Side Barcelona parties collapsed after only eight days in the wake of the Demolition Derby. Their current ecstasy over the Cantona Crisis was to be equally shortlived.)

Down in the Mancunian football underworld, then, Seventies-style plotting was much in vogue. A week before the game, a Red-dominated anti-fascist group had battled with Blue-hued Loyalists and neo-Nazis outside the 'Clarence' pub yards from Maine Road; now it was rumoured that a Red firm would attempt to take the 'Claremont', the main Blue pub. There were reports that an old City firm was being reassembled as a one-off just for this fixture; others predicted a straightforward mass action after the game on Kippax Street. For those interested in seeking such satisfaction, it appeared that they would certainly get it one way or another.

For those who'd rather avoid such physicalities, the prospects were not so encouraging. The United allocation of 1,350 was, of course, pitifully inadequate and many a Red's week was spent chasing spares from Blues who'd managed to grab bundles for themselves. That there would be hundreds of Reds scattered throughout Blue stands was obvious, although not to the officials apparently – any hopes isolated Reds may have had for protection were dashed by the sight of massive expanses of unstewarded, unpoliced Blue sections. This was not a day to wear your colours.

Like many Reds, I'd spent the morning legging around town in the rain, ticket-hunting; I got one for £35 but later touts at OT were asking £50 and, by 2 p.m., some at Maine Road were going for £90. Passing the 'Claremont' on the way to the ground – and noting that it had not yet been razed to the ground as promised – I checked Blue faces for state-of-mind signals. As always before a Nineties derby, their expressions had that mix of aggression and fear that is unique to the Bittermen, who are probably the greatest sado-masochists in football. The environs of Maine Road speak volumes in comparison to Old Trafford; shabby, concrete-jungle public architecture mixed with pre-war slums tell you that this grim patch has 'No Future' stamped all over it. The only times the construction industry has been there were in the Thirties and Sixties – symbolically, the only years that City have had any prospects. Old Trafford, by contrast, is at the centre of regeneration and renewal based on a European future. How apt.

For those who recall that thrilling Cup semi night in April '94, the new Maine Road interior comes as a shock. Bereft of the towering old Kippax, the ground looks half the size, on a par with any of a dozen provincial Endsleigh holes. A ramshackle array of Portakabins in the corner reminds you of Port Vale; pylons and beams are still in place to obstruct the view; body-condoms are provided in the uncovered Kippax, perhaps because the roof-money is needed to pay off the Steve Daley fee. Everything has been repainted in tacky bright blue, just as Sixties council estates once were - like those ill-fated symbols of urban 'rebirth', one hopes Maine Road too is destined to fade and peel as it rots, until the demolition team arrives.

Sadly for City, the rain had restrained itself sufficiently for the pitch to pass a 1.15 inspection and the latest Blue humiliation was on again. If you'd taken your seat early, you could reflect on the exploding of another Blue myth - that Maine Road is still a 'proper' football venue which has escaped the ravages of family gentrification. The abject lack of pre-match atmosphere, the face-painted ten-year-olds, the well-to-do nuclear families complete with thermos . . . it could have been Old Trafford. The City 'boys' were late in, presumably either in the bogs bricking themselves or outside taking part in the skirmish at ten to three. And in every stand were Reds, making furtive eye-contact with each other before nestling amongst the Blue hordes. They would need the self-restraint of the Trappist to survive the day unmolested.

We were without all three of our greatest derby warriors, Hughes, Keane and Cantona, whose influence and goals have done for City over the past six meetings. Yet as City came out fighting – both team and fans – United stood utterly erect and unyielding. You know that archetypal cartoon scene in which some ferocious small creature is kicking and fighting like a dervish, but all to no avail because a big animal is easily holding it off at arm's length? That image sums up the first half. For all their passion and endeavour, City's witlessness and predictability meant that the giants that are Pally, Ince and Bruce were scarcely troubled. From all that fevered application, City made but two chances - Walsh's header and Rosler's missed connection – both of which were trivial in comparison to the golden openings we missed. McClair's over-the-bar blaster after Cole had superbly teed him up was a Pie-eater Classic, even better than the 'goal' Choccy celebrated later which had, in fact, hit the side-netting. He can be a priceless chump but his canny contribution overall that day can't be ignored. That simple McClair trick of turning whilst allowing the ball to run on was enough repeatedly to flummox City's cretinous midfielders all afternoon. Ignore the Hortonian bollock-spiel about City 'shading the half'; to any connoisseur, it was obvious that with a little half-time tinkering, our Red machine would be primed to roll right over the Bluenoses.

In the stands, however, more than a little tinkering would be required to save the day. Surveying the scene just before the kick-off, 'Southy' remarked rather perspicaciously: 'This feels a bit strange. It's not right. Something's gonna happen here.' Within ten minutes, as the first and only sustained City vocal barrage died out, it went off in the Main Stand complimentary section, of all bizarre places. It looked like four or five against two, the only sort of odds City will take presumably. Thus was the day's pattern established: City start on isolated Reds – for no sane Red would kick-off surrounded by nasty-looking blues – a 30-second battering ensues and then the officials eventually turn up with all the speed of a Molby. Such is the modern Maine Road, home of the 'family' club and favoured venue of the friendly, salt-of-the-earth Mancunian . . .

Midway through the half, a larger-scale version of the same sparked off to the left of the Umbro Stand goal. The officials must have displayed City-style efficiency in sorting it out because there was a repeat performance in precisely the same spot half an hour later. Surveying the stands as a whole, it was clear that the ground was woefully undermanned; despite the evident potential for trouble, given the nature of some Blues and the presence of Reds everywhere, parts of the ground appeared to be up to a minute away from the nearest official. It takes rather less than a minute for a pack of Blue savages to put someone in a coma, or worse: is this the standard of protection you should accept at a Premiership 'big club'?

For a few minutes after the break, City could feel they were still in it; once Scholes came on to give Cole some support, United's engine began firing on all cylinders and City became condemned men. Andrei at last got some decent runs on the ball; Giggs took flight whilst Cole produced his most intelligent spell yet in a Red shirt; Ince smashed what was left of City's midfield spirit.

As United found space and opportunities at will, Bluenoses turned white around me – they seemed to know what was coming. Ince drove home on 58 for the opener and good chances were missed by Choccy and Andrei as City frantically tried to get a grip. Quinn came on to give City their old Route One option but was left looking like a lost, orphaned giraffe as United tightened their hold on Blue throats. No amount of City routes and options would have beaten United on this form. Andrei, the Blue-slayer from November, fittingly got the second on 74, slamming through the near-post gap before Cole capped the game's best move with a simple tap-in three minutes later. The slaughter of City that half at least equalled anything we've inflicted upon them before.

As the third went in, City had long since been reduced to silence. They hadn't actually been singing as such – City simply have no songs but *Come on City* and *If You Hate Man U* – but had made enough noise to swamp the efforts of the Red 1,300 in the Kippax pen in the first half. Now, Reds had free reign, with City unable even to rouse themselves to shout 'shit' in reply to our 'United'. At three-nil, they weren't even growling in disgust – they just sat in stunned stupor, punctuated by anguished moans of pain.

Having given up getting behind their atrocious team, City fans had to resort to getting behind their fighters, as that was the only confrontation they had a chance of winning. The Umbro idiots kicked off again after Ince's goal, bringing blood-lusting morons to their feet all around the ground in vocal support. Stewards looked on with smiling approval as Kippax cretins spent the half doing aeroplane impressions and yelling threats to Reds behind them; eventually, the infamous Kippax-North Stand corner exploded, with even the Dibbles getting a few well-deserved smacks. Funny how quickly they can respond when their lot, rather than ordinary Reds, are getting a kicking.

As United threatened to make it four or five, with Cole missing a semi-sitter, devastated Blues streamed out in droves, unable to witness any further torture. Reds in Blue stands began grouping together, plotting escape routes to avoid the packs of purple-faced knobs who were gathering ready to exact vengeance. At the exits, Reds barely able to restrain the howls of joy inside them subtly 'clocked' fellow infiltrators before melting away into the back streets. We passed a swelling growth of Bittermen outside their laughable Social Club, hundreds of seething Magoos waiting impatiently for the main body of Reds to emerge and clearly intent on something other than a round of hearty handshakes. For the first and only time that day, we were glad not to have been in the pen.

I am reliably informed that some sort of ruck did indeed take place on the concourse, and even that the 'Claremont' did get a Red visit after all. Certainly, later that night, Reds and Blues clashed around Deansgate forcing a temporary police seal-off. Derby Day aggro is back: the Eighties revival has spread beyond the confines of pop.

As you can probably tell, I personally find the violence to be both sickening and fascinating. At the risk of sounding immoral, I think it's a fair reflection to say that most true Reds distinguish between two types of aggro. When it consists of isolated Reds being attacked by Blue animals in the stands, it is completely unacceptable and outrageous; I felt like throwing up watching it and intensely angry at the grievously slack 'protection' offered by MCFC. However, when it's gang-based skirmishing, engaged in by totally willing participants and harming no 'innocents', there's undeniably something appealing in it. Indeed, for the fan who is concerned that families and the middle-class are taking over football grounds, the odd bit of public brawling is almost to be welcomed. It may be morally reprehensible to say so, but it's the sort of phenomenon that can help remind interlopers that the game does not yet belong to them and that those who wish to join in should do so on 'our' terms.

As for the football, what can you say? A virtually unprecedented second successive league double; not only two victories, but two absolute spankings. An 8-0 aggregate record that could last for a century and which stands as unimpeachable evidence of our total supremacy. If I was a Blue, I'd leave town. How can they ever live this season down? If their ranks didn't contain so many violent, cowardly bastards, you'd almost feel sorry for them.

Typically, the media chose largely to ignore the City-inspired aggro. Imagine the same scenario at Old Trafford; 'United Savages' would make every front page in the country. Still, that's the price of being the only team in Manchester. Huh? Well, according to both the BBC News later and even John Motson on 'MOTD', who both referred to United in their derby reports simply as 'Manchester', City have become completely negligible. 'City, Man. City - nobody knows your name' indeed. It's a good job that the Blue myth of City being 'Manchester's team' isn't true - what a shame, what a stain on the Manc soul it would be for our city to be represented solely by the Maine Road jokers.

Team: Schmeichel; Irwin, Bruce, Pallister, Neville (Scholes), Kanchelskis (May), Ince, McClair, Sharpe, Cole, Giggs

19 February: LEEDS AT HOME (FA CUP ROUND FIVE)

Final Score: UNITED 3 Scum 1

Scorers: Bruce 1, McClair 4, Hughes 71

Attendance: 42,744

EVER SINCE LEEDS EMERGED from their Yorkshire hovels in the 1960s to join football's top flight, any United fixture against them has held something special, whatever the pertaining circumstances at the time. It is, in many ways, the most fascinating blood feud in football. We could not truly be said to be 'local rivals' in the way that we are with Bolton, Rovers, City and the Scouse; our support does not, to any significant degree, overlap very much (*pace* The Yorkshire Reds). Nor do our clubs really have that much of a history of going head-to-head for honours, at least not in comparison to our struggles with Liverpool; the odd Cup semi apart, we have only been in title contention together twice, in 1965 and 1992. For the best part of a recent decade, we didn't even play each other as Leeds scrabbled around in a lower division, drawing mammoth crowds of 8,000 to Elland Road. And as the Clubs never cease to remind us, the two camps' players and officials are all nauseatingly good mates. Yet, according to the wholly reliable *Red Issue* surveys, within two years of Leeds' last promotion, they have regained their Sixties position as the Club Reds most despise. As for Leeds, their position never waivered: since that first, modern-era meeting in the autumn of 1964, they have loathed Manchester United beyond all others.

The War of the Roses sub-text is self-evident; despite the local government re-organisation of '74, the two Uniteds continue to be seen as the standard-bearers for the ancient counties of Lancashire and Yorkshire. Our club has always stayed true to the essential Lancastrian character – warm, witty, tolerant and open-armed in the welcome of others. Leeds, particularly under Revie, successfully encapsulated all that is Yorkie – dour, suspicious, ruthless and xenophobic. And whereas Lancastrians prefer to look forward without the encumbrance of past resentments, the Tykes are the masters of brooding, festering grudges, ever ready to quote imagined historical injustices and to sulk about the outsider's failure to appreciate their achievements. The nature of our souls sets us apart from the outset.

It hasn't helped matters that Leeds have had no close local rivals to hate – a crucial omission, since any observer of the sheep molesters can testify how important an element of life hate is to the Leeds. Sadly, despite the city's pretensions to greatness, it is barely able to support the one sporadically successful club it has – there's no room for a Leeds City FC. Consequently, we have been co-opted to play the iconic role of demon figures for the scum, a part in which we have enjoyed doing our best to excel.

History refused to follow the Leeds script. When, at last, the glory of our European triumph faded and Leeds' footballing achievements began to outstrip ours, the nation refused to bestow either the love or admiration it had shown to Busby's men. Instead Britain whooped with delight at every last-fence failure as the dominance of Revie's hatchetmen produced only three or four trophies instead of the dozen they felt they deserved. A City-like bitterness suffused Elland Road and has never left it since. Even when silver was won, the football world carped at their negative destructional tendencies, their appalling cynicism and their lack of flair. The revelation that they'd tried to bribe their way to a title seemed to sum them up – they were football's Anti-Christs whose every triumph was tainted by sin.

Moreover, when their moment came to enter Valhalla at last, their return to earth was wonderfully brutal – and largely effected by United. At last a clean, almost-popular Leeds side won a title and did so by pipping us. Yet every Yorkie attempt to celebrate publicly was met with the response that they had been gifted the title by a side whom they had failed to beat in four attempts. With the new season came their opportunity to secure an undisputed place in heaven but within months they were up to their necks in the mud of earthbound swamps – and the foot stamping down on their heads was ours. We robbed them of their one true hero, robbed them of their title and robbed them of their chance to establish a fresh, pure and popular football dynasty. They must have thought they were going to be the Team of the Nineties: to their horror, they now find that it's us. 'Let's all laugh at Leeds – baa, baa, baa.'

No wonder, then, that almost all our meetings have been wracked by tribal tension and hostility; no wonder that even at the height of football's rehabilitation, a United-Leeds fixture still guaranteed seething virulence and indiscriminate aggro. In recent years, it might have been true for a while that their hatred of us dwarfed our contempt for them but the events at subsequent Elland Road clashes have brought us up to something approaching equality of mutual disgust. After all, we have suffered no footballing setbacks at their hands, bar the '92 title race result, since that infamous Cup semi in 1970. Indeed, until last September they hadn't even won a match against us for over 13 years. Our venom has almost entirely resulted from the subhuman and criminal behaviour of a large Leeds fan minority. They are bad enough in our absence, of course; their rioting at Bradford and Bournemouth and their continued dispatch of neo-Nazi morons to England games alone warrant condemnation. But when we are the visitors, all codes of human, or even animal, civilisation are jettisoned. Buttressed by an indolent local constabulary, who have often disgraced an already shame-soaked uniform, and by a slack, limp-wristed Club bureaucracy, the bestial inhabitants of Elland

Road treat a United game as an excuse for a mobhanded man-hunt. United may have their own hoolies still but even they will observe an honour-code of sorts: bricking family coaches and attacking women, as enacted by Leeds vermin last season, does not fall within such parameters. Even when we are there in spirit only, as at the Ewood Park Busby memorial last season, they cannot restrain their pond-life instincts. Their hard-core is such that they are the only fans in the country of whom you would not be ashamed to think the following: you wish it had been them at Hillsborough '89 instead of Liverpool.

So any United-Leeds fixture brings a lot of emotional baggage with it – but this had a context and timing guaranteed to incite blood-lust all round. It was, of course, a Cup tie, a simple matter of sorting the slayer from the slain with no defeated's mitigation about losing battles but winning wars. There was also the small matter of vengeance for the league loss of September which had been celebrated in Scum City with the fervour of a title and milked for months to come. Those who were there hadn't forgotten the agonising detention after the whistle when, for once, the sheep penned in the humans to taunt us from all sides. And finally there was the increasingly central importance of winning the FA Cup for both clubs. For United players, beginning to buzz with self-confidence, there was the realisation that anything less than the Double Double would feel like an anti-climax, even as an insult to such a self-evidently superior team. For Leeds, of course, there was nothing else: as usual, Sgt Wilko's hapless misfits had been 'marching altogether' to another title-free season. Once again, we were being offered the pleasure of ending Leeds' trophy-hunting season.

As if all that were not enough, the events at Maine Road and Lansdowne Road in run-up week had brought any pugilistic feelings right up to the surface. The sight of innocent, isolated Reds getting battered by psychotic Bluenosed beasts, coupled with the sickening TV images from Eire, raised most Red temperatures. We all knew that a large Leeds contingent had gone to Dublin to beat up Oldham and then the Irish; the fact that they had then helped launch missile attacks on *English* fans below and that the Leeds platoon would doubtless be at Old Trafford helped bring some Reds to a state in which they could've started a fight in an empty room.

Of course, such febrile atmospheres bring out the bravado in every bullshit-merchant in town. If every sheep-rustling scheme we heard about had actually come off, the Leeds coaches that had brought 6,500 would have been returning empty but for the odd, multi-apertured, inflatable Flossie. Three planned ambushes in particular did, however, seem to be kosher. The most amusing was the prospective motorway-side party that was due to start with several kegs of ale at 8 a.m., to culminate in a mass coach-bottling as the Leeds turned off for Manchester. The extra 1,300 police ensured that the Wallace Arnold fleet turned up intact though. Another battle-plan involved the storming of the Pier Six pub, where Leeds had drunk before their pathetic Youth Cup Final excursion; the pub was shut for the day but apparently some satisfaction was gained. More bluntly, some just intended a concourse charge at 2.30, knowing that the Leeds would all be in neat files trying to get into the East stand; in the event, Leeds didn't want to know. Their bravura procession up Sir Matt Busby Way, in which the offloaded coach parties massed together under escort, aggressively chanting 'We are Leeds', belied their true intent. In the wake of Wednesday night, the police categorisation of the match as 'C plus' – the highest alert possible – had produced a monitoring operation of impressive scope. West Yorkshire Police, take note and learn for once . . .

(Admittedly, a few coaches who had strayed from the flock and ended up passing slowly by the Chester Road shops received a hail of cans and missiles for their stupidity but it was more symbolic than anything – the glass remained unbroken. A mounted policeman nearby actually burst out laughing; nice to know that a true Manc heart can beat under a pig's skin.)

Inside Old Trafford, the air throbbed with the sort of excitement you get in pre-coitus moments. Keith Fane's best efforts on the fader couldn't quite drown out the unmistakable Yorkie vowel sounds that floated over from the East end as they lumbered repeatedly through their two songs. As the music cut, United fans who'd been keeping their powder dry let rip with a deafening tribute to the missing God. How he would have loved this confrontation . . .

For a bloke, the start of a game is like the start of a sexual encounter. By kick-off, you're at the stage where you've finally got her kit off after hours of building up to the moment. You're buzzing your nuts off, literally: at that moment, you want to shoot and score, so to speak. But of course, you can't yet – you've got to delay to the right moment which could be bloody ages yet. The early ecstasy has to be controlled and never in itself gets to climax. Equally, goals in the first few minutes are rare, for obvious footballing reasons, which is a pity given that a crowd hits one of its greatest peaks in the opening three minutes, especially on a day like this. Sadly, you hardly ever get to explode that excitement into a climax; instead, the crowd settles down and has to build to a peak all over again. So you can appreciate just what it was like for all of us in that opening 250 seconds. The juiciest assignation of the year, you're boiling with desire for a result, the action starts . . . and you get two goals in four minutes. It's the footballing equivalent of getting your mitts on a naked Pamela Anderson and shooting twice before an egg's boiled – and yet she's still totally satisfied . . . Only the last-minute winner can compare.

It was an amusing irony for later reflection that both goals should come from corners. After all, Sgt Wilko is supposed to be a master of both tactics and organisation whose teams are never supposed to be caught cold so comprehensively as this. In fact, the pre-match speculation was that the *Leeds* main threat would be from corners, whereas until recently United could barely keep their corners in play. But the Giggs Revival has included his deadball work, thankfully; on precisely 60 seconds, his centre eschewed its normal destination of the East Lower, to be instead turned into a goal-bound rocket by the granite forehead of Stevie Bruce. Scarcely had the bedlam in the stands begun to abate when, within 200 seconds, another corner flicked onto Choccy who somehow managed to twist his neck and cushion home the ball from the most awkward of positions. 37,000 promptly creamed their keks: the bestial brigades stood transfixed by horror across the East end as their worst paranoid nightmare came roaring to life. Within seconds, the earliest ever rendition of 'You're so shit it's unbelievable' filled the stadium; not a mouth opened in reply from the assembled scum. It was as if they'd been struck dead by lightning on the spot, rows of stiffened corpses ready for burial to the Red undertakers' tune of *Are you City in disguise?!*' It had taken four minutes to avenge the Black September for which Leeds had waited over 13 years. Ain't life sweet?

Sheep-slaughter was now on the minds of every Red. A third at any point in the first-half would surely have inspired us to a historic rout to match the City-drubbings. Leeds players appeared to be shatteringly shell-shocked, some seeming to have thrown in the towel the moment Choccy's header crossed the line. Their tactical plans and their allegedly attacking formation had been demolished; their play for the rest of the half was laughably witless. United contentedly took the piss, knocking the ball around with Cantonesque arrogance; Giggs could easily have added a pair around the quarter-hour mark and narrowly missed connecting with Choccy's ball on 19. 'Two-nil, without Cantona' bayed the Red hordes, ever-mindful of the greater significance. Those Leeds attacks that actually resulted in shots caused only hilarity at the Strettie End – White, Speed, McAllister and Massinga produced, at ten minute intervals, a quartet of the most hopeless 'finishes' you've ever seen. Shortly after Pally's close header on 32, the Tykes finally found some vocal response; a Munich chorus complete with waves, which happily resulted in several ejections. Given the humiliation they were undergoing, you couldn't blame them for wanting to get thrown out. Reds responded in time-honoured fashion with a *Scum/We'll Never Die* medley that was absolutely impassioned; some in J stand no doubt began marking Leeds seat positions for later on, too . . .

We were singing in the toilets and bars at half-time, always a sure indicator of heightened Red pleasure; L, J and F stands had all been particularly vibrant as K standers, spread about the stadium, inspired those around them. As Leeds fans had smartly sabotaged all the normal chants of 'United' by grunting 'Leeds' in between in that primeval way of theirs, we had happily resorted to making 'If you all hate Leeds . . .' the number one chant of the day. Strangely, the Tykes refused to air anti-Manchester songs either out of fear or lack of imagination, both of which explanations would be typical of them. A Leeds version of *Songs From The Bathtub* would be one of the shortest albums ever. For such 'legendary' supporters, their vocal repertoire is pitifully thin. Perhaps it is that their current evolutionary stage is such that they can only remember one or two sets of lyrics at any time, having otherwise to resort to mere grunts and growls?

The appearance of Yeboah as sub after the break was a bad omen for Reds with memories of past black supersubs coming on to wreck Red dreams. On 47, his flash header constituted the first decent Leeds effort of the day. Moments later, a foul by White gave Andrei a chance from the resultant free-kick; within a minute of the ball crashing from Lukic's 'tips to wood, Yeboah had stumbled the ball into the Scoreboard net. In that instant, the game was transformed, temporarily at least, from a procession into a genuine Cup tie. For about 15 minutes United were out of step, dislocated and sporadically under threat. Not that Leeds ever took control but with their support finally coming alive and McAllister showing touches of class, you felt that their moment had come. They peaked around the 67th minute mark, as Sharpe was forced into a life-saving interception to be followed by a narrow White miss, the Bluenose's sole decent contribution of the day and probably a fluke to boot.

Cometh the hour, cometh the Dragon. Hughes, making his first appearance since Newcastle, had been warming to the task all afternoon, revelling in the fevered atmosphere of a clash with his favourite opponents. We all recall his epic displays in the 1992 Trilogy and at Elland Road last April; if Keane and McClair were to be the Men of the Match today, at least Sparky would be ensuring his name made the Roll of Honour by scoring the *de facto* winner. He is a man for the fairytale, storybook headline – as Andrei somehow dug out a supremely crafted cross from the right, who else but Hughes to direct a sublime header into the Strettie net, executed with a technique to match that of his Oldham Wembley volley? The man has his OT detractors, and as a player has his faults, but he can still provide those moments of dramatic flourish upon which United's glorious history is built. When, in 40 years time, you recant the Red legend to your grandchildren, Hughesy's specials will be in there alongside Bill Foulkes in Madrid and Stepney at Wembley. What more do you want?

As Old Trafford roared through a deafening *Que Sera*, Leeds gently expired. Amidst a flurry of Red creativity, their one last hurrah was headed off the line by Incey on 76; the rest belonged to the piss-taking Reds. Kanchelskis continued to give Dorigo – once an England full-back?! – the sort of slaying that Sharpe once gave gypsy Mel in '91. Giggs ran rampant, destroying what remained of Kelly's tattered reputation. Between the Welsh wonder and the Ukrainian, six gilt-edged chances went unconverted in the last 15 minutes. We didn't get the rout that once seemed imminent but, Leeds' mini-comeback notwithstanding, we still gave them a lesson in passing and movement that they'll never live down. As Reds sang *Always Look on the Bright Side* and *So F*ckin' Easy*, even Alan Hansen was purring in admiration up in the box. The viewing nation looked on and gulped nervously.

The ground all but emptied, leaving the 6,000 traumatised Tykes to fester in the bloody juices of defeat in the East stands. Reds in J and L stands stayed on to keep them company and sing them a few songs to keep their spirits down. Those who'd been penned up at Elland Road must have been particularly amused at this point. Rather ungratefully, the Leeds boys reacted badly to this, attempting a mass break-out at the top of K which the police easily quashed before turning their attentions to Reds who were keen to get in amongst the Leeds, presumably to shake a few hands. One or two seats fizzed through the air but this was hardly a Dublin re-run; eventually Reds left them to make their forlorn journey back to Sheep City, although some apparently chose to go via Ordsall to engage in a minor riot for old times sake. The much-hyped Battle of Old Trafford had failed to materialise, the police having given an object lesson to their Irish and

West Yorkie equivalents. The only fatality had been Leeds United's self-esteem – outclassed by the one, true United yet again. Baa, baa, baa . . .

Team: Schmeichel; Irwin, Bruce, Pallister, Sharpe, Keane, Ince, Kanchelskis, McClair, Hughes, Giggs

22 February: NORWICH CITY AWAY

Final Score: Norwich 0 UNITED 2

Scorers: Ince 2, Andrei 16

Attendance: 21,824

OF COURSE IT'S AGGRAVATING that the Premier League forces you to make a 16-hour round-trip to the south-eastern wastelands in the middle of the week for a night kick-off. Who wants to be wandering around Stretford at three in the morning looking for a cabbie when you've got to be up for work at seven? Nevertheless, there is one advantage in this: such fixtures certainly separate the men from the boys, or rather the lads from the part-timers and families. You can guarantee that at least little Andrea and her cohort of face-painted ten-year-olds will be absent, as will the majority of the suit 'n' tie brigade. Thus, for once, you have half a chance of getting a face value ticket from the Club; moreover, the prospect of being in a South Stand full of time-served true Reds lessens the pain of shelling out the £30-plus such expeditions demand. I wonder if Sky could be convinced to make all United aways midnight kick-offs, played on the Orkneys?

Just to add to our discomfort, we arrived in this farming backwater to be greeted by the sort of weather conditions in which Jumping Jack Flash was born. Admittedly, you emerge from a seven-hour coach haul wishing you could have a shower but this wasn't quite what we meant. Bedraggled Reds congregating in local hostelries seemed, understandably, to be in less than the highest of spirits, forcing even the Boyle to beat a retreat; the uniformed inhabitants of the local sty didn't help matters by apparently seeking to pick out terrace songsters for either disbarment or early ejection. As we were to discover from watching the home fans, vocal encouragement of any sort is not the done thing at Carrow Road.

Once under the semi-shelter of the South Stand, however, Reds were soon busy creating some communal warmth. Norwich have a cute little ground, neat and sparkling in a plasticky sort of way, as if built out of Lego by a fastidious child-giant. The South Stand excepted, of course; being the away accommodation, this still resembles an unfinished barn held together by discarded tractor parts. The bar downstairs is clearly somebody's front room that has been transplanted plank-by-plank, complete with dodgy TVs and armchairs, and small enough to make it precisely 100 per cent unsuitable for catering to hundreds of beer-thirsty Reds. I recall that back in the Seventies, the Red Army once took exception to their environment at Carrow Road and promptly demolished it from within. Nowadays, Reds are content merely to grumble and sing 'shit ground . . .' More civilised, perhaps, but rather less effective . . .

I also recall that in darker Eighties days, Norwich were once a United bogey team. A laughable scenario now, of course, as United bid to make it six straight wins there but indicative of the strangeness of those years. For tonight's game, two footballing memories were arguably paramount; the vividly fresh buzz from Sunday's Scum-slaughter and the equally delicious hammering we dished out to the Canaries in '93. Fabulously, United were about to give us reprises of both, on the theme of getting your killer blows in early. It may be very un-United to do things the easy way but we can all do with the odd tension-free match every now and then.

With virtually the first attacking thrust of the night, Cole forced a second minute corner; scarcely had the Andy Cole song died away when, in almost conscious homage to Sunday, a superb corner was headed away only as far as the Guvnor. It is in Ince's contract, one assumes, that he must attempt a 20-yard blinder in every match. Two-out-of-ten hit woodwork, one goes in – tonight the volley lottery hit the earliest-ever jackpot. In the stands, Reds who already had that 'special night' feeling revelled in the second ridiculously premature ejaculation in four days; a classic vocal half ensued.

Norwich, forced straight into fifth gear by this rudest of awakenings, promised some threatening behaviour for a few minutes, Ward even touching the ball onto the bar. Yet United rapidly settled into their most comfortable, Double-winning clothes, those of the counter-attacking Devils. Pally marshalled a defence that contained two midfielders at full-back quite magnificently, easily soaking up Norwich's rather feeble jabs before launching devastating counter-punches. The second goal after a quarter of an hour was a minor classic, if unoriginal, in that it echoed Andrei's epic there back in '93. From defensive header to goal in five seconds via Hughes, Choccy, the pivotal Giggs and the deadliest Ukrainian finish – it was, as the song has it, 'po-etry in motion'. Those Reds in home stand who'd somehow managed to restrain themselves at 1-0 leaped uninhibitedly skywards; the South Stand almost self-combusted. The smell of that vintage Chateau Rouge '94 was back in our nostrils and we'd uncorked it without any Gallic aid. Maybe we really *can* do it, after all.

The South Stand party, *à la* Vale Park, went into full swing. Out came all the City and Leeds songs, with the odd Willie Morgan and Georgie Best standard thrown in for variety. The scoreboard operator, rather inadvisedly, flashed up plaintive pleas such as 'Let's make some noise!' and 'Let's hear it in the South Stand', to which Reds were only too happy to respond with deafening volleys. Presumably the local farmers haven't mastered reading yet as they sat silently brooding throughout.

As Schmeichel superbly saved City's last chance from Bowen on 31, the Red troops let rip with their *pièce de resistance* – a non-stop, full-throated, 13 minutes of *Fergie's Red & White Army*. This chant is not as popular as it once was – indeed, Veg never misses an opportunity to note tartly its banality – but when it's done properly like this, it's still a willy-trembler of the first order. Norwich fans in the Barclay End looked on, open-mouthed in stupefaction, as if realising for the first time how inappropriate it is that their team and fans inhabit the same footballing universe as ours. When we're good, we are still far and away the best in the business.

On the pitch, United had moved into training session mode, drawing on the support's self-confidence and arrogance. Fergie later carped that we spent too much time passing the ball around in midfield but who can blame the lads for taking a midweek breather when it's on offer? Their utter dominance was scarcely questioned for the rest of the 90 minutes; this was piss-taking but without the malice that we'd inflicted on Leeds. Amidst all the passing practice, they made enough chances to be getting on with too, Cole having to settle for a corner, Andrei blazing over in his attempt to emulate Incey's opener and Giggs going just wide from a free-kick. Norwich were turning out to be ideal sparring partners for the heavyweight Reds, doing just enough to keep us awake without ever threatening to put us down. Whilst never being as limp-wristedly supine as a Bruno opponent, Norwich never promised to turn this into a footballing Benn-McClennan . . .

After the break, as Reds rolled through the Cantona canon and various Blue-baiting anthems, United continued to cruise about as a

V12 machine needing only eight cylinders. Hughes, dancing through the box before being scythed down, scarcely bothered to complain about the obvious penalty he'd been denied; Andrei took advantage of the luxurious circumstances to try one of his absurdly acute-angled shots only to find post instead of net. Norwich's attacking threat dwindled to nothingness, with bitter offcast Sheron being particularly, pleasingly useless. As full-time approached, the 100 or so Canaries in the Barclay End who constitute Norwich's singers were finally heard: 'Deehan, Deehan what's the score?' The happy-go-lucky family club seems to be heading for a domestic . . .

Sadly, Blackburn also won, none too convincingly against the Wombles; the fact that we had now delivered up some freshly-plucked Canaries as Rovers' next visitors meant that the weekend's prospects looked less than brilliant. I daresay that an objective review of the highlights would reveal that this had been a good, rather than stunning display by the team and also, perhaps, that Hughes and Cole was not yet a marriage of convenience made in heaven. But no game is just about what happens on the pitch; for most of us, the entire experience is what counts. Why else did we go when we were terrible, back in those days when teams like Norwich were actually a threat? For the real, all-singing, all-dancing, all-drinking Reds, this was a top night. You won't find that truth recorded in the official reviews and annuals, of course. But if you're reading this book as opposed to those, I guess you think, like me, that these things matter, right?

Team: Schmeichel; Keane, Bruce, Pallister, Sharpe, McClair, Ince, Kanchelskis, Cole, Hughes, Giggs

25 February: EVERTON AWAY

Final Score: Everton 1 UNITED 0

Attendance: 40,011

AS ANY EIGHTIES BOY will remind you, the United-Everton rivalry was once within venom-spitting distance of that between us and the other Stanley Knife Park crew. Is it only eight years or so since a visit to Goodison entailed a precarious trek through the Everton Valley of Death, dodging golfballs and other missiles launched from tower blocks whilst keeping a wary eye out for marauding packs of scally hoolies? Back then, Goodison was more than just an honorary embassy of the Ku Klux Klan; it also served as the 'School of Science' to the most formidable team unit of the mid Eighties. Invariably, glamorous Red sides would return humbled, having received yet another lesson in ensemble passing and movement – on one appalling occasion, the instruction consisted of a 5-0 walloping. At least we used to beat Liverpool; in Everton's case, the Stanley knife stood as a symbol not only of their fans' amoral thuggery but also of their team's surgically destructive ability.

Happily, since those grim years whose misery culminated in the sale of Norm to the Blue beasts, Everton's decline has been the mirror-image of our rise. Only a few months before this fixture, Everton FC were the butt of more public ridicule than even Man. City; United had won three in a row at Goodison and would be seeking a league double over them today. Few Everton sides in living memory had been as classless, witless and gutless as the outfit we beat 2-0 in the autumn. Sadly, four months is a long time in football. The arrival of one of Scousedom's less despicable characters, Joe Royle, had effected a dramatic change at Goodison. The team now had balls – and United were about to get screwed.

For Reds en route to Goodison, the Carrow Road buzz had been slightly diminished by Friday's news of Eric's extended ban, a prime example of the FA trying to prove in playground fashion who's the cock of the walk. It was now obvious that rather than United being the ones to have pulled a fast one by banning Eric in a pre-emptive strike, we had in fact been out-trumped. No doubt the blundering warthog Kelly thought he had been very smart but he will surely find that Edwards will never allow himself to be led up the garden path like that again. Let us hope that is the last time United 'co-operate' with the discredited Lancaster Gate junta: next time, a display of Sugary combat would be in order.

There had been some talk of Everton reforming old firms for this match and certainly rumours abounded that the BNP Goodison cell were treating this as showpiece occasion. There was little evidence of this on the walk up the hill to Goodison however; all I saw were the three faces of Murkeyside. The dismal urban wastelands, then, the close-knit terraced streets that huddle close the Park, breeding uncontrolled hordes of Harry Enfield/'Bread' stereotypes; finally the ground itself, which from outside resembles a maximum security prison, cheerily reminding the inhabitants of their inevitable destination. There's nothing as comfortingly amusing as witnessing a living cliché: within three minutes, I clocked a drug-deal going down, two cars without hubcaps and a Red being accosted by three shell-suited, bumfluff teens trying to flog forged tickets. How heartening to see a city's standards being maintained.

Reds filled the left side of the Bullens, with most of the 'lads' appearing to be in the Lower and Paddock; elsewhere, at least a couple of hundred Reds settled uncomfortably down amidst the Hun-loving Blues. For once, Reds in home stands would have little trouble in remaining undetected – there would be little to jump out of your seat for. The pitch glowered grimly; it looked as though Royle had dug up the Boundary Park 'turf' and brought it with him. Full of ruts, rough patches and hard edges, it suited Everton's game down to the ground. The so-called 'Dogs of War' took full advantage of the terrain and the card-shy ref Worrall to come out snarling and biting. For once, we were to be outfought.

It hardly helped that Fergie had decided to 'rotate' Andrei out of the game and play McClair as well as Keane in midfield. This was unpleasant shock enough for us: Andrei's response later was to raise a finger to Alex and say 'rotate on that'. With Giggs playing in fits and starts, United became an unwelcome reminder of Ramsey's wingless wonders - and this on one of the League's widest pitches. The Curse of Tinkerbell returns to haunt again. Everton, needless to say, banged every available ball out to the flank where Barlow was running Sharpe ragged. Fortunately, the hapless Barndoor was crossing as well as he shoots, to the hooting derision of the home crowd. In midfield, Everton's insignificants, whose names I forget, simply bypassed McClair and often outbarked our own dogs of war, Keano and Ince. With Red support in similar fitful vein, it seemed obvious that Everton would not be rolling over as cravenly as our last three opponents.

Had our forwards been even vaguely on form, none of this would have mattered. However, Hughesy's abject air-volley and Cole's wide shot after brilliant initial control typified their day. Still, at least it gave Everton the chance to sing *What a waste of money*, their only song of the first half. It is truly pathetic to see the Gwladys End reduced to such vocal timidity by all-seating and it certainly puts the new Strettie in a much more favourable light. Hard to credit that over 40,000 had turned up; I guess that's the result of having a one-off influx of part-timers for the day. Still, the police must have been happy – the city's crime rate between 3.20 and 5 would surely have been the lowest on record.

Ebbrell should have punished us for our laxity but gently lofted the ball over the bar late in the half. We bayed for Andrei at half-time but the brooding Ukrainian was not yet to be forthcoming. By the time he did emerge, it was too late; Everton had seized the initiative, the game and the lead. In a twenty minute Blue storm, our only chance fell via Incey to Cole, who calmly, deliberately, sidefooted the ball into Southall's ample stomach. At the Gwladys end, Brucey was twice forced into desperate interventions, Horne hit the bar and, inevitably, on 58 Ferguson towered over a dithering defence to head home Hinchcliffe's corner. After a week of profiting hugely from corners, United had been outdone by one themselves. Such is the rub on days like these. Everton even managed to finish the game with eleven men on the pitch. You can't legislate for luck like that can you?

A Schmeichel save handed us a lifeline of sorts at a moment when a second would have been just reward for Everton; even Pally began to gallop forward to try his luck, a sure sign that desperation has set in. Andrei replaced the ineffective Choccy at last but the delay was fatal; with the forwards on such poor form, he would need more than 20 minutes worth of crosses before he could hope to see one converted. Hughes miskicked again, Cole sidefooted harmlessly again – how luminous did the writing on the wall have to be? Even the traditional last-minute hoofing cavalry charge attacks produced nothing but a Cole header that was never going to threaten. The whistle was almost a relief. It was our first away league defeat since Hillsborough and the performance had been uncannily similar. Reds, not held back, emerged gloomily considering the future of Cole and Hughes together and perhaps wondering whether this was a harbinger of life without Eric. How United cried out for that different, inspirational approach to breaking open granite-hewn opponents . . .

As most Reds successfully evaded the few packs of Everton nasties that roamed about post-match, news came through that Rovers had been astonishingly held 0-0 at home by Norwich. The sun that had disappeared behind clouds at half-time emerged to illuminate the valley. Suddenly, the context had changed. After all, many Reds would have realistically expected us to perhaps lose two points to Rovers today; instead, it was only one, and Rovers would appear to have more troubles than us if they couldn't score against such a weedy defence as the Canaries'. The wretched performance of Hughes and Cole was now no longer a doom-laden indicator of permanent incompatibility but could be confidently written off as a mere lowlight; now, you could think that it wasn't the long term absence of Eric that would cost us everything but merely that the temporary absence of Andrei had cost us just one match. David Meek caught the spirit when he wrote that 'Next time, Cole will get the breaks'. Always look on the bright side – and watch out Ipswich.

Team: Schmeichel; Irwin, Bruce, Pallister, Sharpe, Ince, Keane, McClair (Kanchelskis), Giggs, Cole, Hughes

4 March: IPSWICH TOWN AT HOME

Final Score: UNITED 9 Ipswich 0

Scorers: Keane 15, Cole 19, 37, 53, 65, 87, Hughes 55, 59, Ince 72

Attendance: 43,804

(AND TO THINK THAT some approached this game with trepidation . . .)

The day before had been dominated by anxious discussions of the Kanchelskis situation which had opened up the appalling vista of United now losing their two greatest foreign imports within weeks. At first, the source of the transfer request news had been deemed of sufficiently dubious quality to calm fevered Red brows – after all, do even the *Daily Mirror's* executives believe what they read on the London-hacked *MirrorSport* pages? Fergie's appearance on Sky later, however, confirmed our worst fears. In a fit of Slavic pique, Andrei had indeed vented his post-Goodison fury to a *Mirror* hack. Fergie, never the best of screen actors, was clearly finding it difficult to conceal that his anger had reached teacup-chucking proportions. He tersely announced that Andrei, who had signed a three-year deal, would be 'going nowhere', which fell somewhat short of the kiss-and-make-up scenario we watching Reds wanted to hear. Andrei and Fergie do, of course, 'have a history' as they say; twice before, the Ukrainian Mercury had been apparently on his way out, most recently on the eve of his epic Cup semi display. They are said generally not to see eye-to-eye; there is a clear ideological split between the two that will always threaten to rupture the relationship. Fergie, quite correctly in principle at least, believes in the managerial Divine Right which includes a propensity to sacrifice anyone at anytime, however undeservedly, for the sake of that match's Fergie Plan. Andrei's is a typically Continental view: if a great player is fit, on form and willing, he should never be dropped for any reason. At Goodison, this clash of philosophies was evident to all.

Reds I spoke to seemed equally divided. Most had to concede that Fergie's right to manage – this is sounding like a Seventies industrial action – was paramount. Some slammed Andrei for his heresy of seeming to be prepared to quit OT over such a relatively trivial matter; we all expect that no Red should leave us unless dragged kicking and screaming away. Others chided Ferguson for provoking Andrei yet again, having seemingly learned little from past bust-ups – if Cantona gets 'special treatment', doesn't top-scorer and current inspiration Andrei deserve the same? All agreed that Fergie had been wrong to leave him out at Everton. As the bar-room arguments spilled over into Saturday, one desire united almost all Reds: whatever means necessary must be employed to ensure Andrei is happy to stay with us, rather than merely be forced to do so.

Andrei was at least straight back into the team, conventional wisdom being that he, above all, would be vital to break down the expected blanket farmers' defence. Ipswich are, if anything, even more deathly and dreary opponents than Wimbledon or Palace. We'd only won one of five Premiership fixtures with them; the memory of last year's nil-nil sat heavily within, an indigestible defensive stodge, whilst some had still not worked out how Town managed to beat us in September after we made 25 chances. (We were to make another 25 today, albeit at a rather superior conversion ratio.) At kick-off, there was no buzz of anticipation, no sense of impending sensory thrill and not a whisper from the mummified visitors in L stand. We were at Moon Base Old Trafford once more. As far as creating a sense of occasion, a game against sides of Ipswich's standing is simply a non-event over which none of us can get particularly worked up. *Pronto Berlusconi* – get that Euro League up and running, will you?

Thankfully, as against Palace and Wimbledon earlier in the season, United reacted to our disdainful semi-involvement in the manner of the best showbiz troopers. When the Stones were at their peak and faced by a glacial audience, the Glimmer Twins would pull every stagecraft trick in the book to get the joint blazing until the frenzied crowd were baying for more. United did precisely that, as if taking our indifference as a challenge to their manhood. Within minutes, it was obvious that United were as hungry for Ipswich blood as they would've been for Leeds' or Liverpool's. Relentless attacks probed, stretched and strained the Town defence in a masterful softening-up prelude — as Giggs and Andrei yanked from the sides, the rest bulldozed through the middle to wipe out the Ipswich garrison. We'd already made six chances in 15 minutes when the rampant Keane, nominally at full-back but actually at any place he fancied, swung almost lazily from the right to drive home the Strettie End opener. Eight minutes later, Ipswich were already beaten as Giggs ran 70 yards before teeing up the sort of goal that Cole used to score weekly at Newcastle. On 36, five minutes after Town's sole goal attempt, Hughesy's wondrous overhead kick rebounded off the bar to the grateful Cole, who duly secured the points. Three-up and the Red machine hadn't even reached maximum revs yet.

Neither had the crowd. The goals were greeted with almost polite applause before the stands returned to virtual silence. From the Scoreboard, I could at one point hear a small child talking half-way down the North Lower. My neighbour, offered £70 for his ticket by those marauding German backpackers before kick-off, remarked that he should've taken it — 'There's more singing in my bath than in here'. Naturally, he changed his mind later but that doesn't alter the fact that the first-half support shamed the name of Old Trafford. There were several thousand in there that just don't deserve a team like ours. Ipswich were no help either. It's a pity to have to say so, given that Town's fans are the only ones in the Premiership who don't appear to hate us, but they were by some distance the most useless away support bar Wimbledon's this season. What is the point of only singing when you're 8-0 down?! *Incroyable, mais vrai*, as Eric would say.

That this afternoon was transformed into something extraordinary was down to the half-time activities of Fergie and K stand. Rather than take the foot off the pedal, Alex seized the moment and instructed United to hit warp speed and close the goal difference gap with Rovers. Cole and Hughes duly came out with the carnal intent of mass-murderers. K stand, fortified by drink, emerged ready to take on their historic role of stadium-leaders; singing the new 'Swing Low' Cole song from the off, they kick-started the crowd towards the later, unforgettable crescendo.

The break had done little to revive Ipswich — Wark and Chapman looked closer to the grave than ever. As their defence staggered under the attacking weight, with even Brucey coming up to do his Romario impressions, United savagely threw them off the cliff with three goals in six minutes. Cole beat Yallop to head his hat-trick goal, Hughes blasted Giggs' centre in at the right post and then got his head onto a rebounded Giggs effort to make it 6-0. For once, United did indeed literally threaten to score with every attack; in the stands, we could barely catch our breath. There was no time to talk, reflect or turn to watch the scoreboard emit unfamiliar numbers; we were in thrall to the feeding frenzy, a roar of joy permanently in the throat.

Minutes later, Cole reacted brilliantly to bury a Forrest-parried Choccy effort for his fourth. 'What a waste of money' we screamed ironically; Andy beamed the smile of a man who knows his critics are dead in the water. Even the Main Stand was prepared to get to its feet by now – the inevitable Mexican wave, joined by the hapless visitors, was almost welcome in the circumstances. After Ince chipped home the cheekiest free-kick of the year on 72, even Ipswich fans were laughing; moments later, as Town plaintively wailed 'We want one', Ince blazed into the K stand from 40 yards. 'What the f*ckin' hell was that?' bellowed the OT praetorian guard, the sound of smiles evident in the chant as Incey grinned and waved from the circle. We had to wait 15 minutes for the record-breaker – 'Too slack, Reds' yelled an ironic K stand voice – but Cole's fifth was the best of all, a beautiful swivelling snapshot whilst surrounded by blueshirts. Cole's tally was a record; the 9-0 was a Premiership best and United's biggest domestic win since 1892 as Newton Heath. At the whistle, Reds stood transfixed, scarcely able to believe what they'd seen, looking lovingly at the scoreboard for confirmation of the historic massacre. Rovers had won too, despite Hendry's handball, but we had wiped out their goal difference advantage in 90 minutes. It was the equivalent of getting four points, which was the least we deserved for the most phenomenal attacking performance in living memory. Fergie later dubbed it 'A once-in-a-lifetime' display and you would have to be a long-serving Red indeed to recall the last similar rout, 8-1 versus QPR in 1969. But you could argue that, at last, United are beginning to reap goal harvests that match our chance-production. For over 20 years now, we never quite found the perfect striker-midfield combination; in particular, we never had a real goalscoring machine upfront since Law's days. There have been countless games over the years when we've attacked with the fervour we did today and created more than 20 chances but rarely then did we actually threaten to post the rugby score we did today. If the most telling lesson of today does turn out to be that Cole is that yearned-for goal-machine, you can only wonder how many five, six or seven goal routs are to come.

(Incidentally, the win surely seals Ipswich's relegation. Good bloody riddance: that's one less six-hour coach trip . . .)

Team: Schmeichel, Keane (Sharpe), Irwin, Bruce (Butt), Pallister, Kanchelskis, Ince, McClair, Giggs, Hughes, Cole

7 *March*: WIMBLEDON AWAY

Final Score: Wimbledon 0 UNITED 1

Scorer: Bruce 84

Attendance: 18,224

OK, SO THE WOMBLES are hardly Galatasaray, making this less of a 'Return to Hell' than a 'Return to Mildly Uncomfortable Warmth' but this still remained the last place you'd want to go to after hitting Saturday's heights. Not only because of the Dons' giant-slaying pedigree and hodcarrier's application, but also because of the vivid scars left by our last two visits. Last April, we not only lost at a crucial juncture but the overall experience had been an unwelcome milestone in the development of the Nineties United. As ever, United supporters had taken over the entire ground, yet many were hardly what you would term real Reds. In place of the long-suffering, happy hordes who'd filled Selhurst in '93 had arrived legions of bandwaggoners, first-timers and glory-hunters. Andy Mitten, whilst pleased to have broken a 'UWS' sales record that day, noted tartly that the majority around the ground appeared completely clueless, hoovering up merchandise that they'd clearly never seen before, singing the wrong words to outdated songs and generally behaving like day-tripping zombies. The consequence was bitterly paradoxical – United's biggest away support of the season produced the worst possible atmosphere.

Tonight, thankfully, was not quite as bad, although the team, if anything, were even worse. Manchester lads predominated in the west end of the Arthur Wait stand and maintained a constant refrain throughout – well done especially those at the back of Z block – but further east, the response was poor. Our witness, the Boyle, fresh from inciting the troops in the 'King George', later reported balefully on the contents of his section: 'brain-dead f*ckers' he remarked, in best Shaun Ryder accent. As for those in the Main Stand, who later revealed themselves to be 90 per cent United, why did you bother coming? Who are you anyway? Was even one chant of 'United' too much of an effort for you?

The most recent visit had, of course, been Black Wednesday's Palace fixture, producing an indelible memory that is both as vivid as yesterday and yet also like a blast from a different footballing aeon – the Cantona Era. Who, upon taking their Wait Stand seats, could resist a lingering look at that most photographed piece of touchline ever, no doubt summoning up ghostly visions of Eric and Simmons' fateful fisticuffs?

Simmons, unsurprisingly, was said to have given this game a miss and was presumably cowering in some Thornton Heath gaff, encircled by local pigs, praying that the OT T-shirt designers hadn't yet got hold of his new secret address. Also missing were Andrei and Keane, to international duty and injury respectively, the former's absence having come as an eleventh hour surprise to most Reds who were left concocting conspiracy theories about his future. On the night, Keane was perhaps the more damaging loss; with Ince subdued, perhaps due to the previous day's police charging, and the Dons in full fight mode, we could've done with his aggressive influence.

On a quagmire pitch, seemingly designed for the Wombles' anti-football, United lurched into their worst display since the Ullevi Disaster. Clearly, we had used up all the week's attacking rations on Saturday. Despite eight injuries, the Dons' five-man defence coped with our feeble probes quite effortlessly. Warren Barton in particular made Sharpe look like a third-rate has-been, fit only for the Villa Park scrapheap. Ever since God agreed to my prayers before the '88 Cup Final, I've always looked for good things to say about Wimbledon, so allow me to praise their man-marking and pressing. They were so far up our midfield's arses that arrests for public buggery were warranted; any dreams Choccy was enjoying about a Scotland future were rudely interrupted by constant Wombles' rogering.

Our first-half grand total of chances was two: Neville's 20-yarder found only Segers' hands, as did Sparky's later effort after Giggsy's run. All the best opportunities fell to Wimbledon, with male model Puffy Holdsworth going close before Gayle forced saving interventions from Peter and Pally. When Vinny Jones of all people beats Ince and leaves him floundering, you know you've got troubles . . .

At least after the break our possession doubled as United spent 95 per cent of the game encamped in the Dons' half; but if anything, this only increased our anxiety as Wimbledon threatened on the break whilst United continued to linger limply around the box, looking about as likely to penetrate as the Bishop of London. Fortunately, ref Robbie Hart, who according to Kinnear cannot wait to get back into a black shirt (lederhosen optional), was prepared to dish out the cards to Wimbledon's clatterers; this was to be our salvation.

Up in the Wait Stand, the atmosphere grew more feverish by the minute. The Z and Y block lads turned up the volume, interspersing their songs with exhortations to those below, generally along the lines of 'Sing, you sad bastards'. Most of these Reds had been here before, on the mythical, apocryphal 'wet Tuesday night, Wimbledon '89', and knew this was the moment to ratchet up the vocal support. Others, not so well-bred and not so long-serving, are under the apprehension that sitting in silence, waiting for something to sing about, is the way to behave at such junctures. Can you guess which approach helps the team more, dear reader?

Eleven minutes to go. United prepare to waste another corner. Somebody called Kimble – apparently, Afrikaans slang for 'dick' – encroaches by about three inches and puts it out for another corner. Seemingly, Rob Hart carries one of those milli-metric measuring devices used on 'Football Italia' and promptly sends off the bemused Don for a second bookable offence. At last, Reds who've endured this grim evening have something to laugh about; and at last, the team have an unlikely victory in their grasp.

Bruce and Pally, who'd been given acres of room to play in all night to no particular effect, take the bit between their teeth. Pally turns into a Teeside Cantona, knocking balls all over from an advanced midfield position. Bruce, one of life's frustrated would-be centre-forwards, waddles upfield to snuffle for goals. In the stands, we're all on our feet, screaming incoherently for somebody to cross, to shoot, to score. With five minutes left, McClair plays yet another overhit, useless ball. It sticks in the mud, inviting Hans Segers to pluck it out to safety for the nth time. But out of the pack tramples Brucey, chasing the elixir of his '93 Wednesday winner, seeking the transmogrification from dowdy carthorse to glam striker. As Hans bends over and freezes, possibly pondering a Malaysian holiday, Stevie steals in to whip the ball home. There's a nanosecond's delay as Reds' eyes turn to the ref for confirmation of the deliverance . . . then orgasmic release. Even the Main Stand get up for this one. My neighbour, not usually the most emotional of blokes, eschews his normal punched-fist goal celebration and instead goes beserk, kissing most of row 20. The Andy Cole song is hastily reworked in honour of 'Steve the Bruce' and sung by the entire stand – he tried, tried and tried again. God bless you, Mr Ugly.

While Joe Kinnear was busy engaging in his weekly anti-ref pogrom, we spent the last moments baying *United top of the league* and

We shall not be moved; on the whistle, we produced a deafening, heartfelt volley of *Champions* which seemed to draw the players over to us. Bruce, grinning, splayed his hands and shrugged as if to say 'Shit game – three points' whilst a wild-eyed Ince repeatedly punched his fist in the air in time to our chants. We would only be at the top for 24 hours – after all, you couldn't expect drug-snorting, bung-taking Arsenal to be in sufficient shape to halt Rovers – but at least we'd shown that we still have that Champion-like ability to grind out scratty wins in adverse conditions. We can match Rovers in that respect – but can they ever hope to match our Saturday-style flair? A 1967 revival meeting at Upton Park still gleams alluringly at the end of the tunnel . . .

Later that night, a Manchester posse staggering around Thornton Heath accidentally-on-purpose came across Kynaston Avenue, home of the Simmons creature. There were no police around and as they approached, all the lights in Simmons' house went out. As net curtains twitched nervously, one of the group suggested that the living room was in need of an extra brick. 'Nah, don't bother' said another. 'He'll be living in fear for the rest of his life. That'll do, won't it?' Indeed – whatever sentence Eric gets in court, it won't outlast the one Simmons has to serve.

Team: Schmeichel; Irwin, Neville, Bruce, Pallister, Ince, McClair, Giggs, Hughes, Cole, Sharpe

P.S. Less fortunate than Simmons was one Jason Ankers. You might remember him from the Dublin riot, a Catweasely creature dressed in purple Umbro top (yuk!) captured by cameras hurling missiles from the upper deck. He later appeared on TV proclaiming his pride in being English whilst wearing – to our shame – a United hat. Reds were surprised to see him sauntering about under the Wait stand; less surprisingly, Ankers was later dragged out of a pub and supposedly beaten to a pulp, allegedly by *Red Attitude* sympathisers. This new, virulently anti-fascist 'zine had been threatening to make a mark for some time with its pro-aggro hard-line against the BNP, NF and C18; declamatory pieces in the 'News of the Screws' and the *Evening News* soon followed. This re-emergence of blood-feud politicking that smacks of the late Seventies has come as a surprise and promptly divided the world of United fanzines and activists; by the time of the Spurs game, the issue was near the top of the pub-talk agenda.

12 *March:* QUEEN'S PARK RANGERS AT HOME – FA CUP ROUND SIX

Final Score: UNITED 2 QPR 0

Scorers: Sharpe 23, Irwin 52

Attendance: 42,830

'IT'S ALWAYS A GOOD, open game against Man Utd, and we always play well,' opined Ray Wilkins before the game; 'trouble is, we always bloody lose too.' For Rangers, despite much shrill whistling in the wind from Loftus Road, it was the worst possible Cup draw and they scarcely bothered concealing that heavy realisation. For us, it has to be said that Cup quarter-final or not, this was hardly a fixture to compare with, say, Leeds in the willy-trembler stakes. Having been switched back from Monday night to Sunday lunchtime, the match was almost being treated by us as a gentle appetite-builder for the roast and two veg to come. Defeat was simply unthinkable. At Loftus Road before Christmas, United had only bothered playing for about 30 minutes and had still won, despite Ferdinand being at his best: on the day, the young Scholes had outshone him. Under today's balmy sun, which seemed to announce simultaneously the arrival of spring and the beginning of the run-in, Ferdie was again to be comprehensively outclassed by the glimmering, shimmering, heaven-kissed figures of Pally and Hughes.

Like a mouthy challenger about to face Tyson, the Rs were talking a good fight but without much sincerity. They had, of course, dragged every available Shepherd's Bush bod up for this great day out, although still not in sufficient numbers to sell their complete allocation. They were, however, undoubtedly the most replica-topped away support there's been here; as their 6,000 mingled good-naturedly with Reds on the concourses, one could reflect that a support's propensity to cause trouble varies in inverse proportion to the amount of kit they've got on. These, clearly, were not fans who would need to be held back at full-time. I asked one blue-wigged bloke about Ferdie's injury: 'He's back ready to beat you!' he grinned manically. His eyes, however, gave him away. He had come to drink, sing but lose, and he knew that I knew it too. He managed a sheepish expression before staggering off to join his cohorts in a chorus of 'Gallen Wonderland'. Gallen, naturally, had a stinker.

What with the sunshine, low-key atmosphere and lack of Cole 'n' Cantona, you could be forgiven for imagining we were on a re-run of the season's opening day, which had also starred Hughes and finished 2-0. In the Dog & Partridge, always an accurate gauge of Red blood-pressure levels, all was laid-back and easy-going; the absence of Boylie, outside busy selling his new album, and the minimal drinking time saw to that. We were taking the day at a Jamaican tempo – 'It's Sunday, man; sit in de sun, smoke some ganj' and don't worry, it's only QPR.'

Unfortunately, this mindset continued inside the stadium as most seemed content to carry on puffing the metaphorical weed. The North Lower under J stand excepted, however: the Boyle Chorus down there did a fine job in meeting the challenge of the Rangers singers alongside, sporadically joined by L stand to form a vocal pincer movement. Students of oral history will note that the fifteenth minute rendition of *Eric the King* was the first, completely-together, clap-perfect one we've had at OT; all those recording sessions have done the boys some good.

By then, Giggs and Ferdie had already traded the first serious attacking blows. Two bursts of Kanchelskis' Cossackry had set up Ryan's first-timer which glanced wide on 10; the self-styled Black Panther replied by skinning Bruce before pulling hopelessly wide. That was Rangers' last effort for the next half-hour. United effortlessly cruised up to the next gear; Sharpe burst through to force a good block on 19, then beat ex-Strettie Ender Bardsley four minutes later to slam-drive the opener after scintillating centre-forward work by Hughes. Not bad, admittedly, for a 'shagged-out, third-rate has-been'. His new haircut seems to have had a Sampson-in-reverse effect – it was his first goal, in his first decent performance, since the Barcelona 2-2. Nice improvisation of corner-flag as microphone too.

Rangers harried and hustled to almost no discernible effect, beyond the three bookings they clocked up by half-time. Their attempts to turn this into a physical battle, such as the one we endured in '93 at Loftus Road, were met by Reds coolly turning the other cheek, a fact that will naturally go completely unnoticed by the 'United are dirty whingers' media brigade. Rs in K stand were left with little to shout about – Ferdie's poor 40th minute effort being their only other chance – and had to resort to yelling 'Are you Arsenal in disguise?' when their docile forwards were caught offside. Reds replied with 'Are you City/Chelsea . . .', a fair question given that Rangers were even less threatening than either of those poor outfits, if that's possible.

It was blindingly clear to all that a second United goal would kill the game off, and that Rangers were not even going to get a decent sight of goal until that occurred, such was our dictatorial dominance of pace and position. As the eastern North Lower boys finished their half-time vocal entertainment, Keano came on for the injured Giggs and almost scored within 30 seconds of the off. United were going to be merciful: a quick, clean kill followed by an afternoon's defensive practise for our underworked backs. Doubtless, some Rs probably still reckoned they were watching a genuine contest. Poor deluded fools! This game was being played by marionettes, with Alex pulling all the strings with the frightening, effort-saving efficiency of - dare I say it – Liverpool in their prime. This was not a day for full-cylindered nine-nils; the epic battles to come demanded some conservation of resources.

Hughes didn't have to wait long to avenge the utterly unjustified booking he received on 47. He had been battered all day, by Maddix, McDonald and Barker in cynical rotation so as to avoid red cards, but on 51 Maddix was finally undone. Their number 16, like ours, is apparently built out of girders; unlike ours, however, he is like a caricature of a hacking thug. Having been fouled on the edge of the box for the seventh time, Hughes took a bit of a kick at the giant behind him. Other players would have crumpled under the force but Maddix, as if in a cartoon, remained as motionless as though bitten by a gnat. Instead, he simply picked Hughes up and threw him to the ground. For a split-second, it was almost funny, with Hughes looking as stunned as Wily Coyote. Then, of course, 36,000 screamed 'Off! Off!', in certain knowledge that the already-carded Maddix could not possibly remain and should, in fact, take up with the WWF. Remarkably, he escaped unpunished but his team did not. As obscenities filled the air, Denis took up the cudgels on all our behalves, curled the free-kick around the wall, and thus sealed our seventh semi-final of the decade. When Brevitt scuffed wide sixty seconds later, Rangers' last chance went with it; the crowd were not tempting fate as they roared through our favourite Wem-ber-ley songs.

For the last half-hour, United went into cruise mode, cruelly teasing Rangers by giving them some space, even letting them get near Schmeichel, without ever losing overall control. When they could be bothered, Andrei and Sharpe mounted hit and run raids just to keep the muscles warm; Sharpe almost went through for a third on 62, Hughes was denied a blatant penalty on 67, and Denis was inches wide from a free-kick on 83 after Maddix had savaged Hughes yet again. How did that creature stay on the pitch for 90 minutes?

Rangers' two best efforts, by McDonald and Penrice on 67 and 80, found only Schmeichel's steady presence.

Rangers' fans, bereft of on-pitch inspiration, ended up spending ten minutes engaged in a childish but amusing competition with the rest of the stadium as to who could shout 'Paul Ince is a wanker/is the Guvnor' the loudest, the final joke being on Rangers as each mention of his name appeared to make Incey jump twice as high and tackle twice as harder. They even resorted to the last refuge of the footballing scoundrel, anti-patriotism, in the shape of the atrociously dated 'Stoichkov and Romario', and were bemused by the Red response of enthusiastic cheering. Ironic wit has not yet reached the Westway, I think. After the whistle, with another routine day at the office over for United, the Rangers contingent continued to 'celebrate' their loss with indecent gusto. For Reds, I suppose, defeat is always an immensely serious business; for Rangers and their ilk, it's a way of life. No wonder they pretend to get on with City so much.

Our minds had already turned to Wednesday and beyond; the mad scramble for Anfield tickets, the return of the Sheep and, first up, the visit of Spurs, seen by the rest as a Cup Final rehearsal but by us as three of the hardest points yet to be won. Home in time to watch us draw Palace or Wolves at Villa Park for the semi, we know that the 17 days from Spurs to Birmingham will contain most of the answers to the Double Double question. Come in, our own number 17: your time to lead us has come.

Team: Schmeichel; Neville, Irwin, Bruce, Pallister, Ince, McClair, Kanchelskis, Hughes, Giggs (Keane), Sharpe

15 March: TOTTENHAM HOTSPUR AT HOME

Final Score: UNITED 0 Spurs 0

Attendance: 43,803

PERHAPS IT WAS A tad premature to herald the arrival of the gambolling, carefree spring run-in. An icy chill descended on Manchester tonight, gripping our testes (as if the footballing tension were not already discomforting enough), scattering snowflakes like reminders of the traumatic winter of sporadic discontent that we thought had passed. Bad enough that the nation's two most attacking sides couldn't muster a goal between us – in our case, the first home strike-out of the season – without the addition of Keith Fane's astonishing words to the departing masses. 'What a tremendously thrilling game of football' he burbled, drawing a chorus of muttered 'F*ck off, you twat' from aggrieved Scoreboarders. I daresay games such as these do indeed raise the pulse-rate but then so would a spell of Chinese water-torture – it was hardly a 90 minutes of 'excitement' to *celebrate*.

Two dropped home points at the worst possible moment. You don't really want to read about it – especially if you were there – nor do I want to write about it. Bury it deep alongside those nil-nils of recent seasons such as Ipswich and Arsenal. As an exercise in stylism, I summarise it in the fashion of Pinter writing 'haiku', the Jap verse form in 5-7-5 syllable structure (as you do . . .)

> Zeros, Os, circles,
> Symbols of the holes we dig
> When points die in pairs.

> Zero is the score,
> The temperature, our luck,
> (And Spurs target shots)

> An 'O' as in Cole,
> The shape of pursed lips as he
> And Hughes hit woodwork.

> Circles run round Spurs,
> And our fingers' shape as Sharpe
> Fucks up, the wanker.

> Crass, hissing gassing,
> J Stand Hitlers are silenced
> Jew kicks off the line.

> Bugger, bollocks, shit,
> Would fifty-five thousand come
> Watch UEFA Cup?

Team: Schmeichel; Irwin, Bruce, Pallister, Sharpe, Kanchelskis, Ince, McClair (Butt), Giggs, Hughes, Cole

PS: Fifty-five thousand is, of course, the prospective capacity for the new Old Trafford, the plans for which were revealed next day, happily relegating the Spurs match headlines to second place. A behemoth of a North Stand is to be built, reducing capacity at the start of '95/'96 to 31,000, at a cost of £28 million. We had been expecting something like this for several months; once United had stumped up 50 per cent over the odds for the land, the project became unstoppable. No-one would oppose the overall goal of increasing capacity, nor the potential end product of a triple-tiered super-stadium holding 86,000. We could easily fill such a ground several times a season and such a stadium is a prerequisite for a club with pretension to Barcelonian status. Long-term delight comes at the price of short-term suffering, of course; just how much suffering is the contentious question. Half a season at 31,000 brings back unhappy memories of late '92, when poor performances and poor atmospheres had a symbiotic relationship. Essentially, only season-ticket holders and LMTB bearers will be in Old Trafford which, while delivering us temporarily from the day-tripper, will also deprive us of a lot of 'lads'. Moreover, just how much do we have to pay in ticket-price readies for it? A price-hike is inevitable - beyond the implicit 10 per cent increase that the Premiership reduction entails – but will Edwards now take his historic opportunity to match ticket prices to real market values and in so doing, create the middle-class/family-dominated audience he prefers? It might not happen straight away but I cannot help feeling that we are on a two or three stage journey to a doubled ticket price in the long run.

Of course, United were crassly idiotic not to start this third tier at the perfect opportunity, when the Strettie was rebuilt; we could be starting from a base of 50,000 with no extra disruption. Amidst all the Edwards PR bluster about 'long-term vision', he seemed to have forgotten that missed open goal. It is doubly unfortunate that the stadium's sociology, disrupted by the Strettie 'false start', had just begun to settle down; now we are all to be thrown into turmoil once more, finally to end up God-knows-where. What most hope for is that club class, the families and all the other Brigades of the Respectable (sic) will end up in the new giant, leaving the rest to us and the visitors to fill with songs, obscenities and dancing in the aisles. Sadly, the trouble with this Club is that 'we' will be the last to be considered, even though we were here first.

19 March: LIVERPOOL AWAY

Final Score: Liverpool 2 UNITED 0

Attendance: 38,906

THE TROUBLE WITH US and Liverpool – although neither would care to admit it – is that we're just too damn similar; truly, this world ain't big enough for both of us. Consider the parallels for a moment. Two clubs, once city underdogs, that rose on a swell of Irish and Catholic support to dominate their 'Establishment' neighbours as tenants turned landlords. Two sets of supporters that alone in England will be there, en masse, in good times or bad. Two clubs whose appeal has historically stretched far beyond their cities to the furthest corners of the world, these two old centres of Empire now propagating a new cultural imperialism. Both Mancs and Scousers have ongoing love-hate relationships with the rest of Britain, by whom we are seen either as loathsome scallies and jibbers or as the locum of genius that spawned Madchester and the Casuals. Above all, we both carry the burden of tragedy that should bind us together but which we have often used to torture each other. The hard-core, working-class support of the two clubs stands as living disproof of Marxist theory; never have we stood together for common class cause, preferring the certainties and joys of tribalistic antagonism. In English football, there can only be one equivalent of Juve or Barca, only one club that can embody the soul of English football for the rest of the world. The facts that Rovers are apparently Champs-Elect and Leeds are currently more hated doesn't alter the essential primacy of the United-Liverpool rivalry. We two are the only real contenders for that supreme, spiritual, yet un-named Title.

For over thirty years, then, we have both done our best to bury our sole opposition and claim the pedestal for ourselves, with neither succeeding. In the Sixties, we had our Three Gods and the post-Munich sympathy that produced the apogee of '68 – enough to see off most challengers. Yet Liverpool won titles and built legends with sufficient success to stay in the game, at a time when being a Scouse prole living in Beatle City was almost a desirable state of existence. In the Seventies, Liverpool's trophy haul should've done for us but the magnificent emergence of the Red Army kept our own Red flag flying. And in the Eighties, whilst the river of silver continued to flow into Anfield, we did at least become the one team they couldn't beat, allowing us to keep our pride and preventing them winning a couple of titles and Cups into the bargain. Moreover, despite the decline of the 'real' Red Army, we remained the best-supported team in the land.

Now in the Nineties, we're into the fourth decade of this epic tribal bout and there is still no sign of a knock-out blow being applied. On the field, we have now been the superior side for at least four seasons. Where once the pundits would purr over Liverpool's style, they now exalt ours. Old Trafford is feared by visitors as much as Anfield once was. As a team, domestically at least, we are now compared favourably to the cream of Liverpool's sides past. But if, referring to the past two decades, United are now the 'Liverpool of the Nineties', the unwelcome corollary might yet be seen to be that Liverpool have become the 'United of the Nineties.' They, like us in the Eighties, have maintained and even strengthened their hard-core support; they have discovered the pleasures of being underdogs, of not being the team everyone hates; and, most annoyingly for us, they have begun to revel in playing the old United role in East Lancs Road Battles. Now it is they, not us, who come pumped-up for a Final-like clash, now it is they who play out of their skins, now it is they who take the media plaudits. Two titles and a Double to us, but the bastards under our feet won't stay down.

Thus we found ourselves walking up the Everton Valley once more, contemplating the prospect of a make-or-break Sunday match with a team whose recent record against us is, in truth, almost as good as ours was against them in the Eighties. Such is the Mersey-Manc paradox: when at your greatest, you're at your most vulnerable. We once went eight years unbeaten at Anfield, with 'Pool at their peak; after today, the record ran one win in the last eight. More to the point, in the eight meetings since we overtook 'Pool as a team, we only lead three-two; in two of those wins, we were hugely fortunate to win and a couple of the draws were damned lucky too. To be frank, we have only had the better of them once, at Anfield in '93. Are they Man U in disguise?!

Reds who like the traditional ways had already suffered the first disappointment of the day. The habitual rallying point at the Adelphi had been denied them, the owners shutting down after the bottling inflicted upon it by Everton's Klansmen a few weeks back. (Contrary to the Blues' boasts of having 'done' United's boys, their attack had been launched so early that hardly any were actually in at the time.) However, the other tradition of Reds being forced to skulk anxiously around Anfield looking for spares remained, £40 being the going rate.

Scousers strutted around looking appallingly confident; the day's brilliant sunshine was dramatically interrupted by a rampant snowstorm minutes before kick-off, a telling meteorological omen. Bad vibes, man.

Your correspondent found himself in the new Kop along with a few other foolhardy Red souls. It is, admittedly, a magnificent structure, far more inhabitable than most of the Koppites' own homes – a nice touch to leave some grim alleyways round the back in which the locals can lurk with ill intent. And whilst Anfield as a whole does not match Old Trafford vocally as a whole, the Kop on a day such as this remains the equal in decibel-power of our own East end, if not in terms of singing versatility. A letter in *Through the Wind & Rain* bemoaned the fact that the Kop only has two songs (*Liv-er-pool* and *We love you. . .*) plus the occasional, dreaded *You'll never walk alone*; the observation was entirely accurate. Their other songs for the day spoke only of the Scousers' current inferiority, songs that in a more glorious yesteryear they would have been above. *Going to Wembley to win the CocaCola Cup* (!!), *Barcelona*, *Who the f*ck are Man United?* and *Dalglish*: it's a poor state of affairs when you have to rely on tinpot trophies, other teams' managers and foreigners for your 'ammunition'. Whatever happened to that lovable Scouse ragamuffin wit? The only mildly humorous chant was aimed at Sparky: *Useless, useless* to the tune of *Hughesy*. Almost worth a smile, until he missed those two crucial chances . . .

The 3,000 or so Reds, stashed mainly at the Anfield Road end to the right, must have been as mystified as the Scousers to see Cole on the bench. All the would-be Shanklys around me agreed that Fergie had blundered, as he himself later admitted. Just as at Goodison, he had tinkered to entirely negative effect, playing three in midfield, including the lacklustre Sharpe and McClair whilst omitting players who were feared in Andrei and Andy. Ten minutes of play indicated to us that we were on a rerun of Goodison, facing a supremely committed team who were tackling and pressing hard on a poor, dribbler-unfriendly pitch. The difference between the two Mersey sides was that Liverpool can actually pass – thus were they able to dominate us in a way Everton could not. Our counter-attacking strategy foundered on the dodgy individual form of our lads, the bite of Liverpool's defending and our midfield's inability to get a grip. The first half was simply an embarrassment, their excellent mid-point Redknapp goal entirely deserved. We produced nothing I can remember.

159

From the Kop, one could see Anfield Roaders singing, especially those not directly behind the goal, but almost nothing could be heard; the manic frenzy of those around me meant that the slightest United chant was greeted by a volley of Manc-hating abuse. Not that there's anything wrong in that but it was instructive to hear what sort of racial invective is popular in there, given 'Pool's propensity to label Everton as racists (see any fanzine).

In the lower Kop, groups of skinheads sang 'Die Munich scum' and other such nursery rhymes with impunity. One or two Reds gave themselves away at this point by murmuring disapproval. Koppites reacted like zombies from *Invasion of the Body-Snatchers*, turning in packs, arms out-stretched accusingly, screaming 'Manc!' until their faces contorted with purple rage. I felt like David Attenborough observing exotic wildlife, a sane presence amidst gibbering gibbons on heat.

For about a quarter of an hour, with Cole on for Sharpe, we had flashes of potential victory. When we concocted the move of the game, culminating in Giggsy's volley to James' clutches, the tide seemed on the brink of the turn. A moment later, Hughes seemed certain to score from an even better position than Redknapp had had, but James reacted well. The moment had passed; Hughesy's blast over the bar soon after indicated the shape of things to come. Scraping a draw seemed to be the best on offer. Denis got into a great position but slipped onto his arse at the crucial juncture, an emblematic instant for the rest of the game. The luck we had ridden in the Old Trafford fixture was truly exhausted. Poor Brucey's own goal five minutes from time was evidence enough of that, dashing the last slim hopes of escape.

All Reds of both cities understood instantly the historical reference of a 2-0 scoreline – April 1992, that awful, searing afternoon when we lost the Title at Anfield. Liverpool fans, always ready to harp about the past, instantly reprised with heartfelt joy the deathly anthems of that '92 nightmare: *You lost the League on Merseyside* and *Always look on the bright side of life*. Anfield Roaders responded the best they could to those songs that once haunted us for months and which we never thought we'd hear in such circumstances again. And they sang *Champions* rather than *We'll support you ever more*, bravely refusing to admit what some were already thinking, that we've blown the title.

So we are six points behind with eight games left. Blackburn are now, rightly, odds-on favourites. Cole has only scored in three of his ten games. Mass suspensions loom, with Sharpe and Bruce already

Cornered Reds at Elland Road – for once, the humans are penned in by the sheep

The rock-like Pallister prepares to head ball and nut Hammer

*Leading by example: Brucey thinks Hinchcliffe's free kicks
are so puffy that he needn't cover his knackers*

*Poor Choccy: if he's not arseing it up himself,
he's got someone else up his arse*

Doppelganger alert! 'Two Peter Boyles, there's only two...' The terraces' chart-bustin' hero meets his Catalan twin

Southy gives the finger to the Catalonians' scoreline predictions: 3–0? How amusingly optimistic...

The King, already isotonic enough as it is

Eric, truly the new King –
he's even got the Presley pose pat

eric the king

Sleeve of 'Eric The King' record.
Boyle and the K-Standers' cult indie-
hit of the season; forget Oasis and
Take That, this was the best record
out of Manc in '95

The King's flag still flies over Old
Trafford – despite the seagulls above,
out looking for sardines

Red Army! The biggest awayday gathering so far enjoy the vomit-inducing heights of the new Holte End

The familiar sight of Sparky and ref in discussion. On this occasion, Hughesy understandably declines to help Elleray massage his testicles

Wembley at 2:59 – the last happy moment of the season

As Everton go up to lift the Cup, United faces say it all.
Choccy, however, with no pie to hand, settles for a munchy medal

Adrian Longden's portrait of the King, wistfully looking forward to October

definitely banned. Tellingly, this was the first time we've failed to score in successive games since before Eric's arrival; never have we needed him more. If Rovers do win the league this day will live in infamy.

Yet even in the wake of this most shattering of defeats, there is a certain nobility, even greatness of a sort. Chris Eubank, another much-hated Champion beaten this weekend, quoted Kipling: 'Here am I, a mortal man at last'. As he went on to say, 'all men must suffer defeat – it is the way that men become stronger'. In gloomy reflection on the train back from Murkeydive, I remember a passage from *Red Issue*. The author had written about the sheer misery of being on the Kop in '92, being embraced by a disgusting Scouser who mistook his stupefaction for the shock of ecstasy, not horror. It was a vivid recollection of a man who'd waited all his life to see a dream realised, yet even after eventual success, had not lost touch with the sensation of that day. Being a Red is just as much about the pain of moments like this as it is about glory and trophies. For the real Red soul, Anfield '92 – and maybe '95 – are as fundamentally important as Wembley '94 or '85. Only he who has suffered can know true jubilation.

Team: Schmeichel, Irwin, Bruce, Pallister, Sharpe (Cole), Kanchelskis, McClair, Keane (Butt), Ince, Giggs, Hughes

22 March: ARSENAL AT HOME

Final Score: UNITED 3 Arsenal 0

Scorers: Hughes 26, Sharpe 31, Andrei 79

Attendance: 43,623

HOW THE MIGHTY HAVE fallen. Once, an Arsenal fixture stood proudly close to the Liverpool and Leeds games in terms of both glamour and needle; now, post-bungs, post-coke and post-competence, Arsenal are simply points-fodder for us. After the goal-free disasters of the past week, Reds had only the Title race on their mind and treated Gooners' attempts to make us treat them as worthy adversaries in their own right with contemptuous disdain. Indeed, there were signs before kick-off that the return of United's 'Ides of March' syndrome had also put some faint-hearted farts off United altogether for the time being. Plenty outside were attempting to off-load face-value tickets, presumably ordered by glory-hunters weeks ago and now no longer wanted; touts' prices diminished accordingly. Yet again, a cloud bears a silver lining – good riddance to them.

For the first time in living memory, the match programme contained items of interest, making it a rarity on a par with the famed post-Munich edition. In his notes, Fergie had questioned the players' hunger and wondered whether they had lost their cutting edge, thoughts uppermost in the mind of any who witnessed the Anfield débâcle. The phrase of the day was 'fat cats', conjuring up images of bloated Reds resting smugly on past laurels, apparently aimed at several players and not just the literal porkers Brucey and Choccy. (As Fergie would have expected, the Reds responded full-bloodedly, with Keane in particular slamming the dazed Helder over every touchline possible. Welcome to British football Glenn.)

Elsewhere, buried amidst the standard blurb warning against racism and threatening behaviour, nestled an attack on Reds of far more enduring import than Fergie's. 'We at Man United' – meaning the fat-cat junta in charge, not the true-Red membership – 'have become increasingly concerned about the anti-social behaviour at Old Trafford'. What could this mean? The gratuitous offence caused by Fred the Red's every appearance? The aggravating grunts of 'Sit down' from thermos-toting twats? The aural harassment perpetrated by Keith 'Smash' Fane? Afraid not, chaps. They were referring to we hooligans who have the temerity to stand up, sing and support our team. In bald, chilling terms the Club's dictators informed us that any standing up during play would henceforth be punishable by ejection and membership annulment. This had to be an attempt at wacky, Pythonesque humour, right? As the few who bother reading the programme must have said to themselves, you cannot be serious. An enforcedly sedentary football stadium is a surrealistic image worthy of a Bunuel film. 'Shurely shome mishtake, ed.' Sadly, as we were to discover, the mistake was all ours in thinking that those who run this Club have any feeling for the spirit of football in the slightest.

For the first ten minutes or so, Arsenal looked remarkably perky, given who they are. We marvelled at the wholly unaccustomed sight of Gooner players attacking, and doing so in plural number. George Graham must have spun in his bung-built grave. Naturally, they came nowhere near scoring as Bruce and Pally dominated with ease but it was enough to get their fans warmed up. 'One team in Europe' they crowed in hideous Home Counties accents, showing the sort of inability to count that has cost Arsenal FC dear recently. Merson, strangely lingering overmuch near the white lines of touch, blasted a couple of balls higher than he's ever been and that, bar Wright's cheeky attempt to emulate Eric at the Bridge, was the sum of Arsenal's attacking. (You can see where Merse went wrong, can't you? If, like most forwards, he has a pre-match flutter on himself scoring, no wonder his bookie's bill ended up greater than his dealer's.)

United's fat cats took a tigerish grip on midfield and refused to relent for the rest of the match. Remarkably Ince, given this was the eve of his magistrate's appearance, gave a fittingly magisterial display, whilst Keano marauded at will. Hughes and especially Cole gave masterclass displays in playing with backs to goal, an admirable facet easily forgotten in the light of the latter's later misses. Thankfully, the Old Trafford crowd, instead of waiting for the team to warm us up, recalled the old *modus operandi* and took on the work of inspiration themselves. Within minutes of a rousing *Fergie's Red and White Army* – which incidentally silenced the Gooners until the last five minutes – Hughes had netted Sharpe's knock-on, Andrei had come close and Sharpe had resolved a goalmouth scramble with total assurance. At two-nil, the game was won; even a draw would have been beyond Arsenal's talent or ambition. Drenched with pleasure, Reds celebrated the end of the goal famine.

Or we would have done, had not a tannoy announcement blaringly shattered the moment's perfection. In the middle of play, mind you, leading some to think that a fire or some such disaster had begun, the speakers growled to life. 'You are reminded that standing during play is forbidden; resume your seats or you risk being ejected . . .' etc etc ad total bloody nauseam. Like all around me in the East stands, I could hardly believe what I'd heard. It felt like a desecration of this hallowed football temple, not to mention being the most shit-mouthed, enraging insult the Club has hurled at us – and there've been plenty to choose from down the years. Perhaps we erred in dubbing OT 'the Theatre of Dreams' and a place of worship: the Club seems to have taken such descriptions literally and intends replacing the sound and fury of the old Strettie and modern K stand with the hushed expectancy and polite murmuring of the church and play audience. Jesus Christ: even *Songs of Praise* were allowed to stand. (Lucifer – isn't it time to call down your servants from the Board to join you in Hades?)

At such moments, the Red Army's Basic Instinct remains the same – flash your genitals at authority – and so the tannoy succeeded in bringing the rest of the stand to its feet with a chorus of 'f*ck off!' and 'you can stick your seats up yer arse'. But it did not go unnoticed that some stewards were sinisterly pointing out cheerleaders to the video cameras and the subduing effect on the crowd for the rest of the match was noticeable. On the pitch, Arsenal had resorted to a three-booking display of clattering, allegedly carried off-pitch too by Mr Wright, before Andrei − fully engaged in the game for once − narrow-angled a third. Batram had given a better display of goalkeeping than David 'Koeman' Seaman habitually manages although Cole had aided him by missing two sitters.

I make no apology for skimming over the rest of the proceedings. Solid and welcome though this win was, and although Eric was to dominate our thoughts until the weekend, all Reds that I spoke to the following Monday turned to one subject above all − the apparent declaration of war by the Club on the true Red. For many, the timing was no accident, coming so soon after the redevelopment announcement; to us, the Board's agenda seemed transparently obvious. This had been the first shot of their campaign to build a new audience for the new Old Trafford, an audience that would fit their ideal consumer profile and ideal behaviour pattern. 'We' do not fit into that picture. When one Red said to Veg 'I don't care about the Title anymore - the future is what matters now,' he spoke for all who would now be ready to make the Red Army's last stand. Custer's not invited . . .

Team: Schmeichel; Keane, Bruce, Pallister, Irwin, Kanchelskis, Ince, Sharpe, Giggs, Cole, Hughes

PS: Two days after the game, as a direct result of the catalyst effect of the tannoy announcement, the Independent Man Utd Supporters' Association was formed on the initiative of *Red Issue*'s Chris Robinson. Launched with a 'summit meeting' at the 'Gorse Hill', the IMUSA has already become the organisation which any self-respecting self-styled true Red should join. If you've happily read this far, you're probably just the sort of member we'd welcome onboard.

23 March: CROYDON MAGISTRATES AWAY

Final Score: Bench Bastards 1 Cantona 0 (second leg to come)

Scorer: J. Pearch (*pen*)

Attendance: 15 K standers and 200 seagulls

IT WAS SUPPOSED TO be an enjoyable enough wheeze; 15 of us down in London to appear with Boylie on *The Big Breakfast*, promoting *Eric The King*, headed off to Croydon Magistrates' Court for an Eric-supporting singsong. After all, it was going to be a formality, right? The only debate would be how big a fine Eric would get; no harm in us entertaining the media-hounds while the world waited for a decision. Ha. By midday, we were left reflecting not on a successful day's record-PR but on our witnessing first hand one of the most shocking episodes of this increasingly seismic season.

Turning the corner onto the court road just after ten, we marvelled at the sight outside the entrance, a camera-rich sprawl of over 200 hacks, technicians and curious onlookers but with scarcely a Red to be seen. The media vultures were spread across the pavement, along the central reservation and on top of every available roof – as we legged across the road, roaring *Eric the King*, every telephoto lens and video camera swung towards us, capturing Boylie's Boys and the K Stand placards in their full glory. As we dished out press releases and gave interviews, convincing the most sceptical of hacks that ALL Reds are behind Eric, we gleaned that the media were mostly bored. They didn't expect much of a real news story to emerge here, just an anti-climactic fine; this was just a circus of visual images, capturing pix of media scrums and harassed celebs. The guys with the notebooks assumed they'd be in for an underworked afternoon and had nothing better to do than talk to the likes of us, busy reciting lyrics and badmouthing Simmons. They were, at least, grateful that Eric had typically eschewed the limo and walked the three minutes from hotel to court, seemingly none the worse for his night of champagne, clubbing and gig by the Artist Formerly Known As Talented. At least that guaranteed them the 'celeb surrounded by press pack' pictures that papers rather tediously demand these days.

So there we all stood for the best part of two hours, the world's eyes and ears patiently waiting for news from the lucky recipients of Press Pool passes inside. As we sweated gently under the London sun, Pete Boyle clambered up some vacant ladders to lead us through a few terrace classics to the bemusement of assembled hackery; a few shy London Reds turned up to swell our numbers, whilst the half-dozen Palace fans knocking around kept very, very quiet indeed. The Anti-Nazi League, there to make the most of the anti-racist opportunity, pointed these creatures out to us: 'South London Scum', said one succinctly. Later, with us Reds long gone, these vermin suddenly found their tongues when Eric finally emerged: typical standards of

Palace bravery, making a stand only when there's no chance of a comeback. No doubt Simmons had thought himself similarly secure when he stepped forward that fateful night . . .

Getting inside to see how the King was doing – Incey's committal being an early formality – was harder than getting a face-value away ticket. Southy successfully found a way of making repeated ten minute trips to the court bogs without being promptly ejected, thus being able to emerge to tell us how cool Eric was looking, mixing his customary swagger with some required elements of humble penitence. Amidst the steady stream of exiting local crims, bemoaning their latest drug dealing fines on mobile phones, came Red-friendly journos whom we corralled behind our pen to pump for info. Jim White of the Indie seemed cautiously optimistic: 'poor prosecution performance' and 'Eric's behaving himself' gave us heart. Then the BBC North correspondent, attracted by our chorus of 'one Charlie Lambert', told us about the reading of Simmons' uncensored statement and that two of the bench were women. By 11.30, any lingering worries we'd had were dispelled. Eric's brief had been excellent whereas theirs had been lacklustre; Eric had said all the right things and pushed all the right emotional buttons; a female-dominated bench, knowing what your typical prim, twinset mag.-woman is like, would surely be in thrall to Eric's brooding charm and appalled by Simmons' language. The verdict would be at any moment, then down the pub with the hacks for some Boylie buffoonery on table-tops with lager-tops.

But the bench weren't straight back at all. As the delay stretched on past twenty minutes and hacks jostled impatiently for shot-positions, my own alcohol-pangs were replaced by well-founded concern. What could be taking so long to discuss? I turned to a K Stander and remarked that they must be debating more than the mere size of a fine; this was sounding like one mag. arguing for a fine, one undecided and one pressing for something much worse. Having once been in Eric's position myself, I knew the warning signs only too well.

Even so, when the news broke, the 'thrill' of being there at the epicentre of a newsquake (thank you, Chris Morris) was memorable only for the sense of horrified shock. Southy and Peter Peet ran out, whitefaced, to tell us the worst; for a moment, we guffawed at their attempted kidology, only for the sentence to be confirmed by the racing hacks behind them. Journalists are not, by their nature, easily taken aback, but today those correspondents around us were genuinely appalled. For about three minutes, chaos reigned as journos tried to piece together the facts before animated debates about legal processes broke out everywhere. Was Eric going straight down? Could you actually get time for common assault as a first-time offender? Could you appeal against a sentence like that? 'What the f*ck happens now?' screamed a quality journo, 'someone please tell me, now!' For about 60 seconds my head was in pieces, like the rest of the lads, but I recovered sufficiently to dredge up old criminal process lessons and tell the hack that, whatever happened, a judge-in-chambers had to be found immediately to give Eric bail pending appeal. (Such is British justice – our magistrates cannot be allowed to operate unless tended by a fireman-judge, ready to rush in to correct patent miscarriages like this. Thankfully, Maurice Watkins did find one, down the road at the Crown Court, who did the necessary: we, of course, wouldn't have left the scene unless we'd know Eric's freedom was secured.)

Suddenly, the massed media snapped back into gear, looking for someone, anyone, who would go on record to provide confirmation of what the journos clearly felt – that a judicial outrage had just been perpetrated. With evident relief, they remembered they had some genuine Reds from Manchester on hand; the pack descended on us, pulling us all over the pavement to speak to camera, mike and dictaphone. Lads who'd never spoken to the media in their life ended up doing half-a-dozen interviews, to the nationals, radio and TV; how surreal to see Southy, the most down-to-earth, unmetropolitan lad imaginable, going straight from *The Times* to French TV's main news crew. . .

Our duty done, we withdrew from the battleground, staying just long enough to salute The Guvnor when he finally emerged. Some of us had been up for 36 hours already and Mancunian beds were calling. On the journey home, we listened dumbfounded as the media explosion ran its course on every radio station in Christendom, several bulletins opening with comments by Pete and the boys, intermingled with us singing *Eric the King* outside the court. Some of us realised that for once, *we* – not the media or superstore part-timers – had set the agenda. This wasn't like the original kung-fu aftermath, when true Reds had to struggle to rescue the news agenda after sad twats had condemned our King on air, whilst we were all still stuck on coaches returning from Selhurst. We had got on first, and spoken in the most cutting, condemnatory way possible about the crass misjudgment – in doing so, that challenged any naysayers to go against the prevailing orthodoxy, always a difficult task on a running news story once the initial die is cast. Besides, once BBC Radio stations had broadcast us saying that 'the magistrates deserve a good karate-kicking', anyone else going on to defend Eric would sound quite moderate and reasonable in comparison . . .

Now this is sounding a bit self-congratulatory, which was not the intention. It may well be that our presence and contributions made no difference, that the press and media would have taken just such a pro-Eric line in any event, purely on the case's merits. Maybe so, but who can be sure?

I'll put it crudely: the media follows what they think the public wants; the authorities, in turn, follow the media. The media – and therefore the authorities – will follow the lead given by whoever makes the most noise. So we should write angry letters, get onto phone-ins, use faxlines, hassle TV programmes and generally get ourselves involved with the media whenever there is a cause to be fought because otherwise our power as a Red is lost. And if you get the chance to put the true Red view on radio or on TV, do it. It may well be purer, ideologically sounder and cooler to say 'f*ck off' but it doesn't help build a more Red-friendly world.

2nd Leg: A couple of weeks later at his appeal, Eric's sentence was reduced to community service, announced by the Boyle running from the Court bellowing 'The King Is Free!'. The original magistrate remains on the bench . . .

2 April: LEEDS AT HOME

Final Score: UNITED 0 Scum 0

Attendance: 43,712

THANKS TO SKY, UNITED had by now become a Sunday league team – although at least my local park outfit manages to score from time to time – whereas Rovers, whom no TV audience particularly wants to watch, were able to luxuriate in limelight-free atmosphere the previous day. The efforts of those several Manc Reds who went over to abuse Rovers from the Gwladys End were to no avail; Rovers won two-one but had done so to universal disapproval. The boos from the Klansmen don't count for much, given the way Everton barge about these days, but opening the usually mild-mannered and impartial *Guardian*, I found the following in their match report which has an effect analogous to a vicar shouting 'f*ck'. 'The boos arose from disgust at the gamesmanship sustaining Blackburn's challenge,' wrote David Hopps. 'If honesty, the adjective often given to a performance of boundless commitment, is defined as a fair and righteous approach, then forget it. Too many Blackburn players have become practised at the sly challenge and petulant response. Their feigning of injury would bring an Oscar, so long as Tom Hanks took a vacation.' Dalglish, who has stated that he sees Rovers as the nationally-supported side because they promise to stop United, should reflect on the implications of Hopp's coda: 'Rovers' manager said "we were fortunate". He should have said "lucky"; to be fortunate is to be loved.'

Rovers fans who revel in United's current unpopularity will soon discover what it feels like themselves once they are Champions. We have been used to the 'ABU – Anyone But United' syndrome for decades and have thus been able to withstand and even profit from the present record levels of virulent *rubrophobia*. It will be interesting to see how Walker's club will cope with the coming onslaught. They find the minor sniping about their boring style aggravating enough now; let us see how they are affected by the unleashing of all the latent Rovers/Walker-hatred that lies beneath the surface of most genuine football fans who cannot countenance Rovers' fans bandwagonning, their sugar-daddy set-up and their detrimental effect on everyone else's finances. At least United earned as much respect as hatred, for only the most blinkered bigots ever sought to deny we were great Champions playing football. No such approbation will fall Blackburn's way. They will raise an initial cheer for denying us our hat-trick but that is all. Their fate is to be lauded only for their wrecking someone else's dream, not for what they have achieved by and for themselves. History is never kind to the workmanlike Champions: who now recalls fondly the Villa of '81, the Ipswich of '62 or, indeed, the Arsenal of '71 but their own fans? Let Rovers take on some of our burden, let them 'enjoy' the very English process of build 'em up and knock 'em down, let them have a season of being the team to beat, the number ones, the Euro Cup flag-carriers deserted by the nation they purport to represent. Such are the bittersweet fruits of Title victory; if you think Dalglish looks a sourpuss now, wait until he's tasted some of that. It would be enough, to quote his earlier incarnation, 'To make your head explode'. Rovers will, undoubtedly, have deserved their title in a way that Leeds, for example, never did; as such, perhaps beaten Red gladiators should leave the arena hailing *morituri te saltuant* – 'those who are about to perish salute you' – with good grace. We will recharge and return: in the meantime, we shall delight in watching their sweating, squirming discomfort as they discover the laurels of Title victory are far too prickly to rest upon with ease.

As you've probably surmised, I'm writing this just after the whistle at Loftus Road. Rovers have snatched another priceless trio of points, seemingly with an even grimmer display than Goodison's. Fergie's surrender announcement on Sunday may have been two days premature but it was a realistic concession. The Leeds beasts sang 'You're not Champions anymore' and the Red response was to turn away in dejection. Witty responses tend not to spring to the lips at dark moments such as these. For once, Tyke mouths produced a truth.

Two hours earlier, some had been producing screams of terror. It was ironic that the February visit of 6,000 sheep molesters had passed virtually without incident whereas a closely-escorted 1,600 ran straight into vengeance-seeking Reds on the forecourt. As they snaked their way across the concrete behind K stand, a whooping pack of Reds ploughed in, scattering scum in all directions. Not that I'm making a case for these lads but anyone who's endured the tunnel of death at Elland Road – or even the family coach park, actually – would find it as easy to plead mitigation for them as it was for the thug-kicking King, Eric. Horses appeared to restore order and the Reds duly scarpered, giving some Leeds cretins enough of a sense of security to plant themselves under the Munich clock for a chorus of *Who's that lying on the runway.* Not the smartest of moves or the best of timing: the five-minutes-before-kick-off crowd turned up fresh from pub sessions to pile into the Tykes once more. The mounted police, for the first time in years actually earning their exorbitant overtime, returned to the fray which, at one bizarre point, gave rise to the amusing sight of Leeds fans fighting with the horses themselves. Strange creatures, these Leeds mutants: with their ewe-coitus and equine pugilism, is it any wonder we dub them animals? After all, they don't seem to want to have anything to do with humans – every time we approach them, they run away . . .

How inappropriate that such a gorgeous, sun-drenched day should have borne witness to the death-rattle of our Title defence. Those with memories for this sort of thing might have recalled that similar conditions held sway last New Year's Day when Leeds came to town, looking for nothing more than a point and a decent defensive performance. *Plus ça change* in the land of no ambition. It was evident from every pre-match Leeds utterance that their sole goal was to apply some balm to the wounds we inflicted upon them in the Cup. One point would be enough to do just that. I suppose for them it would seem like a twisted poetic justice: we ended their last hopes of a trophy, so all they desired was the opportunity to help dash one of ours. In such circumstances, the dictionary definition of a draw is jettisoned. For us, a point would spell defeat – for Leeds, a victory.

If the weather was inappropriate, the situation behind the scenes was entirely appropriate for the state of our team's position. If the nexus of our season, the Title, was almost lost, so too appeared to be the case with the foreign nexus of our team. Every day's media rumour seemed to confirm that Eric was Inter-bound, that more was going on than the usual pre-contract talk mind games. The eviction of Eric from his Boothstown semi, occasioned by the Club suddenly breaking off purchase negotiations, looked ominous. So too the meeting in Paris between Inter and Eric's agent, both clearly intent on rather more than merely cheering on St Germain against the tedious AC. Meanwhile, Andrei's absence from the team was said to be a result of something other than the aftermath of his pain-killing injections. A Main Stand rumour had it that Andrei and Fergie had had a bust-up that very morning, with Andrei allegedly refusing to adapt his play to suit the new Cole-led attack. Whatever the truth or otherwise of that supposed overheard conversation, the Kanchelskis crisis was clearly far from settlement. For many Reds, Andrei's latest Scottish press outburst had cost him much terrace support. It is bad enough expressing a desire to leave United without compounding the sin by proclaiming a dream to play for the filthy Huns. Having said that, the Club response was mystifying. Fergie's glib comments about possible mistranslations between Ukrainian and Glaswegian-speakers hardly induced confidence. The constant references to 'forthcoming player-club talks' had now been going on for three weeks. Why hadn't someone got a grip, banged heads together and sorted it out? We could do without this running sore squirting bile all over the place – it's bad for the troops' morale, old boy. What is this mysterious stomach injury anyway? Is Andrei some sort of paranoid hypochondriac – in which case, a move to Maine Road would be in order – or is it just the result of the player feeling sick in the pit of his intestines after all the kickings Fergie is supposed to have metaphorically applied? There is little point in telling an unhappy player that he must serve out a contract – I know of no such scenario that has ever worked out to the benefit of Club or player. With 20/20 hindsight, the sale of Gillespie now looks rather ill-advised: perhaps we could do a swap, dear Toons? At the moment, we are in danger of proceeding from a surfeit of right-wingers to a dearth in a matter of months.

The side we had out wasn't quite the one we'd have to rely on in a post-Eric, post-Andrei world – Parker, Bruce and Sharpe were all absent – but it was close enough to make the point. We were good but never great, committed but never truly inspired, dangerous without ever being lethal. David Beckham, slayer of the Turks, managed to both impress yet simultaneously remind us of Andrei's importance; we missed his box incursions and demonic crosses. The packed borders of Leeds' penalty area cried out for the unearthly creative touch of Eric to resolve the impasses. We still had the drive, the passion and the skill that United fans demand of their teams but that extra, imported *je ne sais quoi* that made us vintage Champions was missing. Once Leeds had escaped the first corner, with its inherent flashbacks to their Cup trauma, the game squeezed into the tight straitjacket that Wilkinson had designed for it.

Naturally, all the attacking emanated from us. Forget what Sky's statistician flashed on the screen (seven Leeds goal attempts?! Were they counting United back-passes or what?): nothing scummy threatened our goal in the slightest until the half's last minute. Not that clearcut openings for us were abundant either as sheep successfully threw themselves headlong into everything we fired at them. Cole had a couple of quarter-chances on 6 and 16 but the best opportunity fell to Giggs on 22. Taking Beckham's delicious ball first-time on the volley, Lukic seemed as surprised as any to find the ball safe against his chest. Otherwise, we spent the half trying to batter through the white-walled box; on the occasions that we exploited the right flank spaces, neither the scintillating Neville nor Beckham could produce the killer ball.

Leeds, not content with the appellations 'scum' and 'sheep', were endeavouring to take the title 'dirties' from Liverpool too. Grotesquely late challenges from Yeboah and McAllister were interspersed by petulant touchline outbursts from Kelly, for which he was eventually booked. I heard an exec-type remark that the full-back, last seen mouthing 'f*ck you' to the Strettie in February, was 'a frightful little shit' and who could demur from that? I'd like to see him try squaring up to Cole *off* the field . . . With a minute to go, the sporadically superb Cole was hacked down on the box line; as United players stood in amazement at the ref's failure to penalise his assailant, Wallace shot down to the Strettie to force a remarkable double save from Peter. It was vintage Schmeichel – a brainstormed error more than redeemed by a flash of instinctive brilliance.

For the first twenty minutes, the East stands had been at their vocal best, keen to prevent strains of the god-awful *Marching Altogether* breaking through. An excellent, coherent *Eric The King* – a celebration of its new indie top 10 status? – segued into an enjoyably childish battle with Leeds as to who could bellow 'You're scum . . .' and 'You're gonna win f*ck all' the loudest. Such are the simple pleasures of true fans which the Club is seeking to destroy. For in the minds of many festered the grievance over the Club's anti-standing – and therefore anti-singing – crackdown upon which the new IMUSA sought to capitalise; leaflets distributed to K stand and to some in the East Lower urged Reds to mount a standing, singing protest during the second half. It did not go unnoticed that at least four Reds were ejected from K stand during the first half for the new heinous crime of standing up. Reports from the Strettie told us that stewards were active there too, handing out warnings by the minute. No wonder the West end seemed so subdued. But if we couldn't win the match taking place on the pitch, we could at least secure victory against our oppressors in the stands.

The second half had already exploded into life by the time the East end took to its feet. Presumably, Sergeant Wilko had given his defensive automatons permission to open up a little but the result was a Red tide streaming in to take advantage of the new space. This newly-unleashed mighty Leeds attacking force produced just three serious chances all half, and the first of those was from Schmeichel's own boot on 47. Wallace chipped over on 69, then blasted over on 76: that was it. Otherwise, United were dominant, verging at times on the rampant. At first, we were stymied by Gifford's inability to play advantage or wait for stoppages before allowing injury treatment; the ten minute flurry that followed Cole's 49th smashshot was thus never allowed to reach a climax. We kept our hands on the wheel, despite the provocations, and shifted up to top gear. In an eight minute spell, we promised to win it but three gleaming chances went awry. Cole, at his most panther-like, raced on to tee up Choccy quite exquisitely on 59 but our favourite fat cat pulled an inch wide. Agonisingly, Cole was equally close two minutes later, having turned from Weatherall superbly. On 67, Lukic chose the right spot and was able to clutch the Bogman's free-kick to his weedy bosom. They talk of Rovers' 'Champ's luck' over recent weeks but our failure to convert just one of these three spoke volumes for our own 'Runner's-Up luck'.

By now, the East stands were up and firing with all throats. The scum in the corner, who had moments earlier been overdosing on 'We f*cking hate Man U', at first tired to compete but then retreated into sullen silence. A good 80 per cent of East Lower and a clear majority of K stand stayed up for the rest of the match. It was an alpha and omega moment, a mixture of first and lasts. We were giving our all for what could be our last meaningful contribution, vocally, in the increasingly doomed Title struggle. But for many, it was also a beginning: in responding to the IMUSA appeal, it served as the opening volley of a war for the soul of the Club with the rugger-bugger Cheshire dickheads who see us as exterminable serfs. Perhaps that struggle is doomed too, with us cast as last-stand Luddites, but it's a fight which we cannot shirk.

As time's sands trickled through Red fingers, it was typical that Hughes should be the one desperately trying to gather up the grains. On 72, he worked himself through superbly to fire millimetrically wide; nine minutes later, his fearsome smash veered into lucky Lukic's hands. In between those heart-in-mouth moments, Pally glanced a corner achingly wide and when Ince's goal-bound shot deflected over on 84, our ammo was spent.

As Leeds' fans and players reacted to the whistle as if they'd won a bloody trophy, United faces everywhere told the full story. Fergie's post-match concession simply put those expressions into words. K standers gathered next to the fence separating us from the sheep pen for some ritualistic mutual loathing but their heart didn't seem to be in it. What has happened doesn't approach the 1992 experience in terms of the searing of Red souls and at least we haven't thrown anything away as such – it has always been Blackburn's to lose – but it still hurts to be about to be deposed. The fact that the crucial fence-falls have been against Leeds and Liverpool hardly helps.

Allow me a brief reprise of the Rovers-slagging which commenced this report. After the Spurs game, a bloke rang GMR on their post-match phone-in. He came out with one of the classic clichés you tend to spout in situations like this: 'I'd rather watch United play our way and finish second than watch Rovers play their way and win.' It's an argument we've often had resort to in the past but he said it with such sincerity that the presenters felt unable to take the piss. When you're young, the result is all. At 15, a one-nil win is better than a three-four defeat, even if the latter is a dazzling tour-de-force and the former a Gunnerish bore. But in your late twenties, you begin to see beyond that. I look back, say, to 1978 and can still remember huge chunks of the beautiful three-five West Brom game whilst a host of one-nil victories are lost in the synapses. Style, and a belief in a way of playing, DO matter above all else. The ends do not justify the means after all. I'm with the late-night caller.

Team: Schmeichel; Neville, Keane, Pallister, Irwin, Beckham, McClair, Ince, Giggs, Hughes, Cole

9 April: CRYSTAL PALACE AT VILLA PARK – FA CUP SEMI FINAL

Final Score: UNITED 2 Palace 2

Scorers: Irwin 70, Pallister 96

Attendance: 38,256

ONCE UPON A TIME, United were about as good at winning semi-finals as City now are at winning quarters i.e. total bobbins. Looking through the record of the Busby team reveals the extent of the hoodoo – how we made finals in 1963 and 1968 appears, in retrospect, miraculous. The failure in 1975 was one of the worst, beaten over two legs by Norwich, a team who only just squeezed into Division One that year. Painful defeats against the Sheep in 1970 and 1965 were still fresh in the memory for Reds back then. Yet 1975 was the year our domestic semi fortunes shifted cosmically: we haven't lost one since. What's more, that uniquely successful run has encompassed some of the modern Red's greatest moments, triumphs that equal and often surpassed those of the Finals themselves. Whether beating reigning champs as in '76 and '85 or overcoming tremendous setbacks as in '90 and '94, semi finals are something to be clutched to the Red-shirted bosom. And with United being unbeaten in Villa Park semis since the war, our total self-confidence was forgivable. Though at about ten to six, some would have reflected that hubris does, indeed, come before a fall.

Only semi finals can provide the spine-tingling sight of a decent away ground being taken over by Red hordes (yes, I know we get that at Selhurst Park, but note the adjective is 'decent' not 'shitehole'.) Despite the usual FA misallocation of tickets that meant we had to jump ten hurdles to get seats whilst Palace first-timers could turn up and buy a row-full, and despite the price that represented almost criminal extortion, we were all there. Palace couldn't even sell their stands out: at least Red dominance would be guaranteed in the vocal department, once the stragglers zigzagging their way back from the Irish Centre shindig turned up anyway. The footballing department was, however, quite another matter . . .

As Boyle's Boys sing, 'On the field, it's almost unreal . . .' – indeed, Palace's almost complete first-half domination was unearthly, unexpected and entirely unwelcome. Had Beckham properly connected with Sharpe's 100th second cross, I daresay we would've been spared the ensuing epic. At least his miss carried the happy pay-off of breaking Martyn's finger which would cost him a replay place. There was also the cheeky Giggs attempt to lob home from 50 yards after five minutes, which fell short into Martyn's grateful clutches. The '£10 million' man's chutzpah instantly conjured up memories of past geniuses, to whom Giggs remains inferior, whatever Johann Cruyff might bullshit. Pelé missed the target by inches, Cantona hit the bar and Best, probably, would have scored . . . That moment of inspiration was utterly out of place today, however. United were slow, predictable, lacking in imagination and often exhibiting the signs of players who don't really know their position or role. To be fair, we had one absentee too many; added to the list of Cole, Cantona, Kanchelskis and Parker was the suspended Stevie Bruce. Just for once, Reds hoped David May would be available but typically the Ginger One was hernia'd. (A likely story – more plausible that some enraged Red in a nightclub had applied a critical knee to the bollocks . . .) That left Keano to battle manfully but diminutively against the monstrous Dowie; it also meant Choccy would be free to wreak havoc, to our detriment, in Keane's midfield slot. A Red defence that had kept nine clean sheets in 12 was now to totter dangerously as they strained to repel Palace's ceaseless aerial bombardment.

Notwithstanding Keane's flashing wide header on 18, Palace were dictating the tempo and style as well as putting it about a bit. The clattering Pitcher was in the book after only 11, whilst Shaw, sporting not so much a hair-do as a hair-don't, was as surprised as we were that he escaped a card for a savage scythe on 18. David Elleray was apparently keen to even-up the supposed pro-Red 'mistakes' of the Cup Final: just for today, the Harrovian disciplinarian became a soft-soaper in the Joe Worrall mode.

By the half's mid-point, Palace were in control. As Dowie and Armstrong missed gaping openings on 22 and 23, we even heard the Palace day-trippers sing, the excremental 'We support our local team' being met from the Holte by a barrage of part-timer insults. Within a minute of the unpunished Young elbowing Hughes in the face, Armstrong's snapshot just missed as a prelude to Dowie's opener on 33. Yet another airborne assault was, this time, resolved emphatically as Dowie's hideous eyebrows met the ball Schmeichel had missed. What a horrific sight the celebrating Dowie is, like Frankenstein's monster pursuing Mittel-European villagers. Had Armstrong been on target after his one-on-one with Peter moments later, the Red fright-night would've been complete.

Considering the crap we'd been force-fed, the Red support at least in the packed Holte End had been pretty decent, although in comparison to last year's first semi, even Palace's weedy efforts were superior. The Cantona songs were particularly heart-felt as Reds took the televisual opportunity to remind both Eric and the world of our sympathies. The mixture that you get on these occasions whereby thermos-toters from G & H rub up against lads from the two ends was somewhat combustible however; everywhere, blazing toe-to-toe arguments were breaking out between the standers and sitters, despite the official sanction given to cheerleaders in the match programme. (A copy of that encouragement is on its way to Merrett & Co., of course.) The West Midlands Police, keen to live up to their billing as the nation's filthiest pigs, still found cause enough for multiple ejections: presumably, their blood was up after the day's earlier events in the city and Walsall. Typically, when it went off after the equaliser in the Ellis Upper, they took minutes to react. Presumably, their 'police intelligence' — what a contradiction in terms! — had swallowed the myth of lovable Palace daytrippers being far less likely to cause hassle than the 'animal' Reds.

As the second-half began, the Upper Holte had clearly got used to their vomit-inducing height and had overcome the sensation of being about to fall off Everest's summit. Upping the volume in conjunction with the lower, they seemed to inspire United into an early cavalry charge. To be honest, United were charging with bludgeons rather than rapiers but at least we had Palace on the back foot at last. Our crosses and final balls remained woeful but once Dowie had sent over a warning shot on 63, we sharpened up in response. Both Giggs and Sharpe had good efforts saved on 65 and 67; minutes later we were level. The Bogman's free kick looked too far out even for him but his strike was quite awesome. A nice touch too that the foul should've been committed by ex-Red fanatic Southgate and helped on its way into the net by Scouse reject Houghton. Reds, on their feet and united in song for five minutes afterwards, demonstrated to the Palace bandwaggoners exactly how a semi-final goal should be celebrated: in delirium.

As is always the case in our Cup semis down the years, we have to be made to suffer. If there's a long way around, United will be sure to take it. Within a minute of the equaliser, Armstrong wasted a glittering chance to bury us. The ref's booking of Keane for mild dissent after what he saw as a blatantly incorrect decision was too far out, man. As was Giggsy's shimmering blast on 79, as true and hard as a Side-winder but still leaving Martyn sufficient nanoseconds to adjust and make the save of the tie. So Denis had saved us from execution but we were still condemned to extra-time against one of the few sides that are probably fitter than us. For once, a replay looked alluring, even at FA extortion prices.

Within a minute of the restart, the vision of a rematch became more than merely alluring − it was all you desired in the world. Scarcely had the Holte air cleared of angry epithets after McClair's 20th second one-yard miss (rearrange 'pie-eating', 'fat Scottish' and 'bastard' to make a familiar phrase) than Armstrong was shinning a lob over the flailing Schmeichel for 2-1. It was the sort of spawny-goal-produces-fairytale-ending instant that wins matches like this. 'Dopehead returns from disgrace to weed out dazed Champs': yes, you could picture it all. But Reds were back on their feet, producing an Old Trafford vintage roar I'd last detected against Forest, that mélange of anger, desperation and love that sounds like no other. Nicky Butt was now entering his purplest patch, forcing Young into a carded foul and then having his header cleared from the line. Palace had shot their load too early: 29 minutes would be enough to get back on terms. In the event, we needed only five. Pally rose as slyly as a giant can manage to sneak home Neville's Vinnyish long throw, the ball seeming to cross the line in slow-mo. We sang out the remains as United played for the replay, confident as we were that Palace would never play this well again, nor we so badly. Only Irwin's free-kick on 108 and Armstrong's fizzing first-timer two minutes later ever threatened to trouble the scoreboard operator.

Once again, United had respected their own Cup semi traditions. First, do a Man City impression and escape with a dodgy draw before going on to slam-dunk the rematch. Next time, perhaps they could do it the other way round and save us all £50?

Team: Schmeichel; Neville, Keane, Pallister, Irwin, Beckham (Butt), Ince, Sharpe, Giggs, McClair, Hughes

A COUPLE OF HOURS into the journey back from Villa Park, news began to filter through to the Red Army convoys that a Palace fan had died after a kick-off outside a Walsall pub. What's more, the initial media diagnosis was grim, detailing as it did an almost Leeds-like scenario. The evening bulletins and consequently next day's front pages spoke of murder, of unprovoked assaults, of family-fan targets and family-man victims. This was an entirely different scale of activity to that which had held sway during the day in Birmingham, where several small-scale skirmishes leading to many of the day's 84 arrests had taken place. Could it be true that Irlam Reds, some of the most loyal around, had taken on the behavioural patterns of the vilest sheepshaggers?

Naturally, the truth, as it eventually trickled down to public consciousness, was full of hues of grey rather than the stark black and white that the media and fellow United-haters demand. The 'unprovoked assault' became a standard car-park brawl; the 'vicious stabbing' a simple case of a poor sod falling underneath a bus. Even the victim, at first trailed as a father-of-four, became instead the convicted-of-five. Not that any of this held any significance for either Palace fans or the media/FA sanctimony-pedlars. What should have been seen as the inevitable occasional consequence of the routine lowish-level aggro that still permeates the football experience away from stadia instead became a *cause célèbre*, as such worthy of the full Hillsborian flowers and memorials treatment. Why should this frankly accidental fatality be accorded such hand-wringing, cringing attention when, for example, the lethal stabbing at the Newcastle-Everton match was barely noted? Sadly, the involvement of the name 'United' transforms everything: a football fan's death duly received not a dignified, restrained response but a full media-driven firestorm. Two of the five injuries were Reds' and potentially the death could have been 'ours' too – I wonder just how much indignant coverage such an outcome would have garnered? Is it too cynical to suggest it would have been minuscule?

It would, of course, have been too much to expect the tabloid harlots to peddle anything other than bone-headed, inflammatory turd-words at such a moment. Reading the true-to-form *Sun*, you could be forgiven for gaining the impression that Eric Cantona himself had been down in the carpark, kung-fu-kicking and lobbing brick-halves with the best of them. What you would hope for is that bodies such as the Palace authorities and the National Federation of Football Supporters would have kept their heads whilst the ex-Fleet Street illiterate winos were losing theirs. However, the temptation to make political capital out of the situation proved to be too great, at least for Messrs Noades and Kershaw of Palace and the NFFS respectively. Perhaps we should have known what to expect from past experience. Colin Noades had clearly come from the same loud-mouth gene pool that produced brother Ron, he of the infamous 'blacks in winter' theorem and the demand for equal Cup tickets in 1990; as for the NFFS, the frequent Cantona-slating TV appearances of Monica Hartland had turned many a Red stomach. The NFFS statement that exhorted Eric to leave the UK was surely the most grossly opportunistic appeal to the gutter mentality ever produced by a football interest group. That the media should have slavishly followed the lead of an organisation that appears to represent virtually no-one says a great deal about the anti-Red hysteria that now grips even the most unprejudiced sports desk.

As for Noades and his boycott appeal, you had to credit his footwork. It is just possible he had a sincere motive but how strikingly coincidental that his stay-away call and noble words should have come after a morning during which the Palace box-office only shifted 1,500 replay tickets. If they had truly wanted to make the point, they should have simply refused to sell any replay tickets through their Club and, *in extremis*, refused to turn up for the replay at all. That would have gained the respect of even the most Selhurst-phobic Red. The fact that the usual away-going Palace hard-core duly turned up for the replay told us all we needed to know about the real picture at Selhurst Park. No true Eagle, like no true Red, would boycott a Cup semi final and leave his heroes supportless because of the unfortunate death of one bloke in whatever circumstances.

Wednesday arrived, the day of the replay which the FA and police had quite rightly refused to postpone, and Palace were still agitating. Even their *soi-disant* 'leaders', types who join the FSA and NFFS, were busily helping to construct the witch-hunt ducking-stool. At the same moment that a coroner's report was recording death by wheel-crushing, Palace heads were still insisting like demented Cluedo-nuts that it had been Mr Red, with the dagger, outside the pub – and that the police were hushing it up to lower the temperature. An alleged stabbing from the 1993 match was used as 'proof' that Reds had a history of anti-Palace violence. The fact that hardly any of us had heard of such an incident even being alleged was explained thus: the police hushed it up, again. Either Croydon pigs have been taking instruction courses from the West Midlands force or these Palace conspiracy-theorist paranoids should take up writing Jack Kennedy books. Then, there was the saga of the mysterious Brummies, the most infamous interlopers since the bloke at the door who interrupted the writing of *Khubla Khan*. At first, they were said to be Palace Brummies, up to meet their cohorts; then, they became 'Zulus', looking for a rematch of the NEC kick-off; finally, Palace had them down as Brummie Reds, up to launch an assault on decent Cockneys. What Brummie Reds would be doing in such a place rather weakens the Palace crime-scene configuration, though: it would be akin to the Salford Boys going up to Todmorden for a good time and drink, i.e. hardly credible.

For the Wednesday media, such irresponsible griping as went on down in London was a godsend. A story that had, excuse the phrase, been virtually as dead as the victim by Monday afternoon, was back on course. All the tabloids had to do was hype, hype and hype again, mentioning the buzz-word 'tension' as often as possible. How pathetically easy it is to plot the course of these tabloid running stories: a chimp with an Olivetti could do it. In creating such a fevered atmosphere, the scribblers could not lose. Either the tension that they had done so much to inflate would explode, giving them another week of three-page specials, or else we would all behave despite the circumstances, cueing up a series of heart-warming, sentimental tripe-servings on the stoic forbearance of the footie-loving Eagles. In the event, they got a bit of both: double-overtime and bottles of Scotch all round. A free press makes a free nation but what does the nature of this shower tell us about the state of our country? As outside observers might say, 'These asswipes suck, Beavis'.

12 April: CRYSTAL PALACE AT VILLA PARK – FA CUP SEMI REPLAY

Final Score: UNITED 2 Palace 0

Scorers: Bruce 30, Pallister 41

Attendance: 17,987

WHATEVER TENSION THERE WAS on Wednesday night didn't have much chance to take effect; the Palace turn-out of less than 3,000 gave the impression of there being one on-duty pig for every Eagle in Birmingham. By contrast, enough Reds had somehow scraped together sufficient readies to be able to pack the Holte and most of the Main Stand. There were, of course, no ticket price reductions. The

FA's various serene smugnesses later basked in the glow of media approval for their vaguely nauseating pre-match ceremony and the he-man hard-line they promised afterwards against those who 'brought the game into disrepute'. For any who had coughed up for exorbitant seats or who couldn't afford to do so, such curtain-calls must have resounded rather hollowly. A week before, IMUSA's Andy Mitten had pranged the FA's Commercial Director live on TV, unable to bear the claptrap about 'bringing families into stadia' anymore. 'If that's the aim,' inquired Andy sweetly, ' why are you asking 14-year-old kids to pay £38 for a semi ticket?' Phillips' jaw sagged memorably before he composed himself sufficiently to mutter the free-market credo about supply and demand justifying the extortion. At least that was a defence of some sort, however inadequate; for tonight's game, no such mitigation existed. The FA's grasping, bread-headed attitude robbed the rematch of all sense of occasion and worth. Their crass, cack-handed misjudgment of 'the market' about which they profess to be experts did more, by pricing out thousands and the young above all, to 'bring the game into disrepute' than any player's physical action that night. Truly, an organisation that cannot ensure a showpiece occasion is at least a near sell-out has little right to sit in judgment on the competence of others. They couldn't arrange their own erections . . .

Faced with the surreal sight of two empty stands, Reds sporadically made the most of the vocal open goal; the *Twelve Days of Cantona* in the second-half was particularly clamorous, even though it carried the undertones of a farewell. But with nothing to oppose, and with the team wrapping up a result by half-time, there was little of Sunday's inspiration left over for tonight. The Boyle Boys in the Holte/Main corner provided far more post-break entertainment than the players – bar Keano – as they ran through most of the tracklisting from 'Bathtub Revisited.'

As the last ten minutes trickled away, the Holte seemed to come to its senses, realising that we were in fact at the gates of Wembley and not merely at some Youth Cup match; taking to their feet, they provided some sort of finalé to what was otherwise a night of anti-climax. Even the police had become laid-back, by their standards: when two nine-year-olds mounted a pitch invasion, the WMP managed to keep their truncheons sheathed and, remarkably, backed off when older Reds objected physically to the pigs' attempts to arrest the poor kids. (Is this how the local filth keeps up its arrest rates, by rounding up those infant school menaces by the Maria-load?)

As we had all expected, the restoration of Bruce and Keane to their proper kingdoms had been enough to secure complete United dominance. We were poor up front, as is now customary, yet Palace contrived to be worse. They, like the semi as a whole, had spent up on Sunday and had little left to offer – certainly not any on-target shots, anyway. Everything about the goals was perfectly apt. The brilliant, domineering force of both superbly worked headers reflected our controlling grip on tempo and structure. The reliance on defenders scoring from set pieces yet again told both of our attack's malaise and of the debt we owe to the dependable defenders who, almost alone in these stressed-out weeks, have played as well as ever. That Pally's goal should have put him ahead of Giggs in the domestic scoring stakes writes a regretful little subscript. What it could have meant to have had 17 Giggs goals again this season . . .

In a season such as this, however, it is not enough for us to provide a boring 'United Get To Wembley' story; how can *The Sun* get six pages out of that? Keano didn't neglect United's column-filling duty – in stamping on Southgate, he handed the press vultures a week's worth of fresh meat on which to gorge. As the FA has now explained, Roy's inability to reflect soberly on the wider implications, Sunday's tragedy, the pre-match entreaties and his position as a role-model within a split-second of receiving a career-threatening tackle was reprehensible and punishable by execution – or, failing that, a Cup Final ban. The attempted retaliation by four Palace players in turn who raced up to 'have a go' at Keane was, of course, entirely justifiable; doubtless, the spitting, marauding thug called them all motherf*ckers. As the *News At Ten* trumpeted, Keane is one of the dirtiest players at United, who are themselves the dirtiest Club (well, if you omit Norwich, Arsenal, Wimbledon, Everton etc from the statistics anyhow.) Edwards and Ferguson are the Kray Twins of the Premiership, inciting and excusing violence by their henchmen.

In fact, United are the Anti-Christs of football. As a Club, the worst role-model possible. A generation of kids is being led into a life of thuggery and crime by these despicable villains. If Sir Matt, God bless him, were alive, he'd close down the Club and lock up all the players. And, at the end of the day, it's all that bloody frog Cantona's fault. The tabloids speak for the people – String 'Em Up! It's the only language they understand. And put all those fan-killing, Cantona-cheering Rags up on the scaffold too.

Hey ho. Anyone else think Keane should've stamped harder?

Team: Schmeichel; Neville, Bruce, Pallister, Irwin, Giggs (McClair), Keane, Ince, Butt, Sharpe, Hughes

15 April: LEICESTER CITY AWAY

Final Score: Leicester 0 UNITED 4

Scorers: Sharpe 33, Cole 45 & 52, Ince 90

Attendance: 21,281

FOOTBALL WRITERS IN SEARCH of fresh metaphors and allusions love Easter. Out come all the references to 'resurrections', 'Easter risings' and good old-fashioned Biblical miracles. United, of course, needed all these after their crucifixion by Leeds. To believe or not to believe, that is the question – the cross-section of archetypal hardcore Reds (bar the odd Norwegian) on the fanzine coach, for example, were as split as the Church of England on the issue. Even after the match, one 'zine editor continued to lead the Bishop of Durham school of scientific realists who still thought we'd had it; others, led by St Bert of Foulds, built sophisticated prediction models to demonstrate that the leap of faith was yet worth the jump. The team, it soon transpired, played with the carefree abandon of those who think they have nothing to lose. A pity they couldn't have maintained that mindset for a further 48 hours.

For Leicester, the time of miracles had passed. Relegated a couple of days beforehand, the Filbert Street club was mired in the most funereal of atmospheres. Had we lost, our wake couldn't have asked for a more conducive environment. Only the few hundred Leicester boys tucked into the south-east corner were prepared to shatter the pall-bearing silence with a display of Pythonesque black humour. 'We're crap and we're going down' and 'Endsleigh, Endsleigh' – getting their retaliation in first – enlivened the pre-match 'atmosphere', such as it was. Many Reds, as usual, turned up at the last minute, having wrung every last drink possible out of the local hostelries. Some brought in tales of run-ins with city's 'Babies'; one particular peaceable group of Cockney Reds had come a cropper whereas other individuals had discovered to their cost what the Midlands sense of fair play entails – a gang of twenty kicking in a lone straggler before leaving a 'Kick To Kill' calling card. Such is the morality of the badly brought-up Nineties hoolie: none of your old-style honour codes here.

Still, you almost feel sorry for City. Both their ground and team have 'Endsleigh' stamped irrevocably all over them. The ground has two semi-decent stands alongside two laughable garden sheds; the team is full of honest has-beens and never-will-bes, clustered around the star class of the shaven-headed Draper. The greatest buzz the crowd seems to get here is from the Walker's Crisps girls bunging free bags into the stands before kick-off. How sad life must be when the biggest cheers of the day are to greet the latest scores from the town's rugby team.

Having said all that, City approached us brightly, with admirable commitment. That's the trouble with playing the already-doomed, as we discovered at Upton Park '92: shorn of the relegation-battle tensions, teams get 'gate-happy', as the prison lingo has it. They start playing football, enjoying their last top-flight appearances and generally become arse-munching pains to Title-challengers looking for three easy points. When Draper forced Schmeichel into agile heroics on 12, with Neville having to plough in to rescue the rebound from ex-Red Robins, you were entitled to fear that old history-repeating syndrome.

By then, as is customary, United had already missed their gilded opening chance, Cole blazing wildly over from Choccy's cross. The Draper heart-stopper, however, appeared to be the galvanising moment we required. Lee Sharpe, as he had begun to threaten at Villa Park, burst into splendiforous, pre-meningitis form at last. During a patch as purple as an ejaculating helmet, United peeled off rapid-fire chances like a Cockney disgorging his wad. Sharpe half-volleyed quite deliciously but just over the bar before latching onto Butt's ball only to be thwarted by the keeper. Ince, roaring through as of old, declined the obvious shot and instead fed Sharpe whose effort was beaten away. Then, in a move symptomatic of the Reds' carefree approach, Cole and Sharpe interchanged with balletic flicks and touches until Cole's drive was blocked. This was attacking football of the sort we'd almost forgotten we were capable of; no reliance on set-pieces or defenders-as-strikers today.

Despite the 25th minute shock of Peter needing to make the instinct-save of the week to deny Willis, the first United goal was as inevitable in its arrival as it was in its execution. So familiar a pattern recently: a Neville long-throw, a Pally knock-on, a spectacular Cole miss, all preceding Sharpe's crack finish. Moments later, a pitch bobble denied Cole his opener after he'd burst through; he made amends with a goal-hanging (and slightly offside) finish on half-time as Choccy and Sharpe combined to feed him. The game was won – Peter's point-blank save from Robins just before had been City's last opportunity to salvage some pride. Typically for this season, however, the first-half star was now to be denied us. No sooner had Sharpe's personal resurrection been completed than God had him nailed up on the injury-cross once more. No wonder we're all so paranoid these days.

Our support, to be frank, had been patchy thus far. Given our dominating presence along the East stand, we should have been better. Only about half of us were singing and once the Boyle had been taken off, the victim of a mysterious substance ingested during a Leicester-Red sponsored pub-crawl, the South end lacked an instigator. Tickets had been hard-won for this game. You would think that anyone in possession of a ticket that either cost them close to a ton, or which they could've sold for that amount, would have made the most of their privileged position. The lads, the familiar faces, did their best and got an improved response during the second half procession but there were too many blank, uncomprehending faces amongst us, too many who'd surely have been happier up in the Carling stand with the rest of the mourners.

United emerged after the break seemingly intent on snapping us out of our reverie and finally silencing the last defiant Fox fans. Ince had already come an inch from the third before a 52nd minute corner powered goalwards via Brucey's head; Cole casually forced the ball over the line with some unusual bodily part. Most of us, to be honest, didn't have a clue what had happened, who had scored or whether the ref had given it for what seemed like an eternity; eventually the truth dawned and, almost sheepishly, we burst into the Cole song. Cheeky Bruce, the epitome of the ugly defender who dreams of being a glam striker, ran towards us frantically beating his chest in claim of the goal. As player and fans grinned gormlessly at each other, we switched in a beat to 'Stevie Bruce running down the wing' - the great man applauded us, delighted that for a few moments he'd conned us all into giving him his goalscoring buzz. The goal, of course, was Cole's.

At last, the East Stand had progressed from the funereal; we were now at the reception, getting relievedly pissed on Auntie Hilda's cheap medium-white. An excellent *Twelve Days of Cantona* segued into a five minute, all-encompassing *Fergie's Red And White Army*; a few volleys of *Three-nil to the Youth Team and without Cantona* helped deepen the brooding gloom of the now-silenced Leicester boys. Their mood wasn't much improved by the ref's refusal to penalise Bruce for his basketball flash, nor by our cheerful 'Handball – and you know it was'. McClair had a snapshot smartly saved and Pally had cleared virtually off the line when the afternoon reached an unexpected climax. A South African radio correspondent sitting in our section broke off from his commentary to announce casually that Leeds had equalised against Blackburn in the minute added on for Rovers' time-wasting. Barely had Reds, now on their feet, finished chorusing 'If you STILL hate Leeds . . .' than Scholes, the reserve-team Cantona, lofted the most Eric-ish of balls to the post for Ince to finish succinctly. We had won 4-0, in a stroke putting us in the goal-difference driving seat, and had closed the gap to six points. The mathematical prediction gurus were back in business. And if your head still told you that the post-Leeds surrender was appropriate, hope still sprang eternal in the heart. As long as there is some hope left, even if only there to be extinguished, there is cause to fight. As any who suffered 1992 will tell you, there is nothing like the sight of the last fence for making your head explode – and Kenny's face does look a little taut tonight doesn't it?

Team: Schmeichel; Neville, Bruce, Pallister, Irwin, McClair, Ince, Butt, Cole, Hughes (Scholes), Sharpe (Beckham)

PS: You have to admit that ref Bodenham had an excellent game but surely he should have noticed the offensive weapon of a charred pineapple that Jamie Lawrence had stuck on his head?

17 April: CHELSEA AT HOME

Final score: UNITED 0 Chelsea 0

Attendance: 43,728

FOR THE PAST THREE years now, the Easter home game has been previewed and reviewed as the crux of the season. In '93 and '94, United rose magnificently to overcome adversity, with Brucey's Wednesday double and the post-Ewood bounceback against Oldham returning us onto the Title rails. In '92, the Black Monday against Forest had been the beginning of the end. Now in '95, the optimists had sketched the scenario: beat Chelsea, pray City get something that night at Blackburn and stand by to watch Rovers' arses go. The realists, meanwhile, had both games down as home wins on the inexorable trail to a Ewood title. Whatever, we expected a definitive answer today, just as Easter always provides. What we got instead was the totally unexpected. That meant that this particular Easter egg hunt had no solution yet – all we discovered was an empty tomb.

After the carefree, spring-lamb gambolling at Filbert Street, this was truly a return to the grim North. Well before kick-off, Old Trafford was thoroughly miserable, drenched to brick and skin after the downpour of the year. Fergie was to wonder later about the footballing sympathies of God – the one in Heaven, not the one on community service – and in more ways than one, it appeared He was pissing on us from a great height. If that wasn't enough to dampen the ardour, some had the additional concern of a promised visit from Combat 18, up to wreak vengeance on those who'd attacked Jason Ankers, apparently. *Red Attitude* sellers kept their heads well above the parapet on Warwick Road, secure in the knowledge that their handy young men propped up by the railings were not just there to take the afternoon air.

The bars below the stands were packed, Old Trafford's 'customers' reluctant to linger on forecourt or in stands thanks to the weather. A brief survey of the East lower concourse provided an answer to the mystery of the ticket shortage. The fortnight before had been filled with anguished wails from home-and-awayers who, for the first time this season, had failed to get a ticket. Branches everywhere were short on tickets, long on ballot-failure letters. By some statistical miracle – not! – the nation's first-timers and part-timers had cleaned up. The tell-tale signs were everywhere: a surfeit of eight-year-olds in family groups, prosperous-looking couples in mohair coats, forty-something mothers laden with Megastore carrier-bags. Clearly, the Club had happily made provision to provide Britain's bank holiday-makers with an alternative to Alton Towers. MUFC's attitude to supporters truly seems to be 'never mind the quality – feel the width!' Sadly for us and the team, expansive pockets do not signify expansive vocal capacity. Considering the central importance of this match, and making all due excuses for the rain's effect, the support today was simply not good enough. Even Paul Ince felt compelled to remark upon this on GMR that night. As embarrassed and ashamed as a true Red would be about this lamentable state of affairs, at least it serves to prove to all observers the truth of what Reds have been saying for years. You mess with the OT eco-system at your peril. The hard-core Reds are the brightest blooms in the garden. If you don't nurture and encourage them, they get swamped by weeds. Today, we were strangled by these parasitic invaders, sat there doing nothing to support our battling boys or, worse, complaining about those who *were* doing something. The effect was quite obvious. It used to be said that the United crowd was worth a goal start. Today, tellingly, we failed to score.

Sections of K stand remained as reliable as ever in coming up with instant responses to the Chelsea hordes. Mind you, Chelsea do make it easy. If, as K standers alleged loudly, Chelsea are all rent-boys, then it must be assumed that standing around the Piccadilly Circus meat-rack has caused them to inhale too many brain-damaging fumes, such was their vocal stupidity. *One team in Europe,* they innumerately sang, prompting an instant *Are you Arsenal in disguise?* from K; also *Four-nil, Barcelona* is hardly the smartest tune to pick when you've recently been humiliated by second-rate Spaniards yourselves and, as K reminded them, when a similar Cup Final spanking is still vividly fresh in the memory. As for 'one Johnny Spencer', well, how could we resist a 'Frank Spencer' retort? These were unmissable open goals.

Unfortunately, the team's open goals proved to be eminently missable. When Hughes left-footed laughably wide early on, the die was cast. Cole managed to loft a delicious Hughes flick-up into the stands soon after and a game that should have been already won became touched by malevolent Fate. Despite the fact that Chelsea's first-half marking hit a City-like nadir, neither Butt nor Choccy could put their free headers in the net. Our most impressive effort was Hughesy's drive which the keeper almost dived straight past; Schmeichel then had to be rather more alert to deny Peacock yet another United-beating winner.

The rain that appeared to be threatening to wash United's title hopes away abated somewhat in the second-half yet, if anything, our prospects for success receded even further. In recent weeks, United have been staggering forward like some monster in a teen-scream flick; whatever assaults and attacks we suffer, we have continued to get off the floor and lumber on, dripping blood and losing limbs on the way. But by now, we have lost too many appendages to continue. The absence of Eric, Andrei, Giggs, Sharpe and Keane was too much to bear. We are width-less, wing-less and, frankly, a bit head-less too. The final scene has arrived: the monster is halted. It's time to look forward to the sequel.

Cole had two chances in two minutes on 56 and 58, denied goals from head and foot by timely defensive interventions; United continued to blunder forward, remaining susceptible to the sort of counter-punch from which Stein almost scored. For some unfathomable reason, Davies the half-time sub was hauled off instead of McClair; when Scholesy's chance came in injury-time, he headed uncharacteristically over. By then, we had already received every indication we needed that resistance was useless. We were denied the most blatant penalty I've seen this decade at Old Trafford, a handball so obvious that even Barry Davies gave it. With six to go, Brucey thought he'd reprised his '93 hero role, scoring smartly only to find Hughes had been erroneously given offside. This script sucked.

At one point last season, people had begun to talk of 'lucky' United. That is not a phrase you'll hear these days. When Fergie wondered whether God was a United fan, it was surely a rhetorical question. Of course He's not. He's clearly a bloody bandwagon-jumper like everyone else. Fancied us last season but now prances about with St Peter, wearing a Shearer kit. I'm giving up praying to Him for last-minute winners: now is the time to sacrifice a goat to Satan and do Faustian bargains about selling souls and Rovers' defeats.

Team: Schmeichel, Neville, Irwin, Bruce, Pallister, McClair, Ince, Butt, Cole, Hughes, Beckham (Davies) (Scholes)

PS: THE KING IS NOT DEAD – LONG LIVE THE KING!
THURSDAY 27 APRIL: a date to be burned into every Red cerebral cortex forever. Exactly three months before, every media outlet in the land had been filled with 'that' picture, the portrayal of the act whose consequences threatened to remove the King from his Old Trafford throne for good. Jesus spent forty days in the wilderness: 'Dieu' has had to suffer more than twice as long. But as Thursday's *Evening News* hit the midday streets, Reds all over town rejoiced at the sight of the banner headline over David Meek's exclusive: ERIC WILL STAY WITH THE REDS. As glorious restorations of monarchs go, this beat even Charles the Second's. And as once the Cavaliers stuck two fingers up at the Puritans, so Reds have delighted in our triumph over the rest of Britain, as represented by the media scumbags. They tried their best to force him out and failed: one–nil to the Champions.

How sweet the spectacular misjudgments of, for example, that week's *Daily Mirror*. On Tuesday, they'd announced as fact that Eric was going – even better, that very Thursday morning, the *Mirror's* Nigel Clarke had spent two pages detailing all the reasons why Eric had decided to leave.

A mention too for Patrick Barclay of the *Observer* and a regular on the Red-baiting 'Hold the Back Page', who has come to epitomise all those journalists who hate United's fans as well as players. Only last week, he filled eight columns denouncing United supporters, telling us how disgraceful it was that we should still be singing for Eric at every game, laughing at our 'naïve' belief that such support would encourage Eric to stay. So much for his judgment, then, when Eric made it clear that it was precisely this continued, devoted support that played a huge part in persuading him to stay. To those who risked the ridicule from the cynical by singing *Eric the King* et al at every game since Selhurst Park, take a bow. For once, we were heard.

To all our rivals who've been wetting themselves with excitement at the prospect of Eric leaving, tough break lads. It seems the 'where's yer Cantona' songs will have to be shelved for a few years yet. To City fans in particular, special commiserations. We fully understand how your arses must be collapsing at the thought of more Eric-inspired derby slayings.

In fact, the list of those whose faces we now want to laugh in, spit at and stamp on is endless. The Cantona Affair has polarised the 'us and them' situation like nothing else in living memory. These past three months have brought all true Reds closer together, huddled around our Club and our King: with a few noble exceptions, everyone outside Old Trafford's Red-blooded family has become the enemy. So a simple 'f*ck off, world' will suffice. No-one likes us and we don't care 'cos we've got our King back.

Above all, let us appreciate the bravery of the hero of the hour, of the year, of the decade. He could have doubled his money; he could have made a fresh start; he could have escaped a country which has imprisoned and demonised him; he could have revelled in a great, new challenge in the world's greatest league; he could have enjoyed the fervent worship of a whole new city and country. Instead, he has chosen to stay, at a Club who won't be in the European Cup next season, who still don't pay him properly and who are hated beyond all others. This from a man whose main goal is to be a Euro Champ, who sees a salary level only as an indication of how much a Club really values him and who has often expressed a need to be loved and appreciated by all who see him, not just his Club's fans. Against all the odds, he really has, as the song has it, declared 'This Club's his perfect wife'. What a man.

1 May: COVENTRY CITY AWAY

Final Score: Coventry 2 UNITED 3

Scorers: Scholes 33, Cole 55 & 79

Attendance: 21,885

AS MY MATE ANDY the neo-Marxist remarked later that night, May Day was always a time of celebration for world Reds. The Government stripped this particular day of its Bank Holiday status but for those Reds who made it to Highfield Road, surely no mere holiday could have equalled tonight's 90 minutes for sensual joy. Forget sun, sea 'n' sex – Cole, Scholes 'n' goals is the top tripper's ticket.

There's a small triangular park yards from the ground where the drunk can safely collapse for a pre-match snooze and which, in Coventry's grim urban context, counts as an area of outstanding natural beauty. (Local urchins point at the grass and ask 'what's that?'; the four trees have grade one preservation orders on them.) Once this was a good place for running skirmishes and general ambushes but tonight, bathed in the balmy evening sunlight, it offered a vantage point on arriving, buzzing Reds. Within a week, the most remarkable change in Red demeanour had occurred. The glum, pale visages of the loser that had been everywhere against Chelsea were now browning, healthy, smiling; for the first time in months, every other gang of lads was singing their way to the ground. Coventry is generally a carefree place to go in any event: not only do we always win but not even the police FIU bother sending spotters to this fixture, such is the lack of hostility from the locals these days. But we had something else beside the melanoma weather and good vibes perking us up – in the space of seven days, we'd had a double delight in which to revel. Blackburn's arses had, apparently, collapsed in a style familiar to any who experienced 1992, losing to City (!?) and West Ham, the latter defeat being particularly resonant for those who were at Upton Park three years ago. And in between those two wonderful nights of Sky-high pleasure, Eric had reaffirmed his marriage vows to us. The King was back in his castle and the trophy in the keep was not yet lost. With our hopes for both the short and long term suddenly, shockingly restored, the Red Army was up for the fight once more, ready to go over the top towards the sound of gunfire. There would be no team complaints about a lack of support tonight, for sure.

Ironically, our state of rabid optimism bore no relation to any objective reading of the situation. After all, City were as desperate for points as us and had a decent home record; the presence of United old boys such as Strachan, Dion and Big Ron himself seemed designed for a vengeance scenario; above all, the two teams were unrecognisable in a way that threatened to be to our detriment. We were without Giggs, Bruce, Keane, Eric, Andrei, Parker and Ince, a casualty list of unparalleled proportion that made our eleven look like a Coca Cola team. Coventry, by contrast, may have had the same personnel that our half-Youth team beat in January but were now playing a seductive passing game with skill that had the Atkinson imprimatur stamped all over it. If all that were not sufficient cause for concern, the knowledge that a slip would allow Rovers to claim the title next Monday should have done the trick.

Instead, United's makeshift young team proved what class individual artists they are. Some performers are lost without a script, without the comforting presence of familiar sidekicks; they are life's functional session-men, reliant on routine and rote. United's boys are that special breed, mercurial talents able to improvise and create in any situation, the Hendrixes of football. 'Electric Ladland', *con brio*.

Had Cole's one-yard header gone in faintly the right direction after 60 seconds, we would have surely been spared most of the ensuing drama. Good job he missed then, really. Ignited by a ten minute vocal volley from the 4,000 Reds in the M&B stand, the match broiled and throbbed menacingly for the first half-hour, growing faster, sharper and sleeker by the second – and, if anything, City were having the better of it, until Nicky Butt began to assume an Inceian dominance in midfield. The time for calling him a 'boy' is now passed; tonight he was the complete man. Scholes – an Eric-worshipper who has a massive blow-up of the kung-fu kick on his wall – took on Cantona's old deep-lying role to increasing effect as United traded up-front punches with the Sky Blues. Sharpe's cheeky lob fell just short on 10 but Neville had to be sharp to rob Dion on 13; Choccy blasted wide from Cole on 16 but Wegerle was even closer after May allowed him a freebie on 18. Neville, despite a callous card for a minor infringement on City's headbutting chicken-impersonator, remained an absolute stalwart whilst Cole appeared to be as motivated as a Robson or Moran, even engaging in some crunching back-tackling on 17.

Fittingly, Cole's pantherish box movement provided the opener. On 33, he left two for dead before forcing a despairing parry from Gould, Scholes thrashing the rebound straight back into the net.

For the first time in weeks, the thousands of Reds (swelled by the hundreds that had infiltrated home ends in the best such incursion since Portman Road,) sang *Champions* with the full-throated verve of those who really believe it; a deafening *We Shall not be Moved* followed, seguing into five minutes of roaring passion that promised to inspire a deluge of goals. And they almost came too, as goalmouth scrambles and just-missed crosses abounded in front of the fist-slamming, shrieking Red hordes. This being '94/'95, however, when hopes are raised only to be dashed, no two or three goal rally was forthcoming as we once expected by right. Rather, an isolated City break produced a corner on 39, from which a loose shot was spawnily heeled in by the aforementioned unpronounceable little clucker. We heard City's boys at last, singing *Marching Altogether* after the prompt from the earsplitting tannoy. (I noted in passing that Coventry, the epitome and originator of the 'family club' philosophy, allow all their behind-goal lads and the away fans to stand as much as they like; unlike United, they use their PA to encourage rather than threaten the support. Merrett and Ramsden, take note . . .)

As if to emphasise with heated indignation how much City's goal had been against the run of play, Butt replied on 43 with a gorgeous curling drive that Eric would've been proud of; a minute later, Neville hit the bar with what we are sure was a wholly intentional side-booted bender. At half-time, a bunch of Midland trollops bounced artlessly around with all the sex appeal of Michel Vonk – Gothenberg standard they were not – as we waited impatiently for our destiny to be decided. For about five minutes after the break, as Peter denied Dion, then saved one-handed from the onrushing Cook, we were peering into the abyss. The upper tier responded on 50 with a rousing *Red and White Army* which seemed to galvanise the Red shirts; for the next twenty minutes, both the team and fans were rampant.

Two minutes after Strachan felled Scholes, turning an unsympathetic crowd firmly against him, United launched one of those classic three-man counters that linger in the mind for months. As the ever-alert Cole left Pressley sprawling and addressed the target, I had one of those 'Condor moments' that any Seventies child will understand. This was an archetypal Cole chance, the sort he used to bury with unerring accuracy at Newcastle. It seemed to be a defining moment, that split-second: as he rifled the ball home, didn't we all feel a burden lifted? Light-headed with relief, Reds took to their feet and launched the party, young and old alike. Pensioners dancing on seats is a sight to remember, although it was all too much for one poor old sod who promptly had a stroke – they carried him off gasping, but still grinning. The Cole songs set off a tremendous, non-stop medley of all the fave raves, including the Kippax song and *Forever and Ever* which only come out for an airing when true Reds are the dominant presence. A brief diversion into *We all hate Leeds*, at maximum Fergie-baiting volume, was inevitable once Strachan got Cole an absurd booking. As United applied ceaseless pressure, leavened by the odd piece of possessional piss-taking, we moved on to the night's highlight, a Cantona celebratory medley that drowned out the Coventry boos and apparently led Sky to comment that 'It sounds like 40,000, not 4,000'. We were all, players and fans, rolling home, coasting, cruising . . . and then Coventry scored. The goal, on 71, was dreadful, a Pressley free header on a rare City excursion upfield. For about four minutes, we sat in stunned silence, reeling from yet another typically '95 kick in the teeth. Having already watched United 'lose' the title three times this season, against 'Pool, Leeds and Chelsea, a fourth would have been simply unbearable.

But on 75, the cry of 'Sing yer hearts out' went up once more; gradually, we pulled ourselves together and started to drive the team on for one last push. The lads' heads lifted, none more so than Cole's, and when Richardson headed back from 40 yards, the Black Panther was there to pounce lethally, flicking the ball precisely over Gould before first-touching home. As he reeled away, glorying in both his own and United's resurrection, stabbing the air repeatedly as if he had Blackburn's body to hand, we erupted with the sort of melt-down nuclear ecstasy that you only get two or three times a season. The amount of man-to-man snogging rivalled that of the Oldham Wembley semi; lads raced into the concourses, bellowing to the heavens, roaring bestial howls up to the upper tier. Those few seconds were the best value 17 quid has ever had.

There was, of course, the obligatory last-gasp near-catastrophe as Peter saved wildly before Wegerle headed over with 15 seconds normal time remaining; the 200 agonizing seconds of injury-time, punctuated by a superb Hughes effort, ended with a final, defiant cry of 'champions' as Cole trotted over to salute us. Many said to me later that it had been the greatest awayday of the season and who could argue with that? It had been a perfect symbiosis of team and supporter effort, a vindication of everything true Reds believe. And if the short-term triumph isn't achieved, think of the long-term, when Eric returns to lead Butt, Scholes and Neville to greatness. 'The kids are all right', to say the least . . .

Team: Schmeichel; Neville, Irwin, May, Pallister, Sharpe, McClair, Scholes (Beckham), Butt, Hughes, Cole

7 *May:* SHEFFIELD WEDNESDAY AT HOME

Final Score: UNITED 1 Wednesday 0

Scorer: May 5

Attendance: 43,868

ONE ASSUMES THAT THE Coventry result had done wonders for the players' morale but it's unlikely to have surpassed the euphoric effect it had on us Reds, whose critical faculties now appeared to be as dodgy as a Bluenose's, strung out on the Highfield Road elixir. 'Pink' readers will be wearily familiar with the Blue letter-writer, T. Knott of Droylsden, who weekly proclaims forthcoming Maine Road miracles like a Derby win, a Cup Final or a Blue international call-up: he is the embodiment of the triumph of faith over experience, or rather hubris coming before nemesis. Virtually every Red I spoke to after Coventry proclaimed the inevitability of an Old Trafford Title hat-trick, in proud defiance of both the bookie's odds and the table's mathematics. Every time, I shuddered, thought of Mr Knott and mouthed 'For f*ck's sake shut up'. In a season where disaster has followed victory as invariably as evil fart follows curry, such naked self-confidence is usually asking for trouble.

Still, in such a situation, needing to win lest Rovers clinch the Title on VE night, who better to face than the woeful Sheffield Wednesday? Without Hirst, their autumn trump-card, they looked on paper about as likely to win as a Tory council candidate. So it proved to be on the pitch; Schmeichel's remarkable record of not conceding a home league goal since last Easter was never endangered.

Arriving on the concourse, there was the momentary horror of seeing the place apparently stuffed with Yorkies; on closer inspection, one realised that it was merely a *trompe l'oeil* caused by the preponderance of United third kits. You would think that this would have been the one match for which the terminally tasteless could've worn our true colours. Perhaps they get a kick out of resembling the opposition, a sort of footballing transvestism? How sad it would be if one or two of them had indeed been mistaken for Yorkies and taken a slap during the brief concourse kick-off at ten to four . . .

It soon transpired that Wednesday had sold so pitifully few tickets that they were comfortably accommodated in the back rows of the main stand, leaving 'L' entirely for Reds. It's come to something when a self-styled 'big club' gets out-supported by travelling Wombles. To think that it was once thought that Eric Cantona could have been contained by a club like that! No wonder he left so soon, unless it was the sight of Tango Man's hideous midriff that offended.

The complete lack of away support robbed the fixture of any essential import as a clash of grand old clubs; the fact that we were playing Yorkies became immaterial – it could have been any eleven men out there. This was about nothing but the three points – it was not an afternoon for inflatable sheep or inter-tribal repartee. Nor, as it happened, for good football either.

We all like a decent 90 minutes of value for our ticket money but who wouldn't have settled for a full-time whistle after, say, ten minutes? Two years ago, these two clubs had served up a similarly dire game, rescued at the death by the improbably orgasmic Mr Ugly. This time, the script ran in reverse. All the heroics, the drama and the passion were front-loaded into the blistering, opening salvoes, with Davey 'Bluenose' May emerging as an even more unlikely *homme du jour*. It was Orson Welles' life as a footie match – all Citizen Kane to start, with dribbling sherry commercials at the finalé.

For those first ten minutes we were all, fans and players, men possessed. The East End vocal barrage was monumental, as though inspired by the memory of Highfield Road and incited by the exhortations of Paul Ince and IMUSA, whose leaflet drop that day had urged us to be at our best. The Red-fan/Red-shirt symbiosis functioned beautifully. After only two minutes, Neville had already softened up the Owls' nervy defence; on four, Irwin's blaster was deflected away for a corner. Ten seconds later, David May was in the net, holding his ginger mop in his hands after his header was incredibly saved – fifty seconds later, it was his shot that nestled in the net. Scholes left Bright gawping, pulled back superbly and 'Ooh-ay' himself prissily side-footed past four stranded dummies. Perhaps Wednesday had taken in too much Red anti-May propaganda, considering him so useless as to not need marking; our Davey could not fail to exploit all the space he was given. Old Trafford, just finishing a rousing 'Allo Allo' as the ball nipped smartly home, erupted into that most unforeseen of tributes, 'David May, David May . . .' Two weeks ago, you could have got 500-1 against United doing the Double, odds that were still shorter than those offered on May's name being chorused by the K stand. It all worked out for Davey: his injury and substitution on 23 meant he had no time to do any damage, thus ending the day as an unmitigated hero. 'May'; 'hero'; call Mulder, this constitutes an X-file, Scully.

We were still mounting rallies of *We're gonna win the league* and *Champions* – unthinkable not too long ago – as Sharpe drove badly wide on 17 and Choccy's snapshot after Cole's shimmy was saved on 19. But by the time of the May substitution, bringing two United brothers together in happy recall of the Greenhoffs, the heat and drama had dissipated somewhat – the East Lower had even begun to turn their attention to Mexican waves. We had greedily expected a thorough bum-slapping of the Tykes to ensue but it was clearly not going to materialise. We were almost entirely widthless and a touch slow in the absence of both Giggs and Andrei. Sharpe in particular was as much of a let-down as he had been in our last Wednesday match. Apparently, meningitis can affect the hearing; presumably, the teenbait idol had misheard Fergie's instruction to 'go out and be a winger' as 'go out and be a wanker'. Fergie remarked later that he had picked the wrong team – correct! – but added that he ought to have played Butt instead of Scholes from the start. So much for Scholesy's crucial assist, then. Ask anyone else in the stadium, or indeed the known universe, and they would surely have told him that he ought to have played Butt, Highfield's man of the match, instead of the sodding McClair. The Fergie-McClair love affair was always disgustingly sickly anyway but is now turning stomachs to serious effect. A United 'zine today asked if Choccy had some incriminating pictures of Fergie *in flagrante* with an OT cleaning lady and was blackmailing his way into the team. The truth is that Fergie thinks Choccy is still a good player. Yes, it's hard to believe, dear reader, but it's a strange world; there are also still people who think the earth is flat. Probably the same people who make up the Choccy Fan Club, actually.

The second-half brought increased United pressure and chances but to a backdrop of seeping, insidious tension in the stands. Every minute passed was a minute closer to victory, of course, but equally a minute less for us to fight back should Sheffield snatch a horrendous equaliser. After all, we were playing with a makeshift defence, whose vulnerability would theoretically increase when Waddle eventually lurched onto the pitch. We needed a second, for the sake of our nails and dwindling fag supply.

Consequently, we spent the half switchbacking frenziedly between nervous, chattering, low-level hum and outright, from-the-diaphragm, ensemble bellowing. Hughes had sparked us off on 49, turning to us after winning a corner skirmish to demand a vocal upsurge. For the most part, he got it, although the tension of the moment meant that wit and originality was in short supply; we couldn't manage much more than the obvious, resorting to *Fergie's Red and White Army* whenever we flagged. The team responded with Sharpe and Ince being robbed at the last on 48 and 54; Hughes pulled appallingly wide on 56 but Cole's header on 62 was supreme, forcing a marvellous save from an invidious position.

Seven minutes later Cole was unlucky not to reach Choccy's cross and on 74 we were denied a blatant handball-penalty for the second game in succession. Referee Durkin, so good against Rovers, had appeared to have done an Elleray on us, granting every benefit of the doubt to the visitors. When the admittedly excellent Walker intercepted for the nth time to deny Butt on 78 after the one-touch move of the match, you could sense that the second was not going to come. Indeed, in the last five minute flurry of Yorkie corners and quarter-chances, as frantic whistling coruscated the air, another Red goal was furthest from our minds. We had to put our trust in the resilience of Pally and the bros – and in the guaranteed uselessness of Wednesday's strikers. Bart-Williams, in wasting a free-header with seconds to go, repaid our faith. The final whistle was greeted with a Mafekingian relief not seen since, er, the last United game. Never has the cliché 'It's the points that matter' been more appropriate. And if that last 30 minutes had seemed agonising, what of the next 30 hours wait for the Rovers-Geordies result? It's a shameful thing to admit but there can't have been many Reds spending VE Day reflecting on a struggle of 50 years ago, not with today's battle still raging . . . Elsewhere in this book, Keith Gillespie was described as the present and future of United. Now, in a weird sense, he remains just that. Could this most fondly-remembered of ex-Reds now put us back onto the path to the holy European grail?

Team: Schmeichel; G. Neville, Irwin, Pallister, May, Sharpe (P. Neville), McClair, Ince, Scholes (Butt), Hughes, Cole

10 May: SOUTHAMPTON AT HOME

Final Score: UNITED 2 Southampton 1

Scorers: Cole 21, Irwin (*pen*) 80

Attendance: 43,479

GILLESPIE DID HIS BEST for us, didn't he? But not even his Mickey Thomas impression could swing it: Rovers' 1-0 victory was as close as they could get to a Title-clinching win. On a night which witnessed other proud Title-holders, Arsenal, lose their own particular crown, we were faced with the simplest of duties. Anything less than three points would hand the Title to Rovers. There are many ways to lose a Title but doing so in front of your own kind without taking it to the line is one method to be avoided. The Saints promised to be their usual doughty, grouchy selves, coming in on a good run of form; as at the Dell, we were to need another late show special to pull our nuts from the fire.

They certainly seemed motivated enough, in contrast to their last gooseberry display at Old Trafford. Perhaps they were out to give their old muckers Shearer, Kenna and Flowers a hand. In Le Tissier's case, he appeared to have taken United's lack of interest in him rather bitterly. After months of dropping hints that he wouldn't mind donning a redder shirt, he showed up the previous week on *Fantasy Football* to praise Liverpool, sneer at United and belittle our support: 'I've played at Old Trafford during their bad times when it was only half-full,' he declared. His memory's clearly about as impressive as his work-rate – or as his comedic talents, if his pathetic display with Frank 'n' Dave is anything to go by. Naturally, he was given the bird all night, chants of 'You'll never play for England' mingling with observations on his humungous proboscis.

The pressurised circumstances apart, this was a special night in any event. The last home game of the season always has that sentimental edge to it, sharpened tonight by the realisation that this was the last congregation of this golden era. The 'new Old Trafford', launched at the end of '92, had turned out to be a mere staging post to something much bigger. The demolition crews would be in within days. In truth, we had only just got settled down into this configuration of the ground; now we were all to be uprooted once more, with the shape and sociology of OT '96 a blank page to be filled. This first version of the all-seater OT has had its problems, well-documented elsewhere, but it had been the background to a golden era, reigned over by King Eric. For that reason alone, it will always be fondly remembered, forever intertwined with memories of Blackburn and Wednesday '93, City and Barca '94. Let us just hope that its successor proves to be an improvement and a host to even greater glories rather than a step into a horrendous new world of ultra-sanitised family entertainment. That largely depends on you: get involved now, join the IMUSA or forever hold your peace should the Merrets and Ramsdens of this world succeed in creating a new OT in their own image.

If we're musing upon the future of the ground, it should be noted that tonight's game was not a complete sell-out for the first time since the league season started, as a 'zine editor pointed out with a knowing smile. Perverse though it may seem to take pleasure in 400 unsold tickets, his reasoning was sound. Clearly, the glory-hunters and part-timers at application time had discounted our chances and couldn't be bothered coming to a dead rubber game, which was how it looked when Rovers were six or eight ahead. It simply validated the hard-core fans' argument that United should beware lest they alienate local working-class support with their pricing and behavioural policies; for if less successful seasons are ahead, they will struggle to fill a 55,000 capacity. Will Mr and Mrs fforbes-Smythe from Surrey want to shell out £100 for their family at a midweek game if United are, say, only third in the league? We doubt it. And if the four Salford lads who once would have stepped in to fill the breach, whatever United's position, have long since been discouraged from coming, United will be left clutching batches of unwanted tickets. As enjoyable as it would be to see United's self-styled business experts with copious egg on their fat faces, that would be to the detriment of all United fans, which is why we all have a duty to save the suits from the consequences of their own short-termist stupidity. For if they make mistakes, it's we who'll eventually have to pay for them.

For the first few minutes, all seemed reassuringly in order: a deafening opening vocal assault by both West and East, rewarded by the habitual awful early misses by Hughes and Sharpe. Sparky's was, if anything, even worse than the howler from the last game, as if he was somehow unwilling to give us an easy time, preferring to stoke up last-gasp dramatics. One or two cynics made mention of his record since he agreed a new contract; had a certain complacency replaced a previous raging hunger? Early fouls by Ben Ali and Monkou gave us another familiar indication of what was supposed to come – clogging, blanket away defence punctuated by the odd speculative hoof. Within a minute, however, we witnessed the most unwelcome intervention by a Charlton since Sir Bobby's outburst on *l'affaire Cantona*. Peter could only claw a lob into the lad's path, who became the first to score an Old Trafford league goal against the Dane since April '94. Such was the first appearance of a rare species tonight. The second was the welcome return of traditional United supporting. Instead of allowing our fervour to seep away after the first ten minutes, neither West nor East would relent. Straight up onto their feet after the double-shock opener, Reds kept the terrace hit-mix coming, unfurling rousing renditions of *Forever and Ever, We'll Never Die* and *We Love United*. The lack of part-timers was evident in the passionate sound. No sooner had Watson narrowly missed a chance for a Title-killing second than we were up again with a furious *Red and White Army*, which seemed to drive Pally forward with vicious intent. His header cannoned off the post as United swirled through a flurry of corners, half-chances and cavalry charge drives. The goal attempt tally careered towards double-figures as a trailing United, ironically making one of their best openings for weeks, besieged a quivering Saints defence. On 21, justice was done; as Saints fumbled about in a manner that would induce a stroke in Alan Hansen, Cole demonstrated his velvetish first touch before burying the equaliser. Few could now doubt his application and commitment – and as Trevor Francis would surely have been anxious to point out, Cole had given up witnessing his son's birth in order to join the Red crusade. Footie first, women and children second – a man after our own hearts . . .

Until the half-hour, United looked assured of a second but Sharpe and Bruce were both denied, the former forcing a top save from a curler, the latter finding Andy Cole in the road. Both fans and team took a well-deserved breather as half-time approached which Le Tissier was laughably unable to take advantage of, his efforts on 32 and 37 ballooning hilariously over the bar. Already booked on 30, he slunk out of the game, later to be subbed; Cantona made more of an impact on the night's proceedings than him without even stepping onto the field of play. Seven million quid player? – bunch of arse, mate.

Emboldened by their last ever half-time drink together, J stand came out taunting 'Can you hear the K stand sing?'; within minutes K were back at their best. As Irwin's blaster was pushed into the side-netting on 48, with Ince forcing an even better save seconds later, the crowd re-ignited with a roaring, defiant *We shall not be moved*. Butt and

Sharpe answered with close calls on 52 and 53 as the travelling Saints subsumed into silence, mercifully ending their tediously repetitive *As the Saints*. But once Choccy had miscued atrociously wide on 57, the game seemed to slip from our grasp. Saints began to creep forward, sensing their moment, as our structured songs were replaced by raucous, howling guttural cries. On 66, we even went into the slow, drawled 'Yoo-ni-ted', a classic last-stand sound last heard en masse at the Ullevi. With increasing desperation, even old Brucey was now up, snuffling away around the box, leaving exploitable holes which Peter had to be alert to on 68. Cole sidenetted a good chance from Butt on 69 but it was clearly time for a substitution. Astonishingly, Hughes was the man to come off, in a dark reminder of the '92's tactical errors – surely Fergie had confused the numbers 10 and 9? Brucey, frantically trying to reprise his Wednesday '93 role, couldn't quite punch through an epic goalmouth melée on 75. We needed a miracle and – as the third rarity of the night – got one with ten to go. An Old Trafford penalty for United, that most endangered of species, awarded for the slyest tug on Andy's shirt. Those of us in the East Lower could see it, of course, but scarcely bothered to appeal, knowing full well that an opponent would have to draw a Magnum and blow someone's head away to be penalised by a spot-kick here. However, penalties seem to be Danson's strong point, having already spotted Gordon 'Swan Lake' Watson's dive in our box on 46. As every observer – bar Alan Hansen, of course – later agreed, the ref had done superbly. As Reds everywhere peeped through shaking fingers or looked up to the heavens, Denis came forward in the King's absence to slash home. Just for tonight, Denis was at least the Prince of Old Trafford; the acme of prosaic dependability had saved us at a time when we had lost all those of poetic flair. There could be no more apt saviour.

If the ensuing party wasn't quite at the level of Easter '93, it was at least in the same Premier League of exultation. Right until the 93:13 whistle, Reds in every stand stayed up, bellowing the best *O Me Lads* and *We'll Never Die* for months. As a collared-up Eric made a prodigal return, joining the Red-shirted heroes for the lap of honour, *Glory Glory* rang out resoundingly. Perhaps all we had done was to prolong the tension until 5.45 on Sunday, for the benefit of Sky TV above all; perhaps, as those singing all the way down Warwick Road suspected, our glory would be only in final noble defeat rather than victorious hat-trick. But at least we had departed the Old Trafford stage still as Champions - and next time we salute our end of season boys, we know they'll be Champions again, right?

Team: Schmeichel; Neville, Irwin, Bruce, Pallister, Sharpe, Ince, Butt, McClair, Hughes (Scholes), Cole

14 May: WEST HAM UTD AWAY

Final Score: West Ham 1 UNITED 1

Scorer: McClair 52

Attendance: 24,783

SADLY, THIS BEING LARGELY a work of non-fiction, no happy ending can be guaranteed, at least not for this part of the story anyway. To be honest, the vast majority who travelled across the wastelands of East London to the home of the original neanderthal did so more in slim hope than fervent expectation. The 3,500 Reds packing the North Lower knew the odds as well as Sky TV and the FA: Sky Sports One had laid on the big show treatment for Anfield, not Upton Park, whilst the real trophy was up north too, a replica standing in the Upton bowels should the unexpected occur. Of nine possible result combinations in the simultaneous double-header, only two would give United the title, so that made it 7-2 against for a start. Moreover, a United win at West Ham is a turn-up at the best of times – and being two points adrift with only half our Double team available did not constitute anything like 'the best of times'. Above all, Rovers could not have asked for a more sympathetic venue. Many of us had long since discounted any likelihood of Liverpool doing Rovers and thus half-handing us the Title; once the Coca Cola Cup was in Scouse sticky fingers, the result appeared to be the most foregone of conclusions. As it happened, the Liverpool team showed rather more self-respect than their fans. Murkeydive sports shops reported mass sales of Rovers scarves and shirts in the run-up, with a majority of Dirties seemingly desperate to witness a home defeat. A noble few stood loyal to the cause, prompting a punch-up in the Kop between the two schools in scenes reminiscent of City at Villa in '93. There is, I suppose, a perverse pleasure in seeing the twisted, bitter-soaked effect United's pre-eminence has had on once-proud and still-loathed rivals. There were few other pleasures on offer to Red palates today.

For those who like an extra touch of spice, however, there was at least the prospect of some serious rucking to be had. The temptation to go head-to-head(butt) with London's most fearsome firms was too much to resist for Red Army veterans, especially given the possible bonus of a warm-up kickabout with Leeds' fans down for the Tottenham game. Well-mannered invitations flew around K stand at the previous home games, offering younger lads who'd distinguished themselves on earlier battlefields the chance to join Red *confrères* in London. The result was evident to all with an eye for these things – Upton Park brought together the most impressive reunion of Red warriors for many a year. On the Saturday night, a subsect of Cockney Reds supposedly launched a pre-emptive, King's Cross action against some wandering Sheep, allegedly with the aid of CS gas canisters, an amusingly ironic choice given Leeds' past predilection for this particular weapon; the Red victory was apparently humiliatingly overwhelming. Consequently, much of Sunday morning was filled with the sound of scuffling trainers around Euston's environs as Hammers were joined by aggrieved and vengeful Scum seeking Reds. The local porkers, desperate to remove the problem away from central London (and no doubt quite happy for firms to kick each other to death out in the sticks) spent a frantic few hours setting up buffer zones, clearing pubs and alleyways and conducting mass line-up searches in an attempt to divide and rule the antagonistic tribes. Typically they went spectacularly over the top, giving an object lesson in the iniquities of the Criminal Justice Act.

In the Kennedy Hotel, a respectable place that has a soft spot for big bar-spending Reds, around 150 United fans were quietly supping Sunday pints when scores of police with dogs invaded the lounge at 10.30 in a scene reminiscent of a more nightmarish moment from *Brazil*. Apparently believing a United attack on Leeds was imminent – no doubt on the basis of notoriously crap 'police intelligence' – they affected to arrest all 150 for being 'likely to cause a breach of the peace', without attempting to discriminate between those in attendance. It seems that in modern Britain, more than nine people having a relaxing drink in a four-star hotel is now a criminal offence. Needless to say, the owners were non-plussed; they had certainly not called the police and had had no need to do so. All the lads were carted off, searched, held for up to two hours outside as police videoed them and took names and addresses of everyone, before they were escorted to a commandeered tube for despatch to the east. Now whilst it may have been true that several main United boys were allegedly in this group, the majority were your average, clean-record boys; certainly no assault on Leeds was on the agenda, merely some idle chat about meeting Hammers at the 'Denmark'. Thanks to police hysteria, all these lads now risk being placed on every 'hoolie list' in Europe, to face God knows what travails at future aways and Euro trips. These days, you no longer have to be charged, tried and convicted to become *persona non grata*; on any policeman's whim, your appearance, however innocent, on a video tape or a name and address list is sufficient. Emerging at Upton Park to form a mass escort group, they were met by screeching packs of Hammers who'd rushed out of various vaults and lounge bars; faced by both the police as well as numerically and physically dominant Reds, the London pondlife settled for a vocal, rather than pugilistic assault.

A couple of splinter groups did have a brief engagement by the underground market; the police response was to scarper in panic. Had more discovered that this is what an East London police escort really entails, a mammoth battle would surely have ensued. What a telling contrast to the police's earlier behaviour: they seem keen to act hard when it's entirely unnecessary but less so when actually required to do their duty. 'Pigs' is too mild an epithet for them: and truly, the Criminal Justice Act is simply an Arsehole's Charter.

Red teens, tagging onto their elders as they marched into the away enclosure and jibbed into the ground with imperial swagger, betrayed the excitement they felt that would have been familiar to those of us who started going in the Seventies and Eighties. 'Did you see Big Sam/Mad Mickey/Psycho Barney?' etc etc they gabbled buzzingly. 'It's gonna go off big-style after,' they would exclaim, half in thrilled anticipation, half in terror. The general consensus was that both sides had some of the tastiest-looking, 'scary' boys seen for some time. For many, as full-time approached, the question was not only 'are we gonna get out of here with our Title intact?' but also 'are we gonna escape with our *heads* intact?'

Inside the strangely unimpressive Upton Park, nowhere near as claustrophobically atmospheric as it appears to be on TV, Reds of different generations could reflect on past epochal experiences there. 1992 was, of course, particularly relevant at that moment; those who had been there that dreadful night could at least take comfort in the fact that whatever horrors unfolded, nothing could be worse than that 1-0 defeat and what it signified back then. Some would have been there in 1975, when the Red Army was at its peak and the mother of all riots ensued; perhaps they could taste a similar tang of cordite in the air today. ('Look up there,' chuckled Lance cheerfully as he pointed to the Hammer-filled Upper tier, 'made for a Dublin re-run or what? Same boys, after all.' Thanks, Lance.)

And finally, there were a handful who'd been here in 1967, the last time we needed a final day win for the title and the first time that the Red Army announced itself to both the Hammers and the nation at large by invading the home end with tabloid-filling ferocity. I guess 1995 will now take its place in that historical roll-call, the day when we narrowly missed both the greatest Title and the greatest punch-up of the decade. Hardly the stuff of glory but unforgettable nonetheless.

As the teams prepared for kick-off, Ince received a predictably warm Cockney welcome although at least we were spared last year's banana-chucking exhibition. Self-consciously aware of the media gaze, Hammers eschewed the overt racism of '94; subsequently their hollering and growling lost a lot of its force. Deprived of the incendiary inspiration that black-baiting brings to your average Hammer, their hearts didn't seem to be in it. A clutch of morons in their East Lower waved a collection of pathetic 'Judas' cards, so small as to be almost invisible, whilst throwing the odd aeroplane pose. I noted one or two beefy 30-something Reds carefully committing their visages to memory, no doubt as a prelude to later asking them if they'd care to repeat their opinions of Mr Ince and the Busby Babes . . . We were in our black kit, probably for the last time. Last year, this had been our 'lucky' garb, the black seeming to speak of the magical, devilish arts we expounded on the field. Symbolically, this season it has become a simple funereal black, already the harbinger of disaster at the Nou Camp and Anfield, today to complete a hat trick of tragedy as we buried our title hopes.

Hughes, astonishingly, had been left on the bench, too overt a reminder of 1992 to ignore. To put it mildly, this did not go down too well with the North Lower Reds, who detected the smell of yet another Tinkerbell/Fergie F*ckwit farty selection. Later defending what we mainly considered one 'rotation' too far, Fergie remarked that he wanted a first-half five-man midfield so that we 'wouldn't be swamped'. West Ham disregarded the tactical script and promptly swamped us anyway. For more than half-an-hour, they made us look as nerve-ridden and bottled-out as, say, Blackburn. They already deserved to be ahead when they hit the bar; ex-Bluenose Hughes rectified the injustice with a superb strike on 30. In a day of joy for the nation's every Red-hater, an extra dollop of ecstasy just for our Bitter friends.

As West Ham fans had already kindly informed us, that goal was not the only deficit we faced. For only the second time in my life, I had Radio Five quivering excitedly in my ear which was now, within

30 seconds of telling me 'Pool were 'all over' Rovers, orgasmically reporting Shearer's goal. Looking up, I could instantly see how many Reds were packing ear-pieces – they were the ones with their heads collapsing between their knees as if about to vomit. At least on occasions such as these, when mainly true Reds are in attendance, we behave as we should; within seconds of both Hughes and Shearer goals, we were all on our feet, roaring defiance, launching the fightback. Cole and Bruce both responded, the former smacking the post, the latter playing Romario and almost winning a penalty. Nevertheless, we looked second best as half-time arrived to Red gratitude. Where were two goals going to come from? Even if they miraculously arrived, who could expect Liverpool to do anything but play out time? The half-time singing in the bars below was desultory and remorseful, in marked contrast to the vibrant, almost stupid frenzy of those making the leaps-of-faith at five to four. A passing 'zine editor remarked that three goals in the two games in 45 minutes was hardly beyond the realms of possibility – how right he was. Unfortunately, the division of spoils was another matter. Liverpool got greedy; we were left to starve.

Hughes rumbled onto the pitch and proceeded to transform our game. Back with a familiar pattern, we were now at least able to salvage some pride. Sharpe's header brought, with ominous portent, a class save from Ludo; minutes later, we were level as an unmarked Choccy headed home with unusual accuracy. There was no bedlam in the stands yet, however, as few yet dared to allow any mad hopes to build up within; it was more a chorus of relief in appreciation of a restored self-respect. The bedlam was not long in coming though. Hundreds of heads sprang up, wires and earpieces flailing everywhere, as the transistorised brigades bellowed news of Liverpool's equaliser. As one, the thousands took to their feet, there to stay for the duration, bar the odd trembling exit of those who couldn't take any more – all stood in barely restrained anticipation of a goal that never came.

To be fair, for a ten minute spell, the driven Hammers seemed the likelier to score as Peter and the wondrous Bogman performed last-gasp heroics at the feet of 'Up 'Is Arse' Morley and the excellent Holmes. The last quarter-hour, though, especially when Scholes came on for the big push over the top, was a straightforward medieval siege of increasing barbarity around the Hammers goal. The time for subtleties and art had long since passed; this was pure bayonets-out, hand-to-hand bludgeoning, with Scholes providing the occasional rapier ball through to the hapless Cole. What made the sight of this frantic, grasping, despairing lungefest even worse was that it took place at the south stand end. From our vantage point, every chance looked twice as good, every shot twice as wicked, every save twice as unbelievable as distance played its optical tricks. Miklosko's performance, saving from Hughes and Cole in particular, conjured up horrendous folk memories of another last stand 1-1 draw, when an East European goalie denied England's finest (*sic*) in 1973. Terry Butcher once opined in *All Played Out* that 'all East Europeans smell' but the only whiff with Ludo was of him coming up with the ball once more, smelling of roses – roses that now looked likely to adorn the coffin containing our title's ashes.

Quite simply, our goalscoring knack had deserted us at the worst possible moment. Having climaxed once through Choccy, our frontline resembled a bunch of exhausted guys, frantically bashing their bishops in a doomed attempt to get it up and in the gaping, willing goal-hole just one more time before the game got fed up of waiting, hoisted up her knickers and left in an unsatisfied huff. The Gestapo used to slowly extract fingernails in their torture sessions; here, we were doing it ourselves as the purgatory endured, Reds all around gnawing away down to the cuticles, breaking off for the occasional, strangulated song on Schmeichel's urging. The tunes of noble defeat emerged as the 90 came up: *Forever and Ever, We'll Support . . ., We Love United . . .* et al. For the rubrophobic public watching on TV, our final half-chances to skewer their 'happy ending' must have seemed like the movie villain's last grasping fumbles for the gun as he clings to the edge of a precipice. But in proper Sunday matinee style, the villain is thwarted. The whistle goes (as Liverpool, in a final kick in the teeth, score again) and we are flung into the abyss, the season's life flashing before our eyes. A nation rejoices as Shearer, the clean-cut hero, lifts the trophy. As for us, having been transported by what all have dubbed 'a roller-coaster season' in which triumph has followed disaster with metronomic regularity, the power was cut at just the wrong moment, leaving us trundling in a trough with peaks behind and ahead.

We saluted the forlorn, gallant eleven, metaphorically turned up our collars and set forth to face the hordes outside (and, from there, the rest of the world) without the Champions shield that we'd borne so proudly for two years and twelve days. It hurt – but it wasn't 1992: at least this time we'd had a Title to lose in the first place. And for the first time, the value of the '92 experience became clear. Because if you'd been through that, you could get through this. After all, we hadn't thrown it away; we were always the chasers, reliant on a fall up ahead. Even today, closer than ever with 25 left, we still had a mile to go, still needed our luck to hold elsewhere. Never did we reach that most desirable state of holding our fate in our own hands.

Stepping outside Upton Park was akin to crossing from the maelstrom of a tornado into the calm, still eye of the storm. It felt like the temperature had suddenly plunged 20 degrees after the heat of those final moments. The chill stares of the assembling Hammers added further ice to the ambience. The police had disappeared. Well, actually they were posted every 50 yards but given the terrain and circumstances, they might as well have all gone home, such was the minimal sense of presence they bore. In the event, the fact that the Hammers had their on–pitch end–of–season rigmaroles to attend to meant that all 24,000 did not flood out simultaneously, which reduced the potential for conflict somewhat. Those that wanted to escape could do so; those developing little firms down the High Street didn't really manage to engineer the situation they required. There were the usual skirmishes and verbals, of course, and those heading for coaches had the odd gauntlet to run but it never really kicked off properly. It didn't help those gagging for a bit that identities were a touch confused, thanks to the lack of colours and lack of familiarity; after years of making do with small–scale rucks, it appeared that the mechanics of a mass set–to were beyond them. Everyone seemed a little ring–rusty. Whether this was the last hurrah for a dying tradition or the first faltering steps to a new era of mass aggro remains to be seen. But such was the sense of exhilarated expectancy created amongst some by the mere sight of large firms, you'd suspect that the latter might be the case.

Later, I wandered through central London, around Holborn and the like, stopping for drinks and watching dazed, fazed Reds staggering about the otherwise deserted streets. News came in that West Ham had finally got the fight they wanted so keenly, wrecking a pub in Plaistow and putting nine pigs in hospital. They had, apparently, begun to fight amongst their own kind. When a love of aggro overcomes your love of your own, you've surely lost the plot. We watched some TV coverage of the revolting Anfield love-in and listened to the lack of magnanimity as Wilcox and Shearer belittled United's injury problems and trumpeted their 'bottle'. A Red in the bar noted wryly that Rovers' definition of 'bottle' appeared to include losing three of their last five games. Indeed: it had been the most unconvincing finish by Champions in memory, Rovers stumbling half-crippled to the post, looking back in panic at their hardier rivals to see with relief that they'd got stuck in the thickets of the last hurdle.

A Red-hater swirling drunkenly around the vault lambasted Steve Bruce for complaining about the penalty he should've had, as blatant as the one denied against Chelsea. 'F*ckin' bad loser.' he growled. Nice one, Brucey, I thought. Loathsome 'good losers' are just that - losers. Being 'sporting' in defeat is for passionless old farts like amateur cricketers or for media-conscious, self-promoting sycophants like Liverpool fans clapping Arsenal in '89. As the United song goes, 'We're a right bunch of bastards when we lose'. Are Rovers 'worthy' champions? Limping, bottle-broken to the finish? Beaten three times by us? Never victorious against good opposition? The most boring team outside Highbury? When half our team were out and being denied blatant goals and penalties? When they can't fill their ground or exist without an inflationary sugar-daddy? Would they ever have got within a point of us had *their* star player been banned for five months? 'Well done, Rovers' my arse. Jammy whippet-shagging bastards, more like. As the United fax to Rovers put it: 'Keep it warm – we'll be back for it next season.'

As one of the fanzine coaches pulled out, an old Hammer was stood on the pavement, holding a sign saying 'Hard luck United. Have a safe journey home.' Coach steward Steve, the man with Manchester's best haircut, burst out through the roof flap and yelled at the sad sod: 'And I hope you get f*ckin' run over, you old bastard.' Now *that's* Red attitude for you.

The nation's most hated supporters traipsed back up north to contemplate defeat and their new status of second-best. Typically, all the coaches were delayed in snarled-up traffic and the 8.00 train was not only dry but enormously late. What an end to the day, to be stuck by some dodgy signals past midnight with only a can of coke for comfort. Some would have got home in time for the reruns and masochistically watched the Rovers' celebrations. Perhaps that little bit of them that remains a general 'football supporter' rather than simply a raving Red would have had some twinge of empathy with the Rovers contingent. After all, for your average, non-part-time Rover – and there are a few thousand – what a fairytale this had been. You'd have to be totally soulless not to appreciate that. Moreover, we above all should be able to empathise and identify with genuine supporters who've had to wait decades for a title. Surely we could see in their contorted joyous faces something of what we felt back in '93. And some of them aren't a bad lot, after all; at least they're Lancastrians, the next best thing to being a Mancunian. Above all, better them as Champions than the Scum, Dirties or Bitters.

All these traces of goodwill are fine up to a point, Lord Copper – and they don't remain at the forefront of the mind for long when either Dalglish, Shearer, Batty or any of Rovers' scummier BNP fans are in vision. But when I read this in the *Independent*, I remember why Rovers remain inherently worth hating, at least to some degree: 'Rovers have not bought the title; they have simply played the modern game better'. Firstly, if the 'modern game' entails flair-free percentage football played by battling near-automatons, then God help the game. We're having none of it. As Fergie said, we would not accept winning trophies by playing that way. Secondly – and this is a fundamental existential matter – it isn't so much that Blackburn have bought the title (for, *pace Independent*, they largely have) but that it is specifically Jack Walker who has provided the wherewithal. United spend as much as anyone. We too could be said to have 'bought' trophies both now and in the pre-Fergie past. The difference is that all United's money comes from United fans; there are no external benefactors aside from the secondary sources such as Sky TV and Sharp.

When MUFC buy a player, or build a stand, they do so almost entirely with money that we fans have ourselves worked for and handed over to the Club in exchange for tickets and merchandise. We have literally built this Club and created our success through our own sweat and toil. In common with the nation's other great, mass-supported clubs, we have succeeded honestly. Rovers, who would collapse without Walker's money, have not earned that success. Those who work for and earn success deserve it when it comes. There is no such linkage at Rovers. Left to succeed on their own merits, Blackburn town could only produce a middling first division club. Like Parma and Monaco, Rovers are the worst feature of modern, mogul-dominated sport: the artificial, plastic Club. They are, sadly, well-suited to the coming Brave New World of contrived Superleagues, media-driven competitions and crowds replaced by pay-per-view telespectators. In a sense, they are more repulsive than Leeds, Liverpool or City could ever be; these, at least, are true 'organic' Clubs.

The last word on the loss of our crown must go to one of the Reds of the year. Emerging from Upton Park almost in tears, Paddy Crerand spoke to a couple of gutted lads. 'You know, if we'd won the title this time, I think we'd never have lost it again.' Hyperbolic, perhaps, but containing two tantalising thoughts. If we had won it, given the sheer enormity of the task we faced and the obstacles we had to overcome, it would surely have been an achievement on a par with 1968. And if United could win in such adverse circumstances, what hope for the rest in brighter future days when Eric and the rest return and when United's life resumes a less troubled path? We haven't won it, of course: like all past Double-winners, it has been too much to ask, although we came closer than any other has managed. Yet the warning for the rest remains in force. We are still placed to establish a triumphant dynasty that could dwarf even that once created by Liverpool. Second-place, maybe: second-best, never.

Team: Schmeichel; Neville, Irwin, Bruce, Pallister, Butt (Hughes) Ince, Keane (Scholes), Sharpe, McClair, Cole.

20 May: EVERTON AT WEMBLEY – FA CUP FINAL

Final Score: Everton 1 UNITED 0

Attendance: 79,592

TEN YEARS AGO, WHEN these teams previously met at a Cup Final, was a generation ago in football terms. Pre-Heysel, pre-Hillsboro' and pre-Taylor Wembley Stadium may still, as the song goes, have been 'shit' but at least you could stand up and party. Moreover, for United fans, the FA Cup still had its magic, a creator of glory purely on its own terms; pre-Fergie and post-Busby, it was after all just about all we had. That epic '85 Final, won by Norman's solo brilliance, was surely the last of its kind for us. Since then, the FA Cup Finals in which we've appeared have carried too much baggage and have held too much import to be appreciated solely for their own intrinsic glory. Consequently, the atmosphere and excitement surrounding them have diminished a little at each turn, paralleling the decline in the enjoyment offered by the stadium's features as the 'terraces' disappeared. In 1990, victory was essential to save the Ferguson dynasty and give us a silver-plated base camp from which to attempt the game's summit. In 1994, victory was not for the sake of the Cup itself but for the Double, necessary to top the buzz of 1993. And in 1995, the FA Cup represented simply a piece of silverware, without which we would end this incredible season cruelly empty-handed after five consecutive years of trophies.

In retrospect, it's so obvious: after a season like this, how blind we were not to see that a final week's Double defeat was a perfectly apt finish. Frankly, the vibes in Cup week had been lousy for a start. When the players assembled for the midweek press conference, ostensibly about the players' pool, the blank, sullen looks on their faces were hardly inspirational for Red viewers. The brave talk about 'putting Sunday behind us' scarcely convinced; there seemed to be no relish for the task ahead, rather an apparent dread of what defeat would entail. And when you've just lost the big one, the prospect of an imminent play-off for an inferior consolation prize is understandably less than adequate compensation. Newspaper stories about Giggsy's girl couldn't have helped our appointed saviour much. Nor was the Kanchelskis splash likely to improve morale; the quotes about Fergie being 'unbearable' were supposedly his agent's. In contrast, Everton's squad and fans appeared to be as happy as Scousers in shit. What did they have to lose? Furthermore, with a fit squad, relegation avoided and the memory of a recent 1-0 win over us, why shouldn't they have felt confidently carefree?

There were, of course, predictable howls from Merseyside about tickets. An overnight queue of Blues clutching four - four! - match tokens were denied their 'right' to go to Wembley and filled the media with their whinges. Reds holding 25 tokens in a similar quandary remained less than sympathetic. Despite the FA policy of allocating tickets on the basis of average gates, both Clubs received 26,000 - enough to accommodate Goodison's entire average crowd but only 60 per cent of ours. The usual scandal ensued as the other 27,000 wended their way from the hands of the old fart network via various criminals and shysters to the hard-up hard-core, forced to put up to £400 for a £35 seat. No doubt in a year's time a list of a dozen names will be published, almost all 'normal' fans, to be banned for years from either OT or Wembley whilst the corporate scam-merchants will escape unpunished. Is it any wonder that the FA is held in even less esteem than the Major government? There is, apparently, a rule that FA Cup Final tickets must be held by recipients for a year in case the FA wish to check on their eventual destination. An objective analyst seeking to end this FA Cup Final farrago might prescribe a recall of all 27,000 non-Finalist tickets in order to smoke out the profiteers. What are the chances of this happening? The same as Rovers have of winning the Euro Cup. The Football Association – crap on crime, crap on the causes of crime, as sleazebuster Blair might have said.

Advance parties from the two Clubs' hard-cores were already in town in force on the Friday night. There had been much talk in Blue enclaves of Murkeydive of them 'mobbing up to do United' but in the event, Reds under attack in Leicester Square and Euston acquitted themselves rather successfully, with the alleged help of CS gas canisters in the latter's case. By Saturday, the mood had improved. If the Willesden Green knees-up didn't hit the heights of previous years, the tribal gathering at the Torch was as buzzing as any past. Once MC Boyle had arrived to ego-boosting cheers, Reds put on their own impromptu show for the passing public heading towards Wembley Way as the clutch of silent Evertonians watching open-mouthed at the car park's south end. As those who'd been drinking since seven slammed down the last cans and the exhibitionists clambered all over the roof, buttocks akimbo, we lurched through every terrace classic, pausing to lob the odd harmless bottle at Blue coaches screeching away. Surreal sight of the day: lorries bearing Eric Nike ad billboards cruising slowly past as hundreds of Reds raised their glasses to bellow *Eric The King* at them. Such passion directed at two inanimate dimensions – had Eric himself sauntered past at any point, it would have been spontaneous emissions all round. Sadly, these were the last happy hours to be had of the season but at least some part of the Wembley experience retains a touch of magic. There were even Blues amongst us, those who truly hate Liverpool, pissed up and buzzing, delighted to join the Cantona hosannahs: even amidst swine, there are pearls.

In truth, Evertonians were more imbued with that Final spirit than we were. They had made the effort, dressing up in the regulation stupid gear, carrying as many banners and props as they could steal, tottering around under ridiculous wigs and behaving like country yokels on their first city-trip. For blasé, even tired, Reds, many making their ninth Wembley trip this decade, how could it possibly mean the same? Perhaps this is why so few seemed to begrudge Everton their triumph afterwards, why so few seemed to be as gutted as last Sunday. Nineties United, as opposed to Eighties or Seventies, have bigger fish to fry now. When once a Final defeat such as '79 or '76 was wrist-slittingly catastrophic, now we have our real hopes invested elsewhere, in Titles and Euro triumphs. Such is progress – it's good we have all grown up but the loss of childhood pleasures is tinged with regret.

Three o'clock arrived, with United veterans having already lost to Everton's after dominating the game. 'Hope that's not an omen,' my partner remarked nervously. The atmosphere, it has to be admitted, was unbelievably subdued at both ends. This, then, is the Wembley experience for which some were paying five grand at five minutes to three. Two sets of fans who can barely hear each other watching two sets of players they can barely see – and playing football which was barely good enough to keep you awake. Despite Sharpe's two early openings, a soppy header and a crassly mishit volley, it was evident within minutes that our standard of passing, movement and penetration was woefully below the minimum we expect. Even at nil-nil, we looked tired and dispirited; above all – and not surprisingly given the absence of Giggs, Eric, Andrei and Cole – we totally lacked imagination. Without those players, we just looked like a decent Premiership side, and one that could be beaten if matched for defensive quality, tackling and commitment. Everton, of course could do just that.

When they broke with four against two on the half-hour, the audible intake of breath at our end spoke of the inevitability of what transpired. It was our only serious back four lapse of the day and, fittingly for such an appalling game, was the Cup decider. When Rideout headed home, Brucey was unable to jump for it, having been injured five minutes before. In a season as much thwarted by injury as the more infamous suspensions, this too was entirely appropriate. How pleasing for the nation's Red-haters that all our 'villains' should be found wanting too; Hughes met his match in Unsworth, ironically a Red as a youth and a former Fergie target; Ince, with court case imminent, lacked concentration; Keane, still not fully fit, was never involved enough even to get close to stamping on anyone. More typically, Choccy was missing in action for much of the 90 whilst Sharpe, often accused of coasting through the minor games, was now unable to influence the majors either. Only Nicky Butt and Gary Neville, the latter filling heroically in central defence after the break, enhanced their reputations.

The second half, naturally, was better all round; it couldn't possibly have been worse. For the first time in his career, substitute Giggs blossomed in a Final, providing some of the inspiration and vision so sorely missed beforehand. At first, everything we tried continued to fly wildly over the bar as if someone had infiltrated USA '94 balls but gradually our sights adjusted. As Reds on 60 began the first, great *Red and White Army* of the day on Peter's urging, we closed further in. Sharpe muffed again from Giggs' ball, McClair lofted one onto the bar and then came the crux of the game. When Giggs found Scholes at inside-right, his first-time drive forced Southall into a reaction save that defied his years and belly; somehow Paul failed to push the rebound through the near-post gap. Although Pally too was to come close with a header, the save was easier than showman Neville made it look; to all intents and purposes, our chance had passed. In a year which has seen the kids rescue us so often, it would have been just reward for Scholes to have saved us today; and for our second half siege, allowing Everton but one chance, it would have been justice on the day. As Fergie pointed out, Everton simply refused to play in the second half but then, this wasn't really a day for football as we know it. The dourest United Final since '76 had been won almost by default through a solitary cock-up, a gruel-thin kind of glory for a victor, an experience not long to linger in the memory for the defeated.

As I stumbled out, leaving Blues to sing their two songs at their workmanlike, prosaic heroes, I watched an eight-year-old Red pissing his eyes out, being consoled by his dad: 'C'mon, son, it's only a game.' Not when you're eight, it isn't, as all those of my generation with 'Bobby Stokes' or 'Alan Sunderland' engraved on their heart will attest. Still, when you're young, a Cup Final defeat is a rite of passage that'll stand you in good stead as you age with United. As Steve B. remarked to me at the Torch, in reference to last Sunday but perhaps subconsciously in anticipation of today, this is just as much what it's all about: 'Catharsis and ecstasy; there's no highs without the lows.' As this season has repeatedly taught us to do, we took it on the chin and looked to the future. Some Cockney Reds outside a pub near the tube station worked it out in their own particular way, taking on all-comers in ever increasing numbers aided by the odd blade, refusing to give ground whilst brandishing half a telegraph pole. Others headed for the Metropole, to salute the players in person, before retiring for a night's commiseratory drinking, the hardier souls emerging next morning for a day's session at Lord's to cheer on Old Trafford's other heroes. The Sunday papers' news that Edwards 'couldn't afford' to release any more funds for players for at least two years – who calculated that then, Nick Leeson? – was just a final smack in the mouth in a blood-soaked week.

There was another quote in the papers from Steve Bruce who'd said that losing both our trophies in a week was 'not a nice feeling'. Reading that, you'd be forgiven for thinking that was some understatement, possibly a reflection of a lack of hunger and passion in the team. But later that night at the Metropole, as the players drank away their sorrows, a truer picture emerged. A gatecrasher who'd gone into the bogs for a slash was surprised to hear a sobbing sound in the corner. There he found our captain crumpled and desolate, crying his eyes out as if he were just another defeat-stricken Red. If that is an indication of our team's spirit, then we've nothing to worry about; as the bookies are already saying, the '96 Title is ours.

So, no happy ending, but then you already knew that. As I've said elsewhere, defeat, even this Double Defeat, has its own power, nobility and value but as a true Red you already knew that too. To come as close as we did after all we have been through was close to miraculous; three more goals in this last week and we'd have witnessed the miracle itself. There are myriad minor consolations, of course: perhaps some of the glory-hunters and part-timers will sod off to Ewood; as Eric detailed on *The Bootroom*, we have learned priceless lessons about Europe; the shareholders, happily, might take a beating on their investment; and maybe we'll get a chance to dump on both Galatasaray and Souness in the UEFA Cup. See, even defeat bears its fruits. As a season, it has given us so much; the emergence of the second crop of Fledglings, the promise of a 55,000 capacity, the future of Andy Cole and the rest of Eric Cantona, even the emergence of IMUSA as a force for change. And, of course, the wondrous individual moments that transcend all others; the fifth against City, the opening minutes against Leeds, the ninth against Ipswich and Eric's swansong winner against Rovers.

But above all, this season of burning intensity that has handed out both cruelty and delight on a whim has brought us together. As the nation revels in our downfall, as the Club seeks to disenfranchise us, as so-called Reds let us down whether vocally or politically, *true* Reds have strengthened the bond that keeps us United. At Highfield Road, you could almost touch it, holding us together, taking us forward. Whatever shit-hole the UEFA Cup sends us to, whatever aggravation we have to endure following Eric away next season, whatever obstacles the Club put in our way, we'll all be there next year and forever more, louder and stronger than ever. No one, including God it seems, likes us – and we really don't fucking care, as long as the Reds go marching on, on, on . . .

Team: Schmeichel; Neville, Irwin, Bruce (Giggs), Pallister, Sharpe (Scholes), Keane, Ince, Butt, McClair, Hughes

PS Two days after the Cup Final, one of our favourite ex-players button-holed Paul Ince at a bar and asked him what all the malarkey about an Inter Milan transfer was about. The Guvnor grinned and replied simply 'Why should I leave the greatest Club in the world for anybody else?' A simple choice for Paul, not one over which to waiver: for both King and Guv, the Italian Job remained the preserve of Coward and Caine. End of story? No: the end of an era.

As I write this, the book is about to go to press. The radio is announcing that Andrei is following Ince and Hughes out of Old Trafford. The last report in this book, of the Cup Final, has turned out to mark more than just the end of the season. At IMUSA, we are just beginning to piece together what has really been happening: the full story will not emerge until long after publication. I just hope it'll look better then than it does at this moment. 'To be continued', as they say, in the first *Red Issue* of '95/'96.

AFTERWORD by 'Veg' of Red Issue

BORROWING A LINE FROM Charles Dickens, 'it was the best of times, it was the worst of times'. On a personal basis, the last month of the season, a month in which we managed to contrive to come second in both the league (I'll never learn to call it the FA Carling Premiership) and the FA Cup (sponsored by Littlewoods Pools), a catastrophe of Leeds circa Don Revie proportions, was the month in which my love for football was reconfirmed. The Double of last season had never really captured my imagination; what should have been the crowning moment in any fan's career had left me strangely unaffected, as I suspect it had a lot of fans who might not care to talk in such heretical terms. It had all been too easy. The Cup Final against Chelsea, played on a damp day, had been a damp squib, too easy by far; the second half of the season had been a relatively easy stroll, enlivened only by the destruction of Leeds at Elland Road.

So what was it that captured my imagination in what many would consider a disastrous finish to the season? One word, tension. We might have come second, but the blood flowed at Highfield Road and Upton Park, like it used to; when Andy Cole scored that last gasp winner at Coventry to keep us in with a chance of winning the league, I knew exactly how Uma Thurman's character had felt in *Pulp Fiction* when John Travolta injects her with pure adrenaline. Ryan Giggs reckons that sex is better than scoring a goal; the young Welshman must be a damn sight better in the sack than he is at crossing the ball, to better the buzz we got from Cole's goal that night.

Even at West Ham, I enjoyed myself in a perverse sort of a way. The league was lost and Liverpool's surprise victory over Blackburn meant that we could have pulled off the comeback of the century to overhaul Kenny's mercenaries. For many that day, failure brought tears and desperation but you couldn't buy the atmosphere in the last fifteen minutes at Upton Park for all the Sky TV money in all the football world. As United pressed for a Michael Thomas-style winner in the last fifteen minutes, there were many in the United End, myself included, who looked physically sick, so great was the anxiety running through the collective Red vein. Brought up on years of relative failure at Old Trafford in the late Seventies and early Eighties, like many others caught up in the Ferguson Five Year Trophy run, I had begun to believe that I could only enjoy my football with silverware in it. What I'd forgotten is that there's sometimes more to be enjoyed in glorious and hard fought failure than in easy victory. In years to come the record books will only show Blackburn's and Everton's names, but is that really what you are looking for when, as a diehard supporter, you pays your money and takes your chance at the turnstile of football fate? The sublime moment in a Cup Final is not when the captain lifts the tin pot, but the moment the winning goal is scored. If Andy Cole's goal against a spirited Coventry ending up being irrelevant, we didn't know it at the moment – who can say, now months later, that the moment was any less sweeter because of that?

Of course, those sweet moments came at the end of a season which most would quite rightly want to discard in the dustbin of football history. The worst of times for me came in Gothenburg and at home against Arsenal. Stood with hundreds of Swedes, fenced in, with a running track further distancing us from the action, denied a place in the official United section as 'undesirables', watching United get humiliated by a team that must surely rank as one of the poorest ever to reach the quarter finals of the European Cup, was as low as it can get. The realisation that in the snow, sleet and over-priced alcohol nightmare that is Sweden in November, our European sojourn was over for another year. There would be no more drunken binges in foreign climes, none of the camaraderie that is unique to United supporters in Europe. Yet again the ultimate prize had eluded us at the first hurdle, and the hardest thing to take was the fact that we deserved to go out; we simply weren't good enough, and the realisation of that cold hard truth hurt like hell. The New Year came and went, Gary Walsh dropped a clanger at home to Leicester (how could we have guessed then, that his mistake would be looked back on in May in a much harsher light), we purchased Andy Cole in a transfer coup that could only be bettered by Cantona's defection from Yorkshire for surprise. Eric of course then slipped over the barrier at Selhurst Park and with it in hindsight went our Championship hopes. Still, though, nothing could prepare me personally for the anger and despair I would feel on an innocuous night when we played Arsenal at the 'Theatre of Dreams' in March. A month previously we had humiliated Leeds in a fifth round FA Cup tie at Old Trafford. In terms of atmosphere it was probably the best game at Old Trafford in two or three years. Sat together in J Stand, 'singers' had got together and rocked the stadium to its rafters, revelling in the despair of our most despised opponents. If every man was out of his seat, it didn't matter; there were no executives or stewards to tell us to sit down, it was if the Stretford End of old, the Stretford End of Barcelona '84, the Stretford End of Everton '83, of Sunderland '75 had been transplanted to the all seated atmosphere free Old Trafford of the Nineties for one afternoon and we loved it! Then came that Arsenal game. If I'd felt low in Sweden at the realisation that the season was over in certain respects, at half time on 22 March, I felt as if the football world I'd grown up in, a world of passion, commitment, camaraderie that was envied around the globe, had had the last rites served on it by the officials of the very club that had given me so much and to which I'd given so much in the eighteen years since I first caught the bug against Chelsea on 17 September 1977. When the club decided that they should make a tannoy announcement to the occupants of K Stand telling us to sit down and shut up or we'd be kicked out, at that moment I had drummed into me what I'd suspected but daren't believe for a while. The old time supporter, the supporter who could remember the barren years and didn't measure his support in his collection of Megastore carrier bags just wasn't welcome at Old Trafford any more. The despair of that night has been dissipated though by the reaction of United supporters to that infamous announcement. When Merret and Co. made that announcement, little did they realise the galvanising effect it would have on Reds, disgusted at a club that no longer thinks of its supporters as fans to be nurtured, encouraged and thanked, but as paying customers to be exploited to the full on the wheel of profit. We have finally got around to doing something to rescue this club from the clutches of the money men and marketing executives. Already the IMUSA has had some effect on the club and it has shown supporters that they can make a difference. In years to come, whilst others might look back on '94/'95 as the year Cantona kung-fu kicked a Palace fan and United blew the chance of an historic double double, I hope I look back on it as the year we finally started to reclaim the game. Because without that passion, commitment, camaraderie, and sense of belonging that following a club can engender, all the trophies in the world will mean nothing.

Chris Robinson, *Red Issue*

THE INDEPENDENT MAN U SUPPORTERS ASSOCIATION

THE IMUSA HAS BEEN formed to give the ordinary, match-going fan a voice. There has been a growing discontent amongst United fans for a number of years and supporters' pressure groups have been formed on various issues. But this time, the very essence of being a supporter is under threat and thus a permanent organisation is needed to represent the views of the traditional United fan.

Our members have asked us to campaign on five key points:

1 Redevelopment of OT – take the chance to recreate atmosphere. 2 No standing and singing in seats? – allow us to support our team! 3 Price increases – rebuild from profits, not fans' pockets. 4 Abuse of away match allocations – tickets for fans not fat cats. 5 Dialogue between board and fans – member have right to be heard.

These and many many more issues have already been raised and are being pursued; we approach the Club directly (as well as indirectly through our contacts within) as well as by using the media who are particularly receptive to our cause. If you are concerned for the future of our Club, then join us. This is your Club: this is your fight. We need your help – and we need you to join. Write to: IMUSA, PO BOX 69, MANCHESTER M32 0UZ. (Andy Walsh, secretary)

FURTHER READING

Richard Kurt's *United We Stood* can still be found in decent shops and direct from Sigma Press on 01625-531035.

Red Issue and *United We Stand* are on subscription from PO BOX 16, Urmston, Manchester M31 1LX and PO BOX 45, Manchester M41 1GQ respectively.

United Anti-Fascists can be contacted through PO BOX 83, SWDO, Manchester M15 5NJ.

The author can be reached via Mainstream, 7 Albany Street, Edinburgh EH1 3UG or via the IMUSA.

Peter Boyle's classic *Songs From The Bathtub* albums as well as copies of the *Eric The King* single and the Wembley '95 video are available direct from Pete: phone 0161 431-8953 for details.

Decent coach travel to games with true Reds is available from *Red Issue/United We Stand* on 0161 866 9300.

We are hoping to produce a book on the Red Army Years, 1974–86, in conjunction with Andy Pollard ('You're Supposed To Be At Home'). If you'd like to contribute your memories, or photos, or write a piece for inclusion, please write to Richard Kurt c/o IMUSA.

Other United 'zines: *Red News* c/o PO Box 384, London WC1N 3RJ *Red Attitude* c/o PO Box 83, SWDO, Old Trafford, Manchester M15 5NJ; *WDWRd*, 16 The Quantocks, Flitwick, Bedford MK45 1TQ.

Some pages have already been extracted in *Red Issue*. Any extracts from other publications are included for review purposes under the terms allowed in the 1988 Copyright Act.

Pete Boyle's recordings are available via Exotica Records on 0181 299 2342.